hjfbcit@gmail.com

When Things Happen at Work

A Practitioner's Guide to People, Circumstances and What to do Now

Hugh J. Finlayson

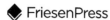 FriesenPress

Suite 300 - 990 Fort St
Victoria, BC, V8V 3K2
Canada

www.friesenpress.com

ISBN
978-1-5255-3113-2 (Hardcover)
978-1-5255-3114-9 (Paperback)
978-1-5255-3115-6 (eBook)

1. BUSINESS & ECONOMICS, HUMAN RESOURCES & PERSONNEL MANAGEMENT

Distributed to the trade by The Ingram Book Company

When Things Happen at Work: A Practitioner's Guide to People, Circumstances and What to do Now is drawn from a variety of sources, workplace experiences and human resource best practices in both public and private workplace settings. The first edition was developed in 1994 and focussed on grievance administration. This was followed by two more editions and a second resource in the early 2000s that examined workplace investigations. In 2016, a consolidation of both publications was published with new content including best practices in communications and interactions. This latest effort adds a new Part Two that focusses on analyzing, understanding, and managing workplace conflict.

"As long as it's woolly I don't ask questions."

Used with permission, The New Yorker Collection/The Cartoon Bank, 2016 by Sam Gross.

Contents

Read with caution with a mind open to persuasion: *Faced with the choice between changing one's mind and proving that there is no need to do so, almost everyone gets busy on the proof.* John Kenneth Galbraith, Canadian-born economist, public official, and diplomat (1908-2006).

Preface

Simply stated, things happen and things happen at work. And there are times when something happens at work that requires further inquiry, which may lead to the initiation of a formal investigation and a disciplinary decision. In unionized workplaces, *grievances* may arise as a result of employer decisions in response to the investigative findings.

When something happens at work, the occurrence is set against a familiar backdrop: the *real* organization, a web of employment rules, a need for information, can be characterized as a conflict of sorts necessitating a measure of negotiation and, of course, requiring a series of informed decisions.

When Things Happen at Work: A Practitioner's Guide to People, Circumstances and What to do Now is based on the notion that you achieve what you achieve through the energy, creativity of those who choose to work with you and what you do together and to understand and manage a workplace, you must understand the nature, structure of employment; when you understand employment you can begin to understand people at work... including yourself. With that understanding you can better manage workplace circumstances including any conflicts that may arise.

It recognizes that organizational change is more the norm than the exception. And more than ever, work roles and organizations are in a state of flux with technological advances, changes in structure, re-deployment, return to work, and redundancy. With people, organizations, and our times being as they are it is necessary for HR professionals to understand the inevitability of conflict and the frameworks, models, structures, and tools that can be employed to best manage that conflict.

When Things Happen at Work: A Practitioner's Guide to People, Circumstances and What to do Now is written for anyone who wants to advance their understanding of people at work, the nature of employment, how conflict happens and what needs to be done to address individuals, events, and circumstances constructively.

Overview of the Structure

When Things Happen at Work: A Practitioner's Guide to People, Circumstances and What to do Now is divided into five parts and is supplemented by additional tools and a comprehensive glossary.

Figure 1 – Overview

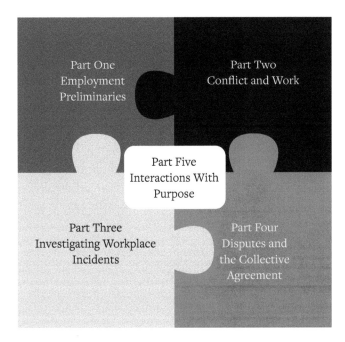

- **Part One: Employment Preliminaries** summarizes employment basics that are the foundation for the ideas, tools, and strategies provided in the next four parts.

- **Part Two: Conflict and Work** introduces conflict concepts and places them in a work context. It is based on the idea that conflict management requires a combination of analytical and people skills and proposes ideas, concepts, and approaches to better understand and best manage workplace conflict. Part Two examines conflict styles, their nature, and how to move from styles to strategies. A comprehensive conflict analysis template is provided.

- **Part Three: Investigating Workplace Incidents** offers practical strategies to prepare for and conduct investigations in the workplace. Chapter 1 examines workplace conduct. Chapters 2 and 3 explore the investigation process and provide guidance on how to make decisions based on that investigation.

- **Part Four: Disputes and the Collective Agreement** focusses on a unionized workplace and is a resource for effectively managing grievances that arise under a collective agreement. Part Four provides ideas and strategies to help you gather and organize the information needed to resolve disputes during the term of the agreement.

- **Part Five: Interactions with Purpose – Skills, Techniques, and Considerations** examines workplace communications and interactions. In addition to general communication best practices, this part explores strategies for conducting interviews and managing what are often stressful or conflict-laden circumstances.

- **Appendices A, B, and C** provide investigation process checklists, and sample expectation, disciplinary, and related letters.

Human resource practitioners face considerable daily pressures and priorities—in both the private and the public sectors—and this book is an attempt to provide a helpful working resource and reference to assist them in their work. Please do not read this book from beginning to end in one sitting. It is too much to take in. It is recommended that if you prefer a purely pragmatic approach, you should start by reading Part One: Employment Preliminaries. Regardless of your experience a measure of reflection is helpful. This first part will serve as an introduction for some and a re-awakening for others. The focus on employment preliminaries, the nature of work, and how organizations really work provides a firm foundation upon which the other concepts in the book are set. You will find concrete examples and helpful guidelines. After that, you might like to go to the theory in Parts Two and Five to examine workplace conflict, its nature, and origin and approaches available to you as a practitioner or leader.

Likewise, if you are more interested in investigating and managing workplace incidents, whether misconduct or other similar circumstance, you may want to go directly to Part Three, which focusses on processes, practices, and frameworks to investigate and manage workplace incidents. If you manage in a unionized workplace, Part Four deals exclusively with disputes and the collective agreement. And finally, Part Five provides a series of resources that can be adopted and customized to improve workplace interactions in different circumstances.

When Things Happen at Work: A Practitioner's Guide to People, Circumstances and What to do Now contains information and guidelines and suggests tools for gathering and organizing information that can help with the investigation and management of incidents that happen at work. However, it only provides a guide and is not a substitute for professional advice in particular situations.

As you journey through the material, remember that at work: *"If you fail to plan, you are planning to fail."* Benjamin Franklin, writer, philosopher, scientist, and inventor (1706–1790).

Part One: Employment Preliminaries

Employment Preliminaries is the foundation for the concepts, resources, and strategies explored in parts two, three, and four. It provides an overview of selected employment topics and is descriptive, not analytical. Readers are encouraged to broaden their understanding of the part one topics as required through further research.

Employment Basics

The field of human resource management is broadly described as decisions and activities involving individuals or groups of individuals that are designed to influence the effectiveness of employees and the organization. It is comprised of transactional and transformational activities. Transactional activities include day-to-day activities that are more administrative in nature such as recruitment and selection, compensation administration, conflict management, statistical analysis and reporting, and the like. Transformational activities include the management of change efforts, leadership development, organizational design, job design, and conflict management process design. As shown in the schematic below, many elements make up the field of human resource management:

Figure 2: Human Resource Management

This resource focusses on *employment relationships*[1] and employee and labour relations. In human resources, *employee relations* refers to the direct employer-employee relationship, and *labour relations* refers to the workings of the continuous relationship between a group of employees (represented by a union) and an employer. The terms and conditions of employment, and the consequent processes or practices that define these terms, exist in both union and non-union workplaces, and many of the principles, processes, and strategies outlined in this resource are largely transferrable between the two.[2]

Understanding more about how employment is regulated in Canada, knowing how an employee is defined, and exploring the many types of employment relationships are important steps for being able to manage workplace incidents. These and other issues are examined below.

How is Employment Regulated? The Web of Rules.

Each province in Canada—and the federal government, in federally regulated industries[3]—has its own legislation to regulate employment matters. These acts, codes, and statutes apply to all employment situations or have employment implications for a specific profession or sector.

The creation, application, and administration of provincial and federal statutes takes place against the backdrop of, and is consistent with, the *Canadian Charter of Rights and Freedoms*. The *Charter* is part of the Canadian Constitution and applies to the actions of government and guarantees such rights as freedom of expression, freedom of association, and equality, within the limits set out in the Charter. Legislation inconsistent with the *Charter* can be struck down as unconstitutional.

1   Defined as social relations among people at work; rights, obligations, expectations, values, and rewards that define interactions in the labour market—the legal link between employers and employees; exists when a person performs work or services under certain terms and conditions in return for remuneration.

2   The terms *adjudicator* and arbitrator are used in connection with conclusions, advice, and considerations resulting from formal-employment-related proceedings. The term adjudicator includes judges, arbitrators, and employment-related tribunal chair/officials; an arbitrator is the neutral third party chosen by the parties to a collective agreement to render binding decisions on collective agreement disputes.

3   As defined by the *Canada Labour Code*, all interprovincial or international air, rail, shipping, and trucking operations fall within federal jurisdiction, as do broadcasting enterprises, banks, uranium mines, and grain elevators. Jurisdiction is determined to be federal when the federal government has specific power over a particular agency (for example, the post office); employees do work that does not fall within the legislative jurisdiction of any province, do work that connects provinces or extends beyond the limits of a province, or do work that the federal government declares to be of "general advantage of Canada" (for example, railways, canals, grain elevators, and atomic energy). In

Legislatures enact legislation commonly called *statutory law*. These statutory laws usurp or extend specific portions of the *common law*—the results of previous court decisions to determine rights and obligations—and may create new rights and obligations for employers and employees. For example, Canadian governments have created a statutory floor of rights regarding wages, hours of work, and vacations by enacting employment standards (sometimes called labour standards). Governments may also create minimum standards around human rights, occupational health and safety, and compensation for workplace injuries. These statutory rights change the common law.

The rules regarding unionization and collective bargaining are another type of statutory law. These *labour laws* substantially alter the common law by making a union the *bargaining agent* for a group of employees. Under labour laws, the common law contract of employment is replaced by a collective agreement negotiated between the union and the employer.

In unionized workplaces, collective agreements define the basic rules that govern the day-to-day relationship between an employer and the union representing the employer's employees. Negotiated through the process of collective bargaining, the collective agreement represents a codification of what the parties have agreed on to regulate their conduct and dealings over a certain period. Management discretion on employment matters is circumscribed; however, as a general proposition, any right to act related to employment and employees that the employer has not expressly bargained away in the agreement is retained by management.[4]

---

the event of a national emergency, all Canadian employees who would provide and maintain "peace, order, and good government" fall within federal jurisdiction.

4   Referred to as *management rights, inherent rights,* and *residual rights.* A shorthand expression for the principle, applied in the interpretation of collective agreements, that any rights that the employer has not expressly bargained away in the agreement are retained by management. For example, if the union cannot point to an explicit clause that prohibits management from contracting out union work to an outside company, management can contract out as part of its management rights.

Who is an Employee?

Is this person an employee? What is the difference between an employee and an independent contractor?

It is not always clear who is, and who is not, an employee of a given organization. There has been a trend in recent years for organizations to hire individuals as *independent contractors* or *sub-contractors* to perform work on a flat-rate or piecework basis rather than as full-fledged employees.

There is often an incomplete understanding of what constitutes an employment relationship, which results in hiring individuals as independent contractors when they are, in fact, employees. This may result in the organization being exposed to unexpected statutory or civil liability.

As described below, four main tests distinguish an employee from an independent contractor: control, ownership of tools, risk of loss, and chance for profits.

1. **Control:** Who controls the actions of the worker while they are on the job? Does the worker have decision-making authority as to how, when, or what work is to be done? Does the employer dictate the method and manner in which work is completed? Does the employer supervise the worker in their activities and to what extent? Does the worker operate independently of the employer, other than for a general description of the work to be done, time frame, and costs? The greater the level of control exerted by the employer, the more likely the relationship is one of employer-employee rather than that of an independent contractor.

2. **Ownership of Tools:** Does the employer provide the means of production or does the worker supply their own tools? Tools includes such items as motor vehicles, computer equipment, personal communication devices, copiers, construction tools, and the like. If the employer tends to own the tools, it is more likely an employer-employee relationship, whereas if the worker provides their own tools, it suggests an independent contractor relationship.

3. **Risk of Loss:** Do the parties share the risk of loss from the proposed business activity? Employees are typically not liable for losses resulting from a failed business venture, while independent contractors may well suffer a loss if the party hiring them is unable to pay the contracted price for the goods or services provided by the independent contractor.

4. **Chance of Profit:** As with risk of loss, employees will typically not participate in the profits of a business venture, whereas independent contracts depend on profitability to realize any revenue.

None of these tests is conclusive in and of itself, and the facts of each case must be considered with a view to determining whose business it is.

What is the Relationship between Employer and Employee?

If an employer-employee relationship exists, what does this mean in terms of the rights and obligations of the parties to each other?

Typically, an individual comes to work under the terms prescribed by an employer. When the employee begins work, the employer and employee have entered a contract. A *contract* is a legally enforceable promise or set of promises made between two parties. This contract between an individual and an employer is called a common law contract of employment. Under common law, both the employee and employer have a number of implied rights and obligations.

Employers

- May not terminate an employee without notice (except for just cause).

- May not force an employee to accept an inferior position within the organization.

- Must deal fairly with the employee.

- Have the right to suspend or terminate employees.

Employees

- Have an obligation to work, including a duty not to be absent or late without a reasonable excuse.

- Must obey the lawful orders of the employer.

- Must perform their duties in a competent manner.

- Must serve the employer honestly and faithfully.

- Must not engage in misconduct that might adversely affect the employer's interest.

- Must not compete against the employer.

- Will sign a written contract of employment if asked at the start of their employment.

When there is a dispute between an employee and employer, the matter is often settled in court. When the dispute is about what precisely was agreed to, and the answer cannot be found in the written employment contract, the courts turn to the common law (i.e., the results of previous legal decisions) to determine the rights and obligations of the employer and employee. Common law rights and obligations are important because few employment contracts contain anything more than the most basic terms of employment (such as job title, salary and benefits, and vacation entitlement).

How Do You Determine if an Employee Has Been Wrongfully Dismissed?

Under common law in a non-union workplace, if an employee is dismissed from employment, the question arises as to whether the employee has been wrongfully dismissed. To determine if a wrongful dismissal has occurred, it is necessary to ask a number of questions:

- **Was the individual an employee?** An individual can only claim to have been wrongfully dismissed if they were in fact an employee of the organization for whom they were working.

- **Was there a dismissal?** Dismissals may be either **direct** (such as an explicit firing or removal from the workplace) or **constructive** (employer behaviour or actions that have the effect of dismissing the employee, although the behaviour or actions do not constitute dismissal in and of themselves). An example of a direct dismissal is if an employee is advised verbally or in writing that their employment has been terminated as of a certain date. An example of constructive dismissal is if an employer unilaterally makes a fundamental or substantial change to an employee's contract that violates the contract's terms.

- **Was the employee dismissed for cause?** The concept of dismissal for *cause* or *just cause* suggests that there are circumstances or situations where an employer may terminate an employee without being accused of wrongful dismissal. There are no hard and fast rules as to what type of employee behaviour constitutes cause; each case must be decided on its own facts. For example, in *R v Arthurs*, [1967] 2 O.R. 49 at 55 (C.A.), rev'd [1969] S.C.R. 85, Schroeder J.A. (in dissent) defined just cause as follows:

    If an employee has been guilty of serious misconduct, habitual neglect of duty, incompetence, or conduct incompatible with his duties, or prejudicial to the employer's business, or if he has been guilty of wilful disobedience to the employer's orders in a matter of substance, the law recognizes the employer's right summarily to dismiss the delinquent employee.

The Supreme Court of Canada made clear in *McKinley v BC Tel*, 2001 SCC 38, that dishonest conduct on the part of an employee does not always amount to cause for dismissal. Whether an employer is justified in dismissing an employee without notice on grounds of dishonesty is a question that requires an assessment of the serious-ness of the misconduct in the context of the particular case in order to determine whether dismissal without notice is a proportionate sanction. For example, where an employer alleges theft as justification for dismissal without notice, it is necessary to determine whether the evidence establishes that the theft actually occurred and, if so, whether the specific nature of the misconduct in the specific circumstances warrants dismissal. The employer bears the onus of establishing both parts of the test on a *balance of probabilities.*

If it is the conclusion that it is likely the employee engaged in the misconduct alleged, the misconduct then must be considered in context to determine whether it has caused an "irreparable breakdown of the employment relationship."5 The principle of *proportionality* is applied to determine whether dismissal is an appropriate sanction or whether, given the nature and seriousness of the misconduct, it remains reconcilable with sustaining the employment relationship. As stated by Justice Iacobucci for the Court in *McKinley* at para. 57:

Such an approach mitigates the possibility that an employee will be unduly punished by the strict application of an unequivocal rule that equates all forms of dishonest behavior with just cause for dismissal. At the same time, it would properly emphasize that dishonesty going to the core of the employment relationship carries the potential to warrant dismissal for just cause.

- **What damage was suffered by the employee?** Once it is determined that the employee was in fact wrongfully dismissed, the court will then consider what measure of damages were suffered by the employee. Factors that may be considered will include the amount of notice (or pay in lieu of notice) that should have been given to the employee, costs for the mental distress imposed on the employee, and punitive damages imposed as a punishment for the employer's wrongful behaviour.

How do Employment Relationships Differ in Employee Relations and Labour Relations Settings?

To contrast union and non-union environments, while non-union workers can be uni-laterally terminated, in unionized workplaces, most collective agreements or, alter-natively, provincial labour statutes, require that employees can only be disciplined or

---

5   *Steel v Coast Capital Savings Credit Union*, 2015 BCCA 127 at para. 27; *Nishima v Azuma Foods (Canada) Co Ltd*, 2010 BCSC 502 at para. 194.

terminated for just and reasonable cause. Over the years, this term has been defined primarily through arbitral case law created in deciding discharge grievances.

It is universally accepted that except in extraordinary circumstances, an employer cannot summarily terminate an employee for misconduct. The concept of *progressive discipline* arises as a consequence of the employer's legal right to terminate an employee in a unionized environment. An employer must build up to termination by invoking stages of lesser forms of discipline; for example, written warnings, suspensions, and demotions. Likewise, except in extraordinary circumstances, an employer cannot invoke a more serious disciplinary penalty—for example, a suspension—before the employer has invoked a lesser form of disciplinary penalty, such as a warning. This is referred to as progressive or corrective discipline.

Employer decisions and grievances under a collective agreement are discussed in detail in "Part Four: Disputes and the Collective Agreement."

Terms and Conditions of Employment

There are three ways to determine the terms and conditions of employment:

1. **Unilateral determination:** Employers unilaterally define the terms and conditions of employment (employee relations).[6]

2. **Collective bargaining:** Unions and employers collectively bargain the terms and conditions of employment (labour relations) under rules codified in labour relations statutes. With bargaining comes the mechanisms to compel the other side to move: the union can *strike*, and the employer can lock out. If the organization is operating in an industry that delivers what are considered essential services, in some jurisdictions, labour code provisions modify the strike/lockout concept.

3. **Third-party processes:** The terms and conditions are determined by a neutral third party through a process codified in a collective agreement, at the direction of government or with the agreement of a union and employer to resolve a bargaining impasse (labour relations).

6   Terms and conditions can also be determined through actions by government (legislative change; union-employer back to work legislation to resolve a collective bargaining dispute). This happens infrequently and is predominantly a public-sector phenomenon.

The Legal Link: Arrangements and Contracts

> There are as many employment arrangements as there are organizations.
>
> Some of these arrangements are codified in formal contracts or articulated in written procedures and roles and responsibilities documents, while others are considered "just understood" and an integral part of the "way things are done around here."

Whether formal, informal, or a combination of both, the existence, operation, and interpretation of these arrangements is subject to applicable provincial or federal employment-related statutes, as well as the acts, codes, or statutes that apply to all employment situations or have employment implications to a specific profession or sector. Some apply strictly to unionized workplaces, while others apply to specific sectors or professions.

Categories of Work Contracts

There are two broad categories of work contracts: transactional and psychological.

Transactional

Transactional work contracts are formal, codified contracts of employment that are generally written and official and which tend to be dominated by employer expectations. Contracts such as these are usually agreed to when someone joins an organization; these contain provisions covering formal terms and conditions of service, including remuneration and other benefits, together with sanctions, if the contract is not satisfactorily fulfilled.

Transactional work contracts exist on the assumption that there is a mutuality of obligation. Employment contracts are legally binding and are often supplemented by organizational job descriptions or unique, person-specific role details.

In unionized workplaces, collective agreements provide the basic rules that govern the day-to-day relationship between an employer and the union representing the employer's employees. Collective agreements are negotiated through the process of collective bargaining, and the collective agreement represents a codification of what the parties have agreed on to regulate their conduct and dealings over a certain period.

As a general proposition, any right to act related to employment and employees that the employer has not expressly bargained away in the agreement is retained by management.

Psychological[7]

Psychological work contracts (or psychosocial contracts) represent the sum of the implicit and explicit agreements we believe we have with key individuals and the organization concerning our employment relationship. These ground our expectations of ourselves and the organization, of terms and conditions, norms, rights, rewards, and obligations.

> Psychological contracts are **essentially relational** and concern the maintenance and quality of emotional and interpersonal relationships between the employer and employee and between peers. These contracts include informal arrangements, mutual beliefs, and common ground and perceptions between the two parties.

Often **tacit or implicit**, psychological contracts tend to be invisible, assumed, unspoken, informal, or at best only partially vocalized; as the unwritten set of expectations of the employment relationship, psychological contracts are distinct from the formal, codified employment contract. These contracts are used as a mental map to help us to navigate our way through our working day.

Like the individuals connected with them, psychological contracts change over time and are, as a consequence, inherently unstable. As we as individuals change, and as the composition of our work team and our operating environment/context changes, so too do our respective psychological contracts. These contracts can become even more complex over time, because each of us tends to project aspects of the psychological contract we think we have negotiated—but may never have explicitly checked out—onto how we think other people should behave towards us and to each other at work.

As **mutual obligations,** these contracts are fragile. People can go from totally excited, actively contributing to the organization and engaged in their work to seriously deflated and disengaged because of a breach of the psychological contract, whether real or perceived. These breaches result for a variety of reasons, including:

- violations of trust, actions that reveal a lack of honesty and integrity, or behaviours that violate ethics or the law

- promises made that are believed to be broken, inconsistency of word and action; misalignment between what a leader says and what a leader does

- incongruity between written and unwritten rules

- assignments that intrude on personal time-specific job responsibilities

7   Originally developed by organizational scholar Denise Rousseau to better describe how employers and employees understand the employment relationship.

- expectations that are ill-defined, and environments, assignments that are considered difficult and unrewarding

- ambiguous reporting relationships and accountabilities

- leaders who unilaterally and/or drastically alter the deal

- inadequate and/or ill-conceived human resource practices, procedures, and structures

Culture, Engagement, and the Like

Taken together, psychological and transactional employment contracts govern employer-employee relationships.

They inform an organization's culture (the combination of shared values and group norms, "the way we do things around here") and have implications for engagement ("how an employee feels about how things are done around here")

Culture: The Way Things are Done Around Here

The *culture* of a group can be defined as the pattern of shared basic assumptions that was learned by a group as it conducted its affairs and solved its problems of external adaption and internal integration. It is the ways of doing things that have worked well enough to be considered valid. These assumptions are taught to new members as the correct way to perceive, think, and feel in relation to circumstances.

To analyze a culture, consider the following:

- visible aspect or artifacts of the organization

- organization's espoused beliefs, values, and strategy

- basic underlying assumptions that have become so much a part of a group's thinking and perspective on the world that they are not questioned and appear extremely difficult to change

And look for demonstrable evidence of the culture, for example:

- Observe the artifacts and workplace norms such as communication styles, how people dress, patterns of socializing, teamwork, professionalism, deference to hierarchy.

- Read documents and talk to people to learn espoused beliefs and values. What does the organization say about itself on the internet, in publications?

- Consider what seems to get rewarded and what gets punished and what appears to be most valued.

Engagement: From the Way Things Are Done to the Degree of Commitment

Engagement is the degree to which employees are committed to their jobs.[8] Engaged employees are seen to be psychologically and emotionally committed to their work and the work of the organization. Above all, they are active and productive. The nature of engagement can be one of engaged, not engaged, or actively disengaged.

Engaged employees work with passion and feel a profound connection to their work and the organization. They drive innovation and move the organization forward.

Employees who are not engaged have checked out, and presenteesim has set in— employees are physically there, but not actively present. They put in time, rather than investing energy and creativity into their work.

Actively disengaged employees aren't just unhappy at work; they act out their unhappiness. These employees may attempt to undermine their engaged colleagues and what they are seeking to accomplish.

> Identifying the attributes that employees perceive as the value they gain through employment is central to understanding the psychological contract and the consequent levels of engagement.
>
> Perceived value attracts prospective employees, and perception of value leads to continuing commitment and engagement once employed.[9]

The attributes of perceived value include:

1. The tangible rewards an employee receives for his/her work— total compensation

   - salary and benefits

   - retirement benefits

---

8   The definition of engagement adopted by the British multi-disciplinary human resource consultancy Chiumento (2004/14).

9   *Competitive Employment Value Proposition Research Initiative* 2006,14, Corporate Leadership Council; an international membership of senior executives with a shared commitment to steward enterprise-wide human resources management and is a leading provider of best practices research, executive education, and decision-support services for senior executives. (CLC Executive Board: Washington DC; London UK).

- annual vacation

2.   The opportunity a job or organization affords an employee—development opportunities and experiences

- development opportunities

- future career opportunities

- organizational growth rate

- meritocracy

- organizational stability

3.   The nature of work itself, the extent to which it matches an employee's interest

- travel

- innovation

- contribution; job impact: making a difference

- job-interests alignment

- location

- recognition

- work-life integration (also referred to as work-life balance)

4.   The characteristics of the organization such as size, structure, and (labour) market position

- reputation (client, public)

- diversity

- empowerment

- environmental responsibility

- ethics

- top employer recognition/designation

- industry or sector

- brand and brand awareness

- standing in the profession (if a regulated profession); profes- sional association

- market position; product/service quality

- respect

- risk taking

- social responsibility

- technology currency/level

5. The characteristics of the organization's people, such as supervisor/ leader quality, nature of colleagues, how people inter-relate/interact

- camaraderie; collegial work

- co-worker quality

- nature and degree of autonomy; professional autonomy

- manager/supervisor/team leader quality

- people management including legitimate voice mechanisms

- senior leadership reputation

Figure 3: Employment Value Proposition (EVP)

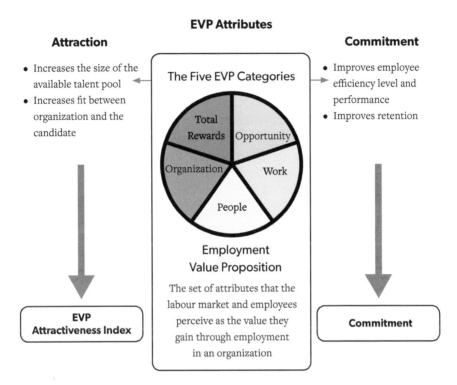

EVP Attributes

Attraction

- Increases the size of the available talent pool
- Increases fit between organization and the candidate

The Five EVP Categories

- Total Rewards
- Opportunity
- Organization
- Work
- People

Commitment

- Improves employee efficiency level and performance
- Improves retention

EVP Attractiveness Index

Employment Value Proposition

The set of attributes that the labour market and employees perceive as the value they gain through employment in an organization

Commitment

Power, Authority, and Rules

Workplaces, like all social organizations, operate according to rules. Generally, workplace rules come from two sources:

- The variety of acts, codes, and statutes that apply to all employment situations or which have employment implications applicable to a specific profession or sector.

- Employment rules, practices, and processes adopted by an organization to manage the workplace.

Organizational rules:

- Are made, interpreted, and applied depending on their context within a statutory framework, the web of rules.

- Are made by those with the power to do so.

- Vary in complexity. Some are simple and easy to follow, others of bewildering complexity.

- May be applied differently to different people.

- Can be waived or bent.

- May be informal, unwritten, and implicit, or formal, written and explicit. Both are equally real in their consequences.

- Are made, interpreted, and applied often by different people.

Rules—Written and Unwritten—and How an Organization Works

An organization's formal structure is defined by how tasks are formally divided, grouped, and coordinated. Formal structures are designed to support the strategic direction by enhancing order, efficiency, effectiveness, and accountability. Formal systems can include: planning systems, control systems, performance management, reward systems, and information systems.

They provide the formal infrastructure structure that operationalizes the organizational structure. Other features of structure and systems include:

- **Differentiation:** The degree to which tasks are subdivided into separated jobs or tasks.

- **Integration:** The coordination of the various tasks or jobs into a department or group; extent to which activities are combined into processes and systems.

- **Chain of command:** Defines how individuals or units within an organizational report to one another up and down the organizational hierarchy

- **Span of control:** The number of individuals report to a supervisor; the ratio of employees to supervisors in an organization.

- **Centralization vs. Decentralization:** How and where decision making is distributed in an organizational structure

- **Formal vs. Informal:** The degree to which organizational charts, job descriptions, and the like exist, are codified, and are followed.

Every organization has a culture that makes it unique, with at least two variants—one that we speak about and one that we do not. Top executives often talk about their organization's vision, values, and organization charts, as well as offer publicity, advertising, and policy manuals about what is most important.

With carefully crafted key messages, headlines, and stories, the visible organization is especially clear and apparent to outsiders and the external public.

What lies beneath the visible organization is what can be characterized as the shadow organization. Frequently invisible to outsiders and often filled with unwritten rules, this version of the organization is usually more powerful than the first. Unwritten rules are:

- Workplace norms such as **acceptable communication styles, dress, assertiveness, socializing, teamwork, professionalism, and deference to hierarchy.**

- Rules that can be found in professional and social interactions, in expectations of managers and employees, in **assumptions** on what makes a good employee or a good work environment, and in many other areas of workplace culture.

- Informal day-to-day **behaviours carried on in the name of tradition, habit, and expectation;** consist of what people actually do rather than what the organizational materials profess.

- **Subtle things in the workplace** that get passed on—or not—by word-of-mouth from employee to employee; norms that everyone seems to know about except those people who are new.

The most successful organizations, those that have a sound employment value proposition and where employees label the organization as a great place to work, have a coherent organizational structure and congruence between written and unwritten rules.

Since employees learn from what they live rather than from what they are taught, new employees experience culture shock when the work climate is different than what they expected. So, when an employee is told one thing and experiences another, they experience what psychologists call *cognitive dissonance,*[10] which often leads to dissatisfaction, low levels of engagement, and reduced productivity.

Observations and Insights on the Workings of an Organization

Businesses exist to succeed, however that may be defined. Any actions we take within our organizations should be designed to contribute towards that success, because otherwise they have no reason and they're a waste of time, energy, and resources.[11]

10   The mental stress or discomfort experienced by an individual who holds two or more contradictory beliefs, ideas, or values at the same time, or is confronted by new information that conflicts with existing beliefs, ideas, or values.

11   Excerpt from author and human resource specialist Andy Swann's November 14, 2017 article, "Why Any Change Must Be Human: How to ensure change in your organization is people-centric."

Consider you organization. Can you describe it, what it does, and what it aspires to? Based on what you know, can you complete the following organizational planning schematic?[12] Why or why not? What does this tell you about you and the organization?

Figure 4: Organizational Schematic

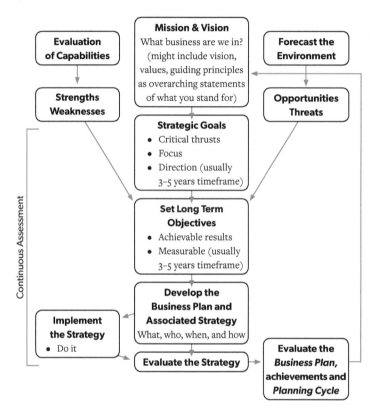

Now consider your organization and its formal and informal structures. Distinguish between what the organization would like to be and what it is in practice.

Does it rely on formal hierarchies with centralized decision making and a clear division of labour, or does it have a flexible approach to work and its organization with fewer rules, and procedures relying less on the hierarchy or authority for centralized decision making? Are there other characteristics that stand out?

Read and consider each group of statements. You have ten points to distribute.

Assign the points to the groups of statements that best describe your organization as evidenced by decision/approach characteristics and action tendencies.

12   In the schematic the term mission describes an organization's reason for being, what it does and *vision*, its preferred future, what it aspires to.

This is not a question of absolutes to define but rather an identification and appreciation of tendencies to describe, inform, and invite further inquiry and analysis. You may find that one group of statements applies fully, attracting all ten points. However, you may believe your organization is best described by elements of each or only some of them. In that case, divide your points proportionally, four to Group A and six to Group B, for example.

Group	10 Pts.	What best describes your organization?
A		A rational enterprise designed and structured to achieve predetermined end. Has routine operations, well-defined structure and job roles, and efficient working inside and between the working parts of the machine (the functional areas). Procedures and standards are clearly defined, and are expected to be adhered to.
B		Organizational politics is a reality. Building support for your approach is essential if you want to make anything happen. There is an important political map that overrides the published organizational structure. Coalitions between individuals are more important than work teams. The most important decisions in an organization concern the allocation of scarce resources (that is, who gets what), and these are reached through bargaining, negotiating, and vying for position.
C		The organization is a living, adaptive system. Congruence with the environment is the key to success. The organization is an open system with sets of interrelated sub-systems designed to balance the requirements of the environment with internal needs of groups and individuals. There is no one best way to design or manage an organization. The flow of information between different parts of the systems and its environment is key to the organization's success. It is important to maximize the fit between individual, team and organizational needs.
D		Form emerges. It cannot be imposed. Order naturally emerges out of chaos. No one is ever in a position to control or design system operations in a comprehensive way. Organizations have a natural capacity to self-renew. Organizational life is not governed by the rules of cause and effect. Key tensions are important in the emergence of new ways of doing things. The formal organizational structure (teams, hierarchies) only represents one of many dimensions of organizational life.

We all have our assumptions about how organizations work, developed through a combination of experience and education. Esther Cameron and Mike Green, in *Making Sense of Change Management,* build on the work of Gareth Morgan to offer an instructive approach using metaphors to illustrate how organizations work. The use of metaphor is an important way in which we can articulate our assumptions. The authors say:

> *Metaphor gives us the opportunity to stretch our thinking and deepen our understanding, thereby allowing us to see things in new ways and act in new ways ... Metaphor always creates distortions too ... We have to accept that any theory or perspective that we bring to the study of organization and management, while capable of creating valuable insights, is also incomplete, biased, and potentially misleading.*

Cameron and Green selected four of Morgan's eight organizational metaphors,[13] which they believe provide the most useful insights into the process of organizational change, to explore the range of assumptions that exist about how organizational change works.

Summarized in the groups of statements above they are: A) organizations as machines; B) organizations as political systems; C) organizations as organisms and D) organizations as flux and transformation.

What can be identified as the organization's institutional attitude, arising from frames of reference taken together with the characteristics best described by a particular metaphor, gives you a sense of the real organization.

An organization operates within that context, including initiatives to initiate, manage, and respond to conflict, change, and organizational life. Note that while individual employees may act differently, the organization as a whole can be characterized by its central philosophy and evidenced by its inclination to particular approaches or courses of action.

Unwritten Rules Inventory

Having examined frames of reference and considered how your organization works, now consider the words, actions, and decisions the organization makes and the congruity between written and unwritten rules.

Review the following questions.

What are your top unwritten rules? What does this say about the organization, how it works, and its employment value proposition?

---

13   Morgan (1986) distinguishes eight metaphors for organizations: machine, organism, brain, culture, political system, psychic prison, flux and transformation, and instrument of domination. Each metaphor highlights other aspects of organizational life.

- What gets rewarded? What gets punished?

- Does your organization promote based on seniority or productivity/results?

- Are people appreciated for bringing up tough questions or is this frowned upon?

- Is gossip an acceptable way to "get in" and "get up" within the organization?

- Are you recognized for the work you accomplish or the hours you work?

- Why do people get promoted?

- Who does the chief executive or executive team favour and why?

- What are the power dynamics in your organization?

- Is there an unofficial hierarchy that differs from the one contemplated by the organization chart?

- What are employees verbally appreciated for?

- Are employees measured on activities or results?

- Are new ideas from employees taken seriously by management?

- Who seems unfireable and why?

- What are the top three factors the chief executive says are important? Shows are important?

- Who benefits from the unwritten rules?

- Why do you think they're unwritten?

- Do you benefit from any of these rules?

- How long should you come to the office each day?

- If you aren't feeling well, is it okay to work from home?

- Do you need to show up on time to meetings or is it okay to be a few minutes late?

- What is a reasonable amount of time to respond to an email?

- Are there development opportunities and how are they accessed?

Power and Rules

To understand how rules operate, we need to know the power positions. But to know these, we must know the rules of the organization (written and unwritten, formal and informal).

> Organizations are political entities to the extent that individuals and groups have conflicting interests that they attempt to reconcile through political manoeuvring, bargaining, and the like.
>
> As a result, life in an organization requires the use of applied politics as employees navigate their way through the written and unwritten rules and personalities. They use social networks and, in some cases, power to influence changes that benefit the organization or individuals within it.

Influence by individuals may serve:

- **Strictly personal** interests, without regard to the effect on the organization, providing personal advantages that may include access to tangible assets, or intangible benefits such as status or pseudo-authority that influences the behaviour of others.

- The **organization and its members** simultaneously, resulting in increased effectiveness/efficiency, development of interpersonal relationships, expedited change, etc.

Power typically provides the capacity to make decisions, shape the agenda, bring about courses of action, and impose sanctions. It is an attribute of positions or roles rather than of individual personalities.

Power is something one has in relation to another and given the nature of organizations is unevenly distributed. Cynthia Hardy in the *British Journal of Management*, December 1996, "Understanding Power: Bringing about Strategic Change" sets out the following dimensions of power possessed by individuals:

- **Resource power:** The access to valued resources in an organization.

- **Process power:** The control over formal decision-making arenas and agendas.

- **Meaning power:** The ability to define the meaning of things.

The bases of power in an organization can be divided into two categories, formal power and personal power.

Formal Power

Formal power is the power conferred on a position by the organization and includes the following:

- **Coercive:** conveyed through fear of losing one's job, being demoted, receiving a poor performance review, having reduced status, or key responsibilities taken away, etc.

- **Reward:** conveyed through rewarding individuals for compliance with one's wishes; may be done through giving bonuses, raises, a promotion, extra time off, etc.

- **Legitimate:** comes from having a position of power in an organization, such as being the chief executive or a key member of a leadership team. This power comes when employees in the organization recognize the authority of the individual.

Personal Power

Personal power is based on an individual's personal traits and includes the following:

- **Positional:** Resides in the legitimate authority of the title and position; includes control and access to resources and the ability to formally reward or punish organizational members.

- **Network:** Results from the informal network of connections of people that permit them to access and pass on information.

- **Knowledge:** Comes from one's experiences, skills, or knowledge. As we gain experience in particular areas, and become thought leaders in those areas, we begin to gather expert power that can be used to get others to help us meet our goals. Knowledge power can be expert and/or information power.

    - Expert power is the possession of a body of knowledge essential to the organization; credentials provide independent certification of expertise and increase one's ability to influence.

    - Information power is influence gained through the flow of facts and data.

- **Personality or Referent:** Results from being trusted and respected. We can gain referent power when others trust what we do and respect us for how we handle situations. It is the ability to inspire trust and enthusiasm from others. Reputation, which comes from people's experience with the person, influences personal power

Remember, to understand the rules we must understand the power, to understand power we must know the rules...

Employment Relationships

Organizations function through relationships. Trust, which is a by-product of integrity and ethical conduct, is the foundation of those relationships.

Simply put, trust means confidence.

Confidence that others' actions are consistent with their words, that the people with whom you work are concerned about your welfare and interests apart from what you can do for them, that the skills you have developed are respected and valued by your co-workers and the larger organization, and that who you are and what you believe truly matter in the workplace.

In an employment contract, the terms and conditions of employment are hierarchical. Most employers understand their relationship with their employees as based on a simple employment contract, developed and amended from time to time by the employer. The employee is provided with a compensation package and certain other benefits, and in return they are expected to fulfil certain functions of the job, usually outlined in statements of expectations, job descriptions, manuals, and the like.

Beyond the employment contract committed to in writing, there is a psychological contract in place between the employer and employee. How the employment contract is administered has implications for the organizational culture and the degree to which an employee is engaged with their work.

Dissatisfaction with the terms and conditions of employment and erosion of the psychological contract leaves employees with two possible mechanisms of adjustment. They can withdraw from the relationship by quitting and seeking employment elsewhere, or they can use their voice to seek change.[14]

The voice mechanism implies that instead of opposing and evading the situation, individuals can, in an attempt to remedy the circumstance, express their concerns, endeavour to repair or improve the relationship through communication of the complaint, or make a proposal for change. Individuals can also use existing institutions to attempt to modify the situation. Inadequate or ineffective internal *voice* processes have potential consequences.

---

14   The concept of exit and voice was first developed by political economist Albert O. Hirschman in his 1970 book, Exit, Voice and Loyalty. Other scholars, such as R.B. Freeman and J.L. Medoff, place the exit and voice concept in a labour relations context

The use of existing institutions can lead employees to seek representation through unionization under labour relations statutes. The existence of a union creates an institutional relationship between a union and an employer and the consequential individual relationships that flow from the change to representative (union)-employer that places an employee's representative in workplace relations.

The collective agreement becomes the employment contract. Formal processes and structures such as on-site union representatives (*shop stewards*/staff representatives), union-management committees, the grievance procedure, and collective bargaining become the predominant voice mechanisms.

Figure 5 illustrates the psychological determinants of the propensity to unionize.[15] The determinants centre on perceptions—a way of regarding, understanding, or interpreting something—and individuals' beliefs.

Figure 5: Propensity to Unionize

Perceptions of work environment
    a. job dissatisfaction
    b. working conditions problems
    c. inequity perceptions

Perceptions of influence
    a. desired influence
    b. difficulty of influencing

Beliefs about unions
    a. image of organized labour
    b. expectations about unions

Propensity to Unionize

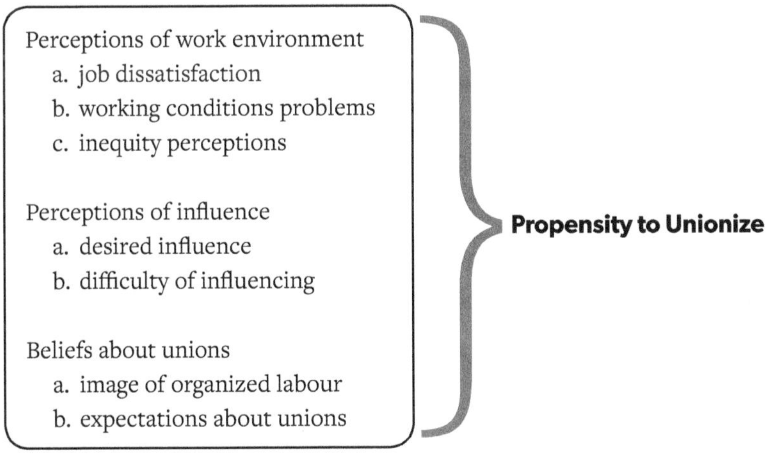

Perceptions may influence actions (exit and voice). Actions may include an investigation by an employee or employees of the value of union representation in their circumstance. The investigation may lead to unionization of the workplace.

Figures 6 and 7 summarize the transition from *employee relations* to *labour relations*[16] and the structure of the relationships that result.

---

15   Thomas Kochan, *Collective Bargaining and Industrial Relations* (Thousand Oaks, CA: Sage Publications, 1980).

16   While not common, an employer may voluntarily recognize the union as the exclusive bargaining agent. This process replaces the Labour Relations Board administered certification process.

Moving from employee relations to labour relations results in a new institutional relationship between the union representing the employer's employees and the employer. This change also has implications for individual work relationships as employees may have differing views on unions and unionization.

Figure 6: The Transition from Employee Relations to Labour Relations

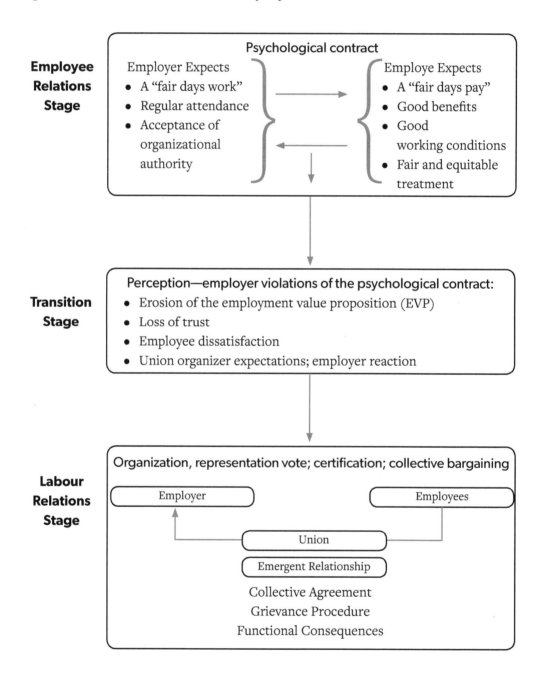

Figure 7: Interrelationship, Interdependence, and New Institutional Relationships

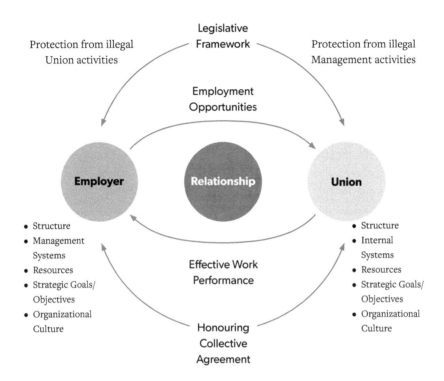

The passage of time plays a role in the transition to a new form of institutional relations. The transition from employee relations to labour relations may be a relatively new phenomenon, necessitating that employees grapple with the change to their current state. However, unionization may date back decades with current employees largely unfamiliar with the workplace events and circumstances that gave rise to unionization. The next section examines organizational philosophies and how union-employer relations evolve.

Organizational Philosophies

Frame of reference: The context, viewpoint, or set of presuppositions or of evaluative criteria within which a person's perception and thinking seem always to occur, and which constrains selectively the course and outcome of these activities. They govern how we think and who we are. Our behavior can be traced to these fundamental values.

Hunter, I.M. *Harper Dictionary of Modern Thought.* New York: Harper and Row, 1988, p. 330.

Our values are based on what we believe to be true about the world. These perceptions shape our attitudes, which in turn shape our behaviours. Over time, these attitudes and behaviours, reinforced through repeated use, shape our habits. Eventually, our habits shape our lives.

Organizations also have philosophies—sets of fundamental values that define how they operate and do business. These philosophies are central to shaping an organization's and an employee's frame of reference. These fundamental values are evident in each employee's words and actions, as well as in the systems developed by the organization.

The beliefs, perceptions, attitudes, and values of all the people in an organization form a culture that makes it unique. While the attitude or perspective of any particular member of an organization may deviate from the institutional pattern, if this perspective lacks sufficient power or political support within the organization, it will not affect the institutional attitude.

An organization's culture is central to understanding the values and beliefs about the legitimacy of its managerial authority and distribution of power. Each individual is socialized by experiences, which result in values and attitudes that come to be regarded as "the way we do things around here." These values are reinforced by the groups the individual moves within, such as people in similar positions and other employees.

> The frame of reference that individuals adopt affects their response to the problems they face—it determines their criteria for making judgements and filters information they receive. The frame of reference is grounded in their beliefs about how the workplace should be organized. Frames are metaphors[17] and conceptual frameworks that we use to interpret and understand the world. They give meaning to the words people hear more than the other way around, because words don't have objective meanings independent of these metaphors.

"A frame is a way of looking at the world that is value laden, and like a metaphor it conjures up all kinds of thoughts and emotions."[18] Frames structure people's thoughts and control the way people act and determine meaning. They are ultimately a blend of

17   A *metaphor* is a figure of speech that describes an object or action in a way that isn't literally true, but helps explain an idea or make a comparison.

18   James Hoggan, *I'm Right and You're an Idiot* (Gabriola Island: New Society Publishers, 2016), 49–50.

feelings, values, and data related to how people see the world.[19] Everything people say, the language they use, and their thoughts are controlled by frames.[20]

Many people hold a metaphor that accurately describes their perception of the organization in which they work. The metaphor also determines the way people perceive, remember, and analyze information they receive. However, any single metaphor limits people's perception by blocking and distorting the information encountered. Much of the conflict in an organization is caused by people holding different metaphors, oblivious to the fact they behave in accordance with their metaphor.[21]

Gibson Burrell and Gareth Morgan, in *Sociological Paradigms and Organizational Analysis*, identify three types of ideological frames—unitary, pluralist, and radical—central to an individual's approach to power and authority.[22] This classification represents the three main theories of workplace organization:

- **Unitary or Unitarist:** Society is seen as an integrated whole where the interests of the individual and society are one. Power can be largely ignored and assumed to be used benevolently by those in authority to further the mutual goals of all parties.

- **Pluralist:** Society is viewed as a place where different groups bargain and compete for a share in the balance of power; it realizes a negotiated order that creates unity out of diversity.

- **Radical (also referred to as critical or Marxist):** Sees society as made up of antagonistic class interests held together as much by coercion as by consent.

The authors observe that each distinct ideological frame engenders its own "structures and expectations" about how individuals respond to issues of power and conflict.

These ideological frames or theories of workplace organization can be used as a framework for understanding why employers approach unionization and unions in the workplace differently. The theories also provide insight into why it can be difficult to resolve workplace disputes and why collective bargaining can be challenging.

---

19   Ibid.

20   ibid.

21   Yair Hamburger and Udi Itzhayek, "Metaphors and Organizational Conflict," *Social Behavior and Personality* 26, no. 4 (1998), 383–398.

22   G. Burrell and G. Morgan, *Sociological Paradigms and Organizational Analysis* (Portsmouth, NH: Heinemann, 1979).

Figure 8: Interrelationship Between Frames of Reference, Ideology,[23] and Organizational Philosophies

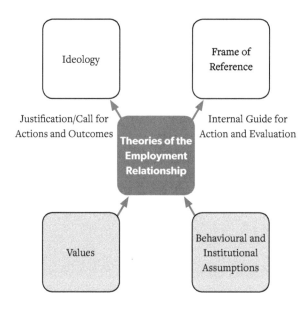

Unitarism

Unitarism is a model of managerial thinking that posits management and employees share the same interests and should work together towards mutual *objectives*. Unitarism rests on the assumption that the work organization is held together by a common ideology that unites all parties.

A unitarist approach implies that employees should have allegiance to only one authority, usually management. Under this approach, any other allegiances by employees, for example, to a union or other institution, are seen as detracting from their commitment to the employer. This approach, common among individuals in management positions, confers legitimacy on managerial authority and treats unions as unnecessary third parties whose presence upsets the "natural order" of the organization.

Unitarists assume that management and workers have cooperative attitudes and values, and often describe the two parties as a team, working together to achieve the organization's *mission* (its reason for being) and *vision* (its preferred future). According to this perspective, all people in an organization are working towards one goal, where

23   *Frame of reference:* how one sees the world; *Ideology:* how one wants others to see the world.

there is one sense of authority. While the two parties' interests may diverge from time to time, the resulting conflict will not be sustained owing to the unifying force of their mutual objective—the survival of the enterprise from which both earn their living.

Unitarism originated with the work of Frederick Taylor (1856–1915), who believed the only way a business can survive is to reduce costs and increase efficiency. According to Taylor's scientific management theory, workers become more productive when their jobs are broken down into simple tasks, and they are given the necessary training to complete these tasks. Employees are prepared to trade off the resulting changes in *working conditions* for the benefit of increased financial rewards. Taylor theorized that the relationship between management and workers is one of mutual interest, rather than inherent conflict. The success of the enterprise benefits both employer and employee.

Scientific management provided a sound theoretical approach, but assumed that workers behave as individuals and do not work together as groups of individuals. However, when workers perceive common workplace problems and act collectively, they can make demands that are inconsistent with the objectives of scientific management.

The unitarist theory was further influenced by the work of Elton Mayo (1880–1949), whose studies at Western Electric's Hawthorne Works in 1927 and 1932 led to the conclusion that workers' productivity is related as much to their motivations as to the scientific organization of work.

In human relations theory, work that is properly managed is an integrated and harmonious activity. Workers behave more rationally if they understand management's need for efficiency and effectiveness, and what management is trying to accomplish through a specific set of actions or initiatives.

The notion of a workplace free of employer-employee conflict emphasizes the following workplace features:

- consensus and workplace harmony

- socialization of individuals into a particular culture, such as a team culture

- respect for the employee

- final decision-making authority rests with management

- conformity with an agenda determined by management

Pluralism

Pluralism is a model that assumes management and employees are more likely to work in conflict than in harmony. The concept of collective bargaining is central to pluralism. Pluralism and collective bargaining rest on the belief that the employee's inferior economic position in relation to the employer makes a mechanism such as the individual employment contract an unsatisfactory way to determine the price for an individual's work.

In a unitarist workplace, management has the unilateral right to set the terms and conditions of employment. Pluralism assumes that the achievement of consensus and the resulting long-term stability in management–employee relations is the best way to resolve the competing interests of the parties. From a pluralist perspective, mechanisms and structures—such as collective bargaining to determine terms and conditions of employment and the grievance procedure to resolve disputes during the agreement's terms—are needed to vent and relieve conflict, rather than repress it and thereby harm the enterprise.

The state plays a major role in pluralist employment relations. If there is a balance of power between management and employees, and if collective bargaining is the mechanism for determining the rights and obligations of both the employer and the union, the state is responsible for ensuring that the rules governing such processes are exercised fairly.

The question invariably arises whether the collective bargaining process and the resulting collective agreement represent a balance from the perspective of both the employer and the union, or whether they are seen as out of balance, favouring the interests of one over the interests of the other.

Pluralist theory has six main assumptions:

1. Collective bargaining leads to the orderly, structured operation of union-management relations.

2. The interests of those involved in creating an organization's wealth and/or success can be balanced.

3. Collective bargaining improves worker consultation and communication.

4. Issues can be raised in a forum where the employer must address them.

5. The union is the best mechanism to represent the interests of employees.

6. The state plays the role of impartial arbiter between the parties.

Those with a pluralist frame of reference see the organization as made up of pluralities of interest groups with differing and sometimes competing interests, which may come together in alliances that shift and change as circumstances dictate. Whatever the long-term interdependence of the interest groups, in their day-to-day struggle for resources and in their operational activities, they assert sectional interests. The employer's role from this frame of reference is to balance the various interests to achieve the objectives of shareholders (and/or stakeholders), customers/clients, government, and employees.

Table 1: Unitarism and Pluralism Compared

Unitarism and Pluralism Compared	
Unitarism	**Pluralism**
• the right of the individual	• the right of the collective
• no inherent conflict between the interests of employees and employers	• inherent conflict of interest between employers and employees
• conflict is abnormal and a sign of bad management	• conflict is unavoidable
• unions are considered evidence of poor workplace relations as management has failed to communicate or provide appropriate leadership	• existence and function of trade unions accepted given the conflicting interest and the power imbalance
• unions encourage workers to perceive their relationship with management in terms of divergent goals: two sides	• presence of a union is evidence of good employment relations: union seeks to address the power imbalance
• emphasis on a family approach to work, mutual respect, open communication, and constructive problem solving; responsibility of the individual	• emphasis on collective bargaining, a belief in the balance of power, and the role of the state as an impartial arbiter
• a focus on leadership, communication, and the right to manage	• a focus on the institution of collective bargaining and ways of managing and institutionalizing conflict

Radicalism

The radical perspective provides a very different perspective than those of the unitarist and pluralist frames. Radicals argue that you can only understand the social relations among people at work by understanding the social, economic, and political relations of society. The structural separation between basic forms of ownership and those who are subject to this control creates irreconcilable differences between employers and workers.

Radicals do not see pluralism as a true attempt to create a balance of power. Although a collective bargaining scheme is clearly preferable to a unitarist model, the power and ownership right of the employer is marginally affected by this approach, and the benefits of collective bargaining are exaggerated. Unions become actors in the capitalist system, negotiating their role while permitting the capitalist ownership and decision-making capacities to remain unchanged. Radicals argue for a fundamental change in the current power structure.

From the radical perspective, the issue of control is at the centre. The radical perspective argues a political-economic philosophy that seeks to explain all aspects not only of work but also of society. Radicals argue that those who exert financial control over organizations form a dominant class in society, with their primary interest being the maintenance and extension of that control. Good employment relations, would thus require change in the basic form of ownership from this dominant class—from the powerful to the powerless. Radical ideologies favour system change.

Table 2: Assumptions About the Three Ideological Fames

Assumptions About....	Unitarism	Pluralism	Radicalism
Workplace relations	• management and employees share common interests • one source of legitimate authority: management	• managers and employees have different objectives • multiple sources of legitimate authority	• reflects a wider class conflict between capital and labour • reflects coercion of working class into dominant capitalist values

Workplace conflict	• abnormal: aberration, destructive, to be avoided • caused by poor management, communication, or dissidents/agitators	• inevitable: caused by different opinions and values; benefit to an organization • can be avoided by accepting union legitimacy and including union in decision making	• inevitable: capital seeks to reduce costs; workers seek fairer price for labour • will only cease by revolutionary change in the distribution of wealth/property
Unions	• competing and illegitimate source of authority • an unwarranted intrusion in the workplace • create conflict where none would otherwise exist	• not the cause of conflict • are expressions of diverse workplace interests that always exist • legitimate part of workplace relations	• should raise revolutionary consciousness of workers • should not limit improving material lot of workers • union leaders who accommodate management betray workers
Role of collective bargaining	• creates and institutionalizes unnecessary divisions of interest • serves to generate workplace conflict rather than resolve it • sows the seeds of and results in inefficiency and bureaucracy	• deals with problems on a collective basis • most efficient means of institutionalizing employment rules • fairer outcomes by balancing employee and employer power	• merely offers temporary accommodations • leaves important employer power intact • poor substitute for real change

Workplaces are an amalgam of perspectives. Although a unitarist manager may work alongside a radical union official or employee, usually one perspective dominates to form the common culture of the organization. The concept of central tendency is in evidence—the inclination to particular approaches or courses of action.

Unionization: Perspectives and Approaches

Employees seek union representation for a variety of reasons and employers react to the possibility of unionization and, if unionized, the reality of unionization in a variety of ways. How and why issues are pursued gives evidence of their perspectives concerning the existence and role of unions in a workplace. Those perspectives, informed by their frames of reference are embedded in their approaches.[24]

Employer approaches and strategies to union representation include:

- **Union acceptance strategy:** The employer views the union and the associated structures like collective bargaining and grievances processes as legitimate and appropriate for their organization and the employee–employer relationship; concerted efforts are made to create constructive, enduring relationships.

- **Union avoidance strategy:** The employer prefers to be non-union and has developed human resource policies and programs that, in their view, create no reason for employees to join or consider joining a union.

  This is sometimes referred to as *union substitution* or a proactive human resource management approach. Should the workplace be unionized, the employer adopts or defaults to an acceptance, suppression, or continued pursuit of a substitution strategy.[25]

- **Union suppression strategy:** The employer grudgingly accepts the presence of the union and its legitimacy. This is a strategy that adopts predominantly competitive, position based approaches to workplace issues, including collective bargaining.

  The employer goes about its affairs with little or no regard for the union and its role, and may adopt hard-ball tactics: for example, frustrating the successful *negotiation* of a first-contract post-certification, hoping that the modest outcomes will lead employees to consider decertification; or using replacement workers during strikes or *lockouts* and contracting work out, if legal. Each subsequent round of bargaining is positional and conflictual and is *normalized* to become the way it is.

- **Union substitution strategy:** The adoption of what the employer believes are proactive, positive, effective human resource management strategies with the goal of eliminating the desire among employees for a union.

---

24   G.E. Phillips, *Labour Relations and the Collective Bargaining Cycle* (Toronto: Butterworths, 1981).

25   Variants of this strategy include the union resistance strategy—seek to limit the spread of unionism to unorganized parts of the firm—and the union removal strategy, which seeks to eliminate unions where they exist in the firm.

This strategy is based on the proposition that employer processes, practices, and policies provide for a defensible and acceptable substitute for what unionization could provide.

When a labour relations board grants a union *certification*, the union becomes the sole and exclusive bargaining agent for the group of employees designated in the certification.

Labour legislation establishes a duty for unions referred to as the *duty of fair representation* that requires a union to represent all employees in the *bargaining unit*, whether or not they are union members, in a manner that is not arbitrary, discriminatory, or in bad faith.

Unions approach their responsibilities from a variety of perspectives, including:

- **Business unionism:** A union philosophy whereby the union recognizes that it is a business (the representation and advocacy business) and should be structured as such, and understands that it can only survive if it delivers needed services to members in a business-like manner. The usual focus of a business union is on producing constant and immediate improvements in the material conditions of member's lives—higher wages, competitive benefits, better working conditions, and job security.

- **Grass roots unionism:** A socio-political movement that is driven from the bottom up and is characterized by union locals having a high degree of autonomy. Issues that people themselves identify are the focus. The organization of non-union workers and the administration of collective agreements are consistent with general union values.

- **Social/reform unionism:** Unionism that attempts to integrate workers, unions, and the labour movement into a broader coalition for social and economic justice. Activity is directed at influencing the social and economic policies of governments, and workplace matters are tied to and integrated with larger social goals.

One description may not fit a union or employer perfectly. Remember, as noted before, unions, employers, and workplaces are an amalgam of perspectives in which one perspective usually dominates. The actions, reactions, and attitudes within that frame give evidence as to how we do things around here and why.

Unions and Their Members: Not All Are Created Equal

Unions are representative organizations and the lifeblood of any union is its membership. Simply put, unions have power because they are, in effect, amalgamations of the collective strength of their membership. Members' perceptions of their unions' effectiveness in obtaining both extrinsic and intrinsic benefits and the unions' responsiveness to the membership are evidenced by member participation in union activities.

The strength of a union depends, in part, on its ability to mobilize its members not only in strikes but also in policing the collective agreement, filing grievances, and serving in the capacity of union stewards or committee members. Satisfied, highly committed members are more likely to support their union in strikes or political activities and to assist in organizing campaigns. Further, satisfied members serve as living advertisements to members and the public generally of the advantages of union membership. The reverse occurs when member are unhappy.

Like all representative organizations, union members are varied shaped by their frames of reference. Review Organizational Philosophies in Part One: *Employment Preliminaries*, particularly the discussion of frames of reference.

Reflect on the union you are familiar with:

- Circle the **description** that represents the people you know, including yourself.

- What are the implications for the operation of the union and the management of the workplace, given the nature of the union's members?[26]

Extremely enthusiastic and loyal to the union; regards management as an *oppressor* and the union as a vehicle for class struggle.	Ideological Union Member
Extremely enthusiastic and loyal; regards management not as a class enemy but rather as an adversary at the bargaining table.	"Good" Union Member
Staunch supporter of unionism in general; differs from ideological and good union members in their attitude towards their local.	Loyal but Critical Member
Passive supporter of the union who generally allows other commitments to come before union activities; will participate in meetings and other union activities when a crisis develops in negotiations.	Crisis Activist Member

26   Adapted from G.E. Phillips, Labour Relations and the Collective Bargaining Cycle (Toronto: Butterworths, 1981).

Tends to hold the union in high regard and support its policies; develops a managerial point of view towards productivity, efficiency, and the operation of the workplace.	Dually Oriented Member
Does not have any strong feelings for or against unionism; joins the union because everyone else does; does not feel obligated to participate in or keep informed of union activities.	Indifferent Member
Forced to join the union against their will by legal requirements or social pressures; if given the opportunity, would readily revoke their union status.	Unwilling Unionist Member

Understanding Employment Relationships in a Unionized Setting

Collective bargaining is defined as a process whereby a union and an employer seek to negotiate a collective agreement, or the renewal or revision of an existing collective agreement; labour relations legislation generally requires the parties to bargain in good faith with a view to concluding a collective agreement.

> Beyond this basic definition, collective bargaining is also a process of "applied politics, a means to reach a result, namely, the resolution or suspension of competing interests for the length of time covered by the collective agreement.
>
> It is an opportunity for an employer and a union to discuss mutual problems, issues, concerns, and priorities, and to fashion appropriate compromises and solutions."[27]

Given the nature of this form of negotiation, relationships[28] are central and understanding relationships in the context of collective bargaining is essential.

This section makes core assumptions about union–management relationships—specifically, that they emerge over time, based on a particular set of factors and further,

27   John P. Sanderson, *The Art of Collective Bargaining*, 2nd ed. (Aurora, ON: Canada Law Book, 1989).

28   For the purposes of this section, a relationship is the meaning assigned by two or more individuals to their connectedness or coexistence. (Lewicki et al, *Essentials of Negotiation*, (McGraw-Hill Irwin, 2007), 194.)

that relationships are influenced by the mixed-motive nature of the relationship—in other words, a mixed-motive dynamic.[29]

The mixed-motive dynamic is largely driven by the *who of it all*. Who plays what role, who has influence, and who leads what and for what purpose? The interactions among those that comprise this composite are complex, multi-dimensional, and with the negotiated terms, subject to *ratification*.

> While the mixture of common and competing interests can be most evident in the relationship between the union and employer, there are multiple interest groups within the union (for example, groups representing specific skills or types of work, internal political structures) and within the employer (for example, line vs. staff functions, board members).
>
> Others with an interest in the workplace or sector (for example, associations, government, the public) also bring a mix of common and competing interests to their interactions with the union and the employer.
>
> As we examine relationships and collective bargaining structures, it is important to keep in mind the fluid nature of the mixed-motive dynamic and the influence it has on how the relationship emerges. This includes the functional consequences experienced by the workplace—operational implications, nature of conflict, disputes, and their disposition—that flow from the relationship.

The close personal interaction between a union and an employer that occurs during the bargaining process provides the opportunity for the parties to either build trust (and therefore move towards a more constructive, cooperative, and less conflict-laden relationship) or reinforce a traditional, predominantly unitarist view of union-employer relations (a relationship seen as inherently conflictual with a large measure of what are believed to be irreconcilable differences). This latter perspective has emerged as the default response given their perspectives concerning workplace authority, and it can be partly attributed to what we have come to believe negotiations are about: a competitive, positioning exercise.[30]

---

29   In contrast to the mixed-motive assumption, some scholars and practitioners operate from assumptions that employment relations are inherently and primarily conflictual in nature with a focus on the economic, social, or legal implications of conflict. Others operate from assumptions that employment relations are essentially cooperative with a focus on building consensus, shared vision, and the most effective organizational design. An exclusive focus just on conflict or just on cooperation will bring the risk of discounting the negotiated nature of change. (J. Cutcher-Gershenfeld, R.B. McKersie, and R.E. Walton. *Pathways to Change: Case Studies of Strategic Negotiations* (Kalamazoo: W.E. Upjohn Institute for Employment Research, 1995).

30   Authors Lewicki, Saunders, Barry and Tasa, in *Essentials of Negotiation* (Toronto, ON: McGraw-Hill Ryerson, 2017), 79, observe it is possible for negotiators to have "traditional" views of negotiation

In *A Behavioral Theory of Labor Negotiations: An Analysis of a Social Interaction System,* Richard Walton and Robert McKersie provide a useful framework to examine collective bargaining and employment relationships.

The authors offer the proposition that collective bargaining is a form of social negotiations—the deliberate interaction of two or more multi-faceted social units attempting to define or redefine the terms of their interdependence and which are comprised of four sub-systems, each with its own function for the interacting parties, internal logics, and identifiable set of instrumental acts or tactics. In social negotiations, the resolution goal can relate to the reconciliation of several values and can involve allocation of resources such as economic resources, power, or status symbols. The sub-systems described by the authors help us understand the complexity of collective bargaining and the employer-employee/union relationships that result after bargaining.

The first, **distributive bargaining,** functions to resolve pure conflicts of interest, the process of dividing up a resource or array of resources that parties have identified. It is the system of activities central to the attainment of one party's goals when they are in basic conflict with those of the other party. Characterized by position taking and positioning, it is bargaining in the strictest sense of the word.

The second, **integrative bargaining,** functions to find common or complementary interests and solve problems confronting both parties. It is instrumental in attaining objectives that are not, upon examination, in fundamental conflict with those of the other party. There is a potential for the parties' interests to be combined or elements incorporated in ways that create joint value. In other words, parties could join forces to achieve something together that cannot be achieved independently.

Integrative bargaining and distributive bargaining are both joint decision-making processes. These processes, however, are quite different and yet rational responses to different situations. A distributive negotiation involves dividing identified resources and is most often associated with a single issue in which one gains at the expense of the other. *Integrative potential* exists when the nature of a problem permits solutions that benefit both parties, or at least when the gains of one party do not represent equal sacrifices of the other.

When parties bargain collectively, there is more than one matter at issue. To varying degrees, each party values the issues differently, necessitating a measure of creative problem-solving to develop solutions. The solutions are not comparable to a fixed pie to be divided between the parties; rather, given the issues, interests, and *options* identified through discussions, an agreement can be crafted that is better for both parties than what they would have achieved through distributive bargaining.

---

that lead them to assume the distributive bargaining process is the only way to approach negotiations.

However, some bargainers approach collective bargaining as essentially a distributive exercise. This orientation may be grounded in their ideologies or social belief systems, bargaining experiences, or "just the way we see how negotiations are done!"

This approach leads negotiators to interpret bargaining interactions as inherently competitive and the dominant bargaining approach to be positional and distributive. They assume that their interests directly conflict with those of the other party ("if it's good for them, it must be bad for us") with the result that the negotiation becomes a debate over who gets what in relation to the fixed positions advanced.

Walton and McKersie identify the dilemmas inherent in reconciling the requirements of the two polar, yet interdependent, decision-making processes of distributive and integrative bargaining:

> The test of time has confirmed the usefulness of conceptualizing the dilemmas that arise between distributive and integrative bargaining because the tactical requirements of one sub-process are opposite of the other sub-process.
>
> If distributive bargaining is pursued too vigorously and/or at the wrong time, then a negotiator may gain a greater share, but a smaller set of joint gains, or worse, may generate an outcome in which both parties lose. Similarly, if the negotiator pursues integrative bargaining in a single-minded manner; for example, being totally candid and completely forthcoming with information, he or she can be taken advantage of by the other party. In practice, collective bargaining is a hybrid of sorts influenced by perspectives, personalities and practices. That said, wise negotiators realize that bargaining is about identifying or creating value and claiming value. The interrelationship between distributive bargaining and the integrative approach is discussed in detail in Chapters 5 and 6.

The third approach, **attitudinal structuring,** refers to the activities of union and management that affect the general attitude one party has towards the other—events and circumstances experienced by union and management and their reactions to them. The attitudes of each party towards the other, taken together, define the attitudinal relationship. Attitudinal structuring aims to influence the attitudes of the participants towards each other and to affect the basic bonds that relate the two parties they represent.

The three processes of distributive bargaining, integrative bargaining, and attitudinal structuring impact the reconciliation process that takes place between the union and the employer. During negotiations, another system of activities is in motion—***intra-organizational bargaining***. This form of internal negotiations is designed to achieve consensus within the union and within the employer with respect to the *what and how* of the negotiations.

Intra-organizational bargaining brings the expectations of the principals into alignment with those of the bargaining team and chief spokesperson so that bargaining between the union and management bargaining teams can occur. This approach has the function of achieving consensus within each of the interacting constituent groups on courses of action.

Intra-organizational bargaining is bargaining in a broader context. In a sense, the bargaining team, and, in particular, the chief spokesperson, is the recipient of two sets of demands—one from across the table and one from his or her own organization.

This circumstance results from conflict at two levels: differing aspirations about issues and differing expectations about behaviour and the conduct of negotiations.

Constituents hold a variety of interests and motivations. While they are not present during negotiations they are, to varying degrees, concerned with what happens at the bargaining table. The union negotiator faces unique challenges and is arguably subject to more organizational constraints than their employer counterpart.

Evolving Union–Employer Relationships

Union–management relationships develop over time. The attitudinal relationship between union and management is exclusive to those particular parties; given the nature of union-management relations, it is a continuing relationship. Does the relationship provide a foundation for productive bargaining through constructive *dialogue* and exchange of views?

Attitudes are fluid, changing with the dynamics of the union-management relationship. Given the sometimes-volatile nature of the relationship, however, and the potential for adversity, it usually takes considerable time to develop an attitude of confidence and mutual respect. Trust and confidence can collapse quickly, given a particular set of circumstances and the parties' actions and reactions to those circumstances.

Figure 9: Emergent Employment Relationships in a Unionized Environment

Four Major Factors (Attitudinal Relationship Factors)	• Acceptance of legitimacy of other party • Degree of trust • Degree of friendliness or hostility • Degree of competitiveness, individualism, cooperation
Pre-determined Factors (Antecedent Determinants)	• Basic personality disposition • Union-employer ideologies • External factors
Events/Circumstances (Attitudinal Structuring Activities)	• How the employees came to have union representation • Grievance and arbitration history • Administration of the collective agreement • Ongoing relations • Approach to workplace issues and dispute resolution
Emergent Relationship	• Conflict • Containment-Aggression • Accommodation • Cooperation • Collusion
Functional Consequences	• Operational implications • Nature of workplace disputes and their disposition • Implications for collective bargaining

Attitudinal Relationship Factors

Many factors shape the union-management relationship. Some factors are matters the parties have little or no control over. Others are variables that the parties do have some control over and which parties might attempt to vary so as to change their relationship.

Four main factors affect the relationship between union and management and can help us understand "why things are as they are."

Acceptance of legitimacy: The willingness of one party to accept the legitimacy of the other party in fulfilling the roles and objectives of the organization; the degree to which one party believes and demonstrates, through thought, word, and action, that the other party has a legitimate role to play.

Degree of trust: The degree to which the parties have a firm belief in the other party's honesty, integrity, reliability, and competence.

Prevailing attitude of friendliness, respect, or hostility: The degree to which the parties have cordial feelings towards one another; whether the parties, although not necessarily friendly towards one another, respect each other as individuals and the job they must do; or the degree to which the parties' relationship is one of hostility and bitterness—the parties develop an actual dislike or hatred for each other.

Prevailing attitude or motivational orientation and action: Tendencies towards each other, the degree of competitiveness, individualism, cooperation; whether the parties' attitudes are competitive—they evaluate each encounter as one of winning or defeating the other party and each side seeks to maximize their relative advantage over the other, even though in the process they may incur some sacrifice to their own interests. May be individualistic—each party pursues its own goals and objectives and ignores the other party in their pursuit of their objectives—or may be characterized as cooperative, where the parties actually work together in pursuit of common goals and objectives and each party is concerned about the other's welfare in addition to their own.

Predetermined Factors or Antecedent Determinants

Certain predetermined factors, also referred to as *antecedent determinants,* also influence the existing relationship pattern.

Basic personality of the key individuals in the relationship. The frame of reference the individuals hold that informs their decisions, actions, and reactions. Union and management leaders may have personalities that make them more or less friendly, trusting, and cooperative. Authoritarian personality types are typically more competitive, have lower levels of trust, and are less tolerant to the views of others.

The union-management ideologies or social belief systems. The prevailing social belief reflected in the organization. Review unitarism, pluralism, and radical frames of reference presented in Part One: Employment Preliminaries. The social beliefs of union and management leaders may also be important. Some employers have a predominance of individuals who do not believe in the legitimacy of unions (a unitarist ideology). Some union leaders may have a basic mistrust of the market system, which extends to resentment towards those in management positions.

External factors, including market forces, legislative initiatives, and technological developments. The implications that arise from the economic environment the employer faces might affect the relationship with the union. If the employer faces an economic downturn, increased competition, or demands for increased services without increased resources, there will be pressure to be more demanding of the union. The evolving legislative environment might affect the relationship. Technological innovation might also lead to hostility when the employer seeks to implement changes that threaten job security.

Actual bargaining experiences that the parties have shared, including how the parties negotiate resolution to workplace disputes. The relationship might also be affected by past experiences with collective bargaining. If either of the parties has had a negative experience with previous negotiations or the administration of a collective agreement, the relationship could be more hostile.

Someone who has had a decision challenged through the grievance process and experienced cross-examination at an arbitration hearing may have a particular view of what they see as the consequences of collective bargaining.

Events and circumstances experienced by both parties will also affect the nature of the relationship. These include the actions and reactions of the parties to workplace issues, how the parties resolve issues and disputes, collective bargaining experiences, and both what was achieved (the outcomes of bargaining) and how the outcomes were achieved (the process of bargaining). Experiences such as strikes or lockouts, legislatively imposed agreements, and the parties' reactions to them also contribute to shaping the relationship.

Emergent Relationships

Attitudinal relationship factors, certain predetermined factors (antecedent determinants), and the parties' actions/reactions in response to events (attitudinal structuring activities) taken together influence the relationship. Defined as the emergent relationship, it is a general characterization of the relationship between the parties.

The emergent relationship is illustrated through five models that help explain how parties approach collective bargaining, dispute management, and day-to-day relationships.

- **Conflict:** In the *conflict* model, the parties are in constant competition. The union vilifies the employer as a way of building itself up and the employer competes for the hearts and minds of its employees by disparaging, undermining, or ignoring the union.

Each party denies the legitimacy of the other party—the union's role as the exclusive representative of its members and the employer's responsibility for the management of the enterprise. The relationship is typified by distrust and, in some cases, even hatred. Management refuses to deal with the union whenever possible, and the union sees management as the enemy.

Containment-Aggression: In the *containment-aggression* model, the presence of the union and its legitimacy is accepted grudgingly by management—the law permits unionization and management accepts it, but does not necessarily like it! The parties have little respect for each other, and are suspicious and mutually antagonistic. The union is determined to extend its scope of influence, and the employer is determined to limit the union's scope of influence.

- **Accommodation:** In the *accommodation* model, while each party fully recognizes the legitimacy of the other party, they are still individualistic in their orientation in that they pursue their own goals, giving no thought or consideration to the goals of the other party. The parties have adjusted to each other and have evolved routines for performing functions and settling disputes.

Each party has a moderate amount of respect for the other party's officials and adopts a hands-off approach to the other's internal affairs. There is little competition for the allegiance of employees. Although they do not adopt an alarmist approach to every demand, the parties adopt what is described as "alert watchfulness."[31] The parties go about their business, interacting in a courteous but informal manner.

- **Cooperation:** In the *cooperation* model, both parties completely accept the other's legitimacy, and have developed a mutual trust and respect. While some interests of the parties are different, some are not.

When faced with a problem or negotiation, the parties engage in discussions in an attempt to clarify the matter at issue, or enlarge the range of alternatives so that the needs of both parties are addressed and met to the greatest extent possible. Discussions extend beyond typical issues such as wages and working conditions to issues such as productivity, organizational efficiency, and use of technology.

There is full respect for each other's organization and officials. The union accepts managerial success as being of concern to the union; management recognizes its stake in stable, effective unionism. The parties, while pursuing their own

31   Benjamin Selekmann et al., *Problems in Labor Relations*, 2nd ed. (New York: McGraw-Hill, 1958).

objectives, act in ways that strengthen the other organization. There is mutual trust and a friendly attitude between the parties.

- **Collusion:** In the *collusion* model, the parties form a coalition to pursue common, often illegitimate goals, inconsistent with their true mandate and statutory responsibilities. At times, the union will conspire with management in violation of the rights of their members. Collusion, depending on the degree, could constitute a breach of the statutory duty of fair representation.

When you examine the evolving union–management relationship, dominant bargaining and issues management approaches are often in evidence. In relationships characterized by conflict and containment-aggression, a positional, distributive bargaining stance is dominant.

As you move to relationships of accommodation, a greater degree of integrative bargaining is in evidence, and in relationships where the cooperation approach dominates, parties predominantly adopt an integrative approach.

The following schematic provides a useful summary of the emergent relationship model and its interrelated components.

Figure 10: Emergent Relationship Model

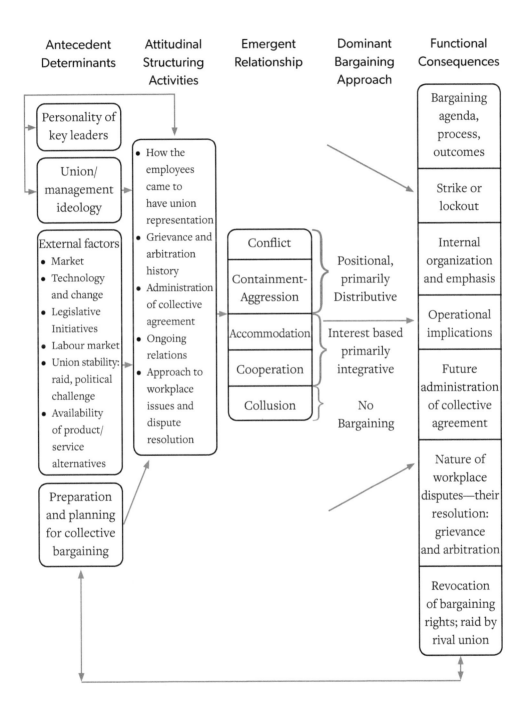

Emergent Relationship Quick Test[32]

Consider a union–employer relationship you have been part of or are familiar with. To evaluate the relationship:

1. Assess each of the four Main Factors in the first column—Legitimacy, Trust, Attitude and respect, Motivational orientation. Determine a rating for each factor on a scale of 1 to 4 that best describes the relationship. Use the descriptions to assist your analysis.

2. Sum these numbers and divide by four to determine an overall score.

In the following example, a rating for each factor has been circled, resulting in an overall rating of 2.75.

- What does the resulting score tell you about the central tendency of the relationship?

- Would the analysis differ when applied to individual vs. institutional relationships? Why?

- Would the analysis have produced a different result five years, three years, or one year ago?

- Remember, this is your perspective. How would a union representative rate the relationship?

Note: This is an adaptation of the Walton-McKersie *Emergent Relationship Model*[33] The use of a numerical scoring system is not part of the model and is used for discussion purposes only.

32   Although there are five models, collusion is not included in the quick test because it is not bargaining or a relationship in the same sense as the other four.

33   Adapted from R.E. Walton and R.B. McKersie, *A Behavioral Theory of Labor Negotiations: An Analysis of a Social Interaction System* (New York: McGraw-Hill, 1993), 208.

50

The Quick Test

Main Factors	Conflict	Containment–Aggression	Accommodation	Cooperation
Legitimacy	Denial 1	Grudging acknowledgement 2	Acceptance of status quo (3)	Complete 4
Trust	Extreme distrust 1	Distrust 2	Limited trust (3)	Extended trust 4
Attitude and respect	Hatred 1	Antagonism (2)	Neutralism courteousness 3	Friendly and respectful 4
Motivational orientation	Competitive tendencies to destroy or weaken 1	Competitive tendencies to destroy or weaken 2	Individualistic (3)	Cooperative tendencies to assist or preserve 4
2.75				

Part Two: Conflict and Work

Conflict is a form of friction, disagreement, or discord arising within a group when the beliefs or actions of one or more members of the group are either resisted by or unacceptable to one or more members of another group; a disagreement when people (or other parties) perceive that, because of a disagreement, there is a threat to their interests.

> Conflict is a human resources reality, and it exists in every organization. While to a certain extent, conflict indicates the presence of a healthy exchange of ideas and creativity, it can also be destructive and has implications for both employee and organizational effectiveness.
>
> As a human resources professional, it is your responsibility to identify and manage conflict within the workplace. By developing your skills in effective conflict management, you can help position yourself as a valuable leader in your organization

Conflict management is the practice of being able to identify and handle conflicts fairly, effectively, and efficiently. Since conflicts are a natural part of the workplace, it is important that there are people who understand conflicts and know how best to resolve them.

> Many people have negative attitudes towards conflict and try to avoid it at all costs. Peace and harmony are held up as ideals. Yet the desire for peace and harmony often represents a desire that others will hold our same values, interests, and needs.
>
> Paradoxically, this kind of thinking generates conflict, since it does not allow for real differences in needs and interests among individuals, systems, and cultures.
>
> The desire to remain in a single state, even a peaceful one, is unrealistic. Life is not static, and everything changes and develops. The attempt to keep change from occurring creates its own dynamics for conflict. Conflict is inevitable; how we respond influences our experience. Phases of conflict are as natural as phases of peace and harmony; however, all are temporary states.[34]

Workplace conflict is a form of interpersonal conflict. It is an expressed struggle between at least two interdependent parties who perceive that incompatible goals, scarce resources, and/or interference from the other party are preventing them from achieving their goals.

---

34   K. Haddigan, *Conflict Resolution* (JIBC, 1999).

Finding strategies to identify, understand, and manage conflict effectively are central to organizational success. It is often the role of the human resource practitioner to discern when a conflict is a normal part of the work day and work relationships or whether there is a need to engage an alternative method of inquiry/resolution and/or refer the matter to a more formal conflict or dispute resolution policy and/or procedure.

Potential benefits of conflict include:

- increases awareness of what problem situations exist

- motivates organizational members to consider problems

- enhances morale and cohesion

- leads to high-quality decisions if conflict is discussed openly

- stimulates interest and creativity

- legitimizes people's interests

- strengthens relationships

- promotes change

Change can be defined as *a process of causing a function, practice, or thing to become different somehow compared to what it is at present or what it was in the past.* Change can be characterized as either minor or major.

Minor changes are typically periodic adaptations and modifications of a function, practice, or thing focussed on improving the current state.

In contrast, major change is generally the result of significant disruption in established expectations, and occurs when people believe they have lost control over some important aspect of their lives or their environment. A loss of control is when expectations are out of sync with reality as the individual knows it to be.

The difference between major and minor change is one of perception. Change is considered major when it is perceived to be so by those affected. Whether major or minor, change necessitates management. Conflict that is not managed inappropriately can:

Cause high levels of tension among the members of a group; may create anxiety, uncertainty, hostility, and frustration.

- Result in escalation if conflict responses are unplanned.

- Lead to increased employee absenteeism, *presenteeism,* and/or turnover.

- Increase employees' dissatisfaction, low levels of engagement, and reduced productivity.

- Engender distrust among employees; lead to costly disputes such as grievances and litigation.

- Erode the psychological contract (employee relations) or cause a shift in the emergent relationship (labour relations), with implications for the *employment value proposition.*

- Distract from organizational goals and purpose.

- Create an unflattering perception in the eyes of employees and the labour market of the organization as a good place to work, with implications for recruitment, retention, and engagement.

Conflict may be viewed as occurring along **cognitive (perception), emotional (feeling), and behavioural (action) dimensions.** This three-dimensional perspective can help us understand the complexities of conflict and why a conflict sometimes seems to proceed in contradictory directions. Several common cognitive and emotional traps, many of them unconscious, can exacerbate conflict.

- **Self-serving fairness interpretations.** Rather than deciding what's fair from a position of neutrality, we interpret what would be most fair to us and then justify this preference on the basis of fairness.

- **Overconfidence.** We tend to be overconfident in our judgement, a tendency that leads us to unrealistic expectations.

- **Escalation of commitment.** This is the tendency to irrationally escalate commitment to a chosen course of action, long after it has proven useful. We desperately try to recoup our past investments in a dispute (such as money spent on legal fees), failing to recognize that such sunk costs should play no role in our decisions about the future.

- **Conflict avoidance and the practice of *lidism.*** This takes the form of measures aimed not to address the underlying issues but to keep the lid on. Because negative emotions can cause discomfort and distress, we may try to minimize them, hoping that our feelings will dissipate with time. In fact, conflict tends to become more entrenched, and parties have a greater need for conflict reconciliation, when they avoid dealing with their strong emotions.

Part Two: *Conflict and Work* is based on the following ideas, which focus on skills and strategies displayed by good managers of conflict and incorporate integrative potential, reconciliation of interests, and recognition of value. As such, conflict management requires a combination of analytical and people skills.

Good managers of conflict focus on the source of conflict, and to resolve it permanently, they address the cause of the conflict and not just its symptoms. They concentrate on building an atmosphere designed to reduce destructive conflict and deal with routine friction and minor differences before they become unmanageable.

Good conflict managers seek to and understand the organization, the real organization—its culture and shadow culture and its written and unwritten rules—and are *historically alert* (they understand the organization's history and how relationships have evolved) and *contextually grounded* (the frame in which events occur).

In conflict situations, there is a tension between behaviours: those that are competitive and those that are cooperative/collaborative. When a situation contains integrative potential,[35] one should adopt a cooperative, constructive orientation: seek and exchange information, attempt to understand the other parties' interests and search for solutions that reconcile the interests of all parties.

Reconciliation of interests involves creating value to facilitate problem-solving, creating packages of matters to maximize value and finally claiming value to conclude the matters at issue. Effective conflict managers instinctively know to use integrative strategies to identify/create value and deploy distributive strategies to claim it.

Processes to create value should precede those to claim value. Every negotiation has the potential to require distributive skills when at the claiming value stage. Processes to create value are effective when done collaboratively and without a focus on who gets what. And, claiming value involves distributive bargaining processes that must be introduced carefully so as not to harm the relationship and derail the progress made to date.

Part Two offers *one* approach to understanding and managing workplace conflict—it does not present *the* approach. Readers are encouraged to continue broadening their understanding of managing workplace conflict by applying the ideas and tools presented here, reflecting on theory in practice and their own further research.

35   Refers to the potential for the parties' interests to be combined in ways that create joint value. Potential for integration only exists when there are multiple issues in the negotiation and parties are able to make trade-offs and/or meet priorities across issues for both sides to be satisfied with the outcome. Positional bargaining, in contrast, is based on fixed, opposing viewpoints (positions) and tends to result in compromise or no agreement at all.

Chapter 1: A Primer on Conflict

Scholars' Views

There are three general schools of thought relating to *conflict:* the traditional view, the human relations view, and the interactionist view.[36] The *traditional view* of conflict (first developed in the late 1930s and early 1940s) assumes that all disagreement is harmful and should be avoided.

The *human relations* view (which emerged in the late 1940s and predominated through the 1970s) is also referred to as the behavioural, contemporary, or managed view. It argues that conflict is a natural occurrence in all groups and, as such, it should be managed and not eliminated.

The latest, the *interactionist* view, proposes that conflict can be a positive force in a group and explicitly argues that some conflict is necessary for a group to perform effectively. According to the interactionist view, conflict can be functional or dysfunctional. Functional conflict supports the goals of the group and improves it performance while dysfunctional conflict hinders group performance. The interactionist view is the one that will be used throughout Part Two: *Conflict and Work.*

With these three schools of thought in mind, consider the following scholars' views about conflict:

> Conflict is the interaction of interdependent people who perceive incompatible goals and interference from each other in achieving those goals. (Joseph P. Folger, M. S. Poole, & R. K. Stutman, *Working Through Conflict,* 1993)

> A conflict exists whenever incompatible activities occur . . . one party is interfering, disrupting, obstructing, or in some other way making another party's actions less effective. (Morton Deutsch, *The Resolution of Conflict,* 1973)

> Social conflict is a struggle between opponents over values and claims to scarce status, power and resources. (Lewis Coser, *The Functions of Social Conflict,* 1956)

> Conflicts that are strategic are essentially bargaining situations in which the ability of one participant to gain his ends is dependent on the choices or decisions that the other participant will make. (Thomas Schelling, *The Strategy of Conflict,* 1960)

---

36   See Rawaf Khaiyat, "Differences among the three views of Organizational Conflict," *International Journal of Scientific and Engineering Research* 7, no.4 (April 2016).

Conflict means perceived divergence of interest, or a belief that the parties' current aspirations cannot be achieved simultaneously. (Dean Pruitt & Jeffrey Rubin, *Social Conflict, Stalemate and Settlement*, 1986)

Conflict occurs within cooperative as well as competitive contexts; conflict parties can hold cooperative or competitive goals. (Dean Tjosvold, van de Vliert, E., *Mediation Quarterly*, 1994)

Well-managed conflicts can lead to better decisions, improve social cohesion, stimulate innovation, and increase morale. (Dean Tjosvold, *The Conflict Positive Organization*, 1990).

Workplaces function through relationships and relationships have their share of conflicts both functional and dysfunctional. Conflict management is not about *just getting along* for the sake of the relationship. Consider Fisher and Brown's observations concerning *good* relationships.

> At the outset, we need to clarify what we mean by a "good" relationship. What each of us wants from a relationship varies greatly. But whether I hope, through my relationship with you, to gain love, money, security, or something else, we are bound to face conflicting interests, perceptions, and values.
>
> Differences are inevitable. And we will not get to what we want unless we can handle those differences. In each of our relationships, whether between individuals, businesses, religious groups, or governments, we should seek to establish and maintain those qualities that will make it a good "working" relationship—one that is able to deal well with differences. (Roger Fisher, Brown, S., *Getting Together, Building Relationships as We Negotiate*, 1988).

Conflicts

Conflicts are inevitable, constructive or destructive, and potentially beneficial, if appropriate management strategies are used. Conflicts can exist without disputes, but disputes do not exist without conflict. Disputes are merely a by-product of conflict. They are the outward articulation of conflict.

Conflict can have a positive side: it can promote *collaboration*, improve performance, foster creativity and innovation, and build deeper relationships. The more skilled individuals are in handling differences and change without creating or getting involved in conflict, the more successful their teams and organizations will become.

Conflict exists in every workplace; however, if it doesn't turn into a dispute, it might not be so easily noticed.

Typical disputes can come in a variety of forms, including disagreements specific to particular issues, arguments, threats and counter threats, grievances filed pursuant to a collective agreement, or formal proceedings such as *arbitration* and litigation.

Conflicts originate with people, and different relationships can result in similar and different types of conflict, depending on each situation.

Conflict and Positions

In conflict, a *position* is a stance taken on an issue and what we assert we want as an outcome. A position is typically a simple statement and can come across as a demand. Positions are defended and there can be a "rightness" of a view that is defended vigorously and which typically does not consider other parties' perspectives. A position be perceived as an all or nothing view.

Conflict and Interests

Every conflict involves *interests.* Interests are the things that people want to satisfy or achieve in a conflict situation, the reasons a party takes a particular stance on an issue or demands something. There is a rationale as to why the interests are important and other parties may be taken into account. Positions can be reframed into interests by focussing on which interests underlie a position and answering either of the following questions:

- "**Why** do you want that?" [37] or

- "**Why** do you feel that way?"

Interests include positive and negative objectives, needs, desires, concerns, fears, aversions, and the like. They may be substantive, procedural, or relational in nature:

- *Substantive interests* include objective interests (which are tangible, quantitative, and rational) and subjective interests (which are intangible, qualitative, and emotional).

- *Procedural interests* are those related to the quality of the process of achieving an acceptable outcome or selecting objective standards of legitimacy and fairness (i.e., negotiators not only want to achieve a fair outcome, but they also want to feel they were treated fairly in getting there).

- *Relational interests* are those pertaining to the strength, nature, and type of both individual relationships (between individuals or groups of individuals)

---

37   For observations on interests, see Lewicki, et al., *Essentials of Negotiations,* 3rd ed. (Toronto, ON: McGraw-Hill Ryerson, 2017), 63.

and institutional relationships (between, for example, representatives of the employer and representatives of the union).

Further observations on interests:

- There may be more than one type of interest at stake (substantive, process, or relationship), based on intangibles such as principles, standards the parties wish to adhere to, informal norms by which they will negotiate, or benchmarks that will guide them.

  Note that interests as principles may cut across the other three types so that the categories are not necessarily exclusive.

- Sometimes we are not sure of our own interests.

- Parties can differ on the types of interests at stake.

- Interests are often based on deeply rooted human needs or values.

- Powerful interests are basic human needs—security, economic well-being, a sense of belonging, recognition, and control over one's life.[38]

- Interests can change over time.

There are a number of ways to identify, clarify, and understand interests.

Issues in Conflict

An issue is a matter, point, subject or something people are thinking and talking about. Imbedded in issues are people's interests.

Another way to look at conflict is to decide the relative importance of the issue and to consider the extent to which priorities, principles, relationships, or values are at stake. There are three types of *issues* in any conflict: substantive, procedural, and relation-ship. Note that interests are at the centre of the three.

38   Abraham Maslow (1908-1970) was an American psychologist who was best known for cre-ating Maslow's hierarchy of needs, a theory of psychological health predicated on fulfilling innate human needs in priority, culminating in self-actualization. Maslow stated that people are motivated to achieve certain needs and that some needs take precedence over others. Our most basic need is for physical survival, and this will be the first thing that motivates our behavior he posited. Once that level is fulfilled the next level up is what motivates us, and so on.

Figure 11: Issues in Conflict

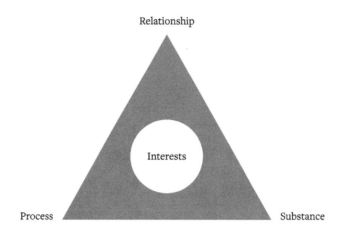

- *Substantive issues* are the concrete content of the conflict and are directly related to the matters at issue—the *what*. For example, level of performance.

- *Procedural issues* are related to the manner, process, and procedures used to settle the matters at issue and are how we talk to and treat each other—the *how*.

- *Relationship issues* are the matters pertaining to the relationship (power, legitimacy, respect) at the individual level (between individuals or groups of individuals) and the institutional level (between, for example, representatives of the employer and representatives of the union).

Conflict, Perception, Influence, and Communication

The way individuals communicate and influence each other underpins conflict and conflict management. We influence and respond with communication that is typically based on our thoughts and feelings, which are a result of our perceptions, values, and beliefs. In conflict, feelings are facts to the person experiencing them, and when we feel threatened we tend to react with blame and self-defence rather than with attempts to understand.

Perception

To communicate and influence others more effectively, you must first change your perception of them. Perception is a way of regarding, understanding or interpreting something. It is individual to each person and while some people may share a mostly common perception of an event, there will always be some subtle differences. Often, people will have different perceptions of what occurred based on their assumptions, expectations, experience and history.[39] Your biased, subjective, personal perceptions of people have the effect of programming how you communicate and seek to influence them, because perceptions determine how you feel, how you communicate, and how you behave.

If you do not first change your perception of the person with whom you want to communicate and influence, trying harder will probably only reinforce your preconceived feelings and behaviour.

People respond to their perceptions as if these are their reality; your perceptions may lead you to a different reality.

- To be understood, you must be sensitive to the perceptions of the person you want to influence. People filter others' communication through their own one-sided, limited, preconceived perceptions.

- To communicate and influence others, listen to understand their perspective or point of view. You do not have to agree or disagree with, or like or dislike their perspective. Simply attempt to understand it. This listening for understanding suspends judgement on your part and enables you, in turn, to seek to be understood.

Being open to understanding how others perceive a conflict and to adjusting our own perception when new information is received is key to managing conflict with others.

Assumptions

An assumption is something that you suppose or assume to be the case without proof. As human beings, we often make assumptions. At any given time, you can only see part of the whole puzzle of positions, interests, options, and intentions. To be constructive, think through your assumptions and verify your perceptions against realities (i.e., demonstrable evidence).

39   Adapted from mediator, trainer Joseph Favick, Human Rights and Equity Services, Dalhousie University, Halifax, Nova Scotia, 2018.

When presented with a problem or faced with a particular circumstance consider the assumptions you are making. Ask yourself:

- What are your assumptions?

- Are they important enough that you need to clarify what you have assumed with the other party?

- What key phrases from the other party should you listen for that might lead you to question your assumptions?

- Are you really suspending judgement?

Influence

How much influence you have is determined by how well you communicate. Personally, and professionally, your relationships with others determine the quality of your living. How well you communicate determines how well you interrelate with others and how much influence you have.

People do not care how smart you are if they cannot benefit from your intelligence. Human beings do not lack for great ideas; they lack for great ideas that are understood and put to use. Therefore, how well you communicate your ideas determines how well others understand and use them.

Communication

In communications, it is key to understand that *how* you say something communicates and influences people more than *what* you say. Your tone of voice and body language have been shown to communicate more than your actual words.[40]

For example, actions like raising your eyebrows, rolling your eyes, and shrugging your shoulders convey way more than your words.

Effective communication requires a considered, reasoned approach. It is more than talking and reacting! Effective communication includes:

---

40   In the book *Silent Messages* (1971) psychologist Albert Mehrabian wrote of his research on non-verbal communications, the results of which are still often quoted today. He found that communication, on a face-to-face basis, consists of three separate elements.

Words (the literal meaning) account for 7%, Tone of voice accounts for 38% and Body Language accounts for 55% of the overall message. Further, Mehrabian concluded that when words and non-verbal messages are in conflict, people believe the non-verbal.

- Being self-aware: Be aware of your own behaviour, emotions, and intentions; be aware of the other person's behaviour and emotions; and be aware of the nature of the other person's responses in comparison to your intentions. Are you getting the response you intended? If not, change your choice of behaviour and try again.

- Using self-discipline: Exercise self-control and control your emotions.

- Suspending judgement and disciplining your word choices to avoid positional language and specific outcome engendering statements.

- Listening and acknowledging: Choose to listen and acknowledge that you understand the other person's point of view (this does not mean you agree with it).

- Engaging in conversational turn-taking: Commit to follow conversational ground rules, conventions, and protocols, and take turns talking and listening.

- Shifting the time focus: Ask questions and make statements that put the time focus on the present instead of the past (e.g., "If I did X, would you be willing to do Y?").

- Using "I" and "we" declaratory statements instead of "you" accusatory statements.

- Taking responsibility for what you are saying and holding others responsible for what they are saying. Don't hide behind or let others hide behind *We*, speak in terms of I and press others to do the same.

- Beginning problem-solving: Encouraging the free flow of information. Don't worry or argue about who was right or wrong, or who is to blame. Diagnose what kind of negotiation situation this is, and begin trying to find a feasible way to solve the problem.

Certain approaches can exacerbate conflict and need to be top of mind when developing a considered, reasoned approach:

- Judging or criticizing, blaming, name-calling: Focussing on their fault(s) instead of your feelings.

- Acting superior or condescending: Putting yourself above others and distancing yourself from others' experiences.

- Defending or excuse-making, justifying, rationalizing: Attempting to make yourself "right" when others disagree with you or give you feedback or criticism.

- Ordering or convincing, suggesting, demanding, pressuring, manipulating: Trying to make someone change, think, feel, or behave the way you want them to.

- Arguing or debating, disagreeing, attacking: Pushing your own point of view without really listening to or integrating someone else's, or listening to find fault.

- Diagnosing or interpreting, assuming, mind-reading: Assuming an understanding of another person's motives or intentions.

- Deflecting or diverting, avoiding: Discounting another's feelings or experience, trying to make the problem disappear or claim it does not exist.

- Placating: Pleasing, even when you disagree; keeping conflict away by compromising self.

- Stockpiling: Collecting grievances and then using them as ammunition, building up resentment, continually revisiting the past.

- Being right: Closed to other ideas, opinions, feedback, and criticism; can't be wrong.

Power as a Factor in Conflict

Power can be defined as the degree to which we are able to advance our own goals and to influence the ability of others to meet their goals in a given conflict.

Power is largely a matter of perception and it is not something we own. Rather, it is about how we perceive our own power and how others perceive our power. Each person in a conflict approaches the other with an idea of the degree of power each person has.

Perceptions of the power relationship may differ and, as a result, the actual power relationship may play out quite differently than expected. If your power source is of no consequence or importance to the other person, it will not be effective.

Power is dynamic rather than static. The power relationship between people in conflict shifts throughout the conflict as the parties evaluate, test, and re-evaluate power base(s) and strategies. The power relationship can shift in one exchange or action. How much power do you have relative to the other person?

A person's effectiveness depends on actual access to power sources, self-awareness of power sources, and their ability to use power effectively.[41]

Power is often defined as a lack of dependence on others. This corresponds to one's alternatives. If an individual has credible alternatives when addressing a matter, they are less dependent on the other party to reach an agreement than they would be if they had a weak alternative or no alternative at all.

Some positions, roles, and titles grant power simply due to the authority or control they exert over a wide range of important outcomes. This type of power, referred to as *role power,* is often found in organizational hierarchies.

It is possible for you to have a psychological sense of power even when you lack objective power. Professor Cameron Anderson of the Haas School of Business at the University of California, Berkeley, has shown that although people differ in the degree to which they feel psychologically powerful in the world, they can create a temporary sense of power.[42]

How Power as a Factor Works in Conflict

Power is central to conflict. As soon as the features or needs of one person impact another person, conflict emerges and power dynamics come into play. People can use their power constructively or destructively to attain their goals.

Constructive uses of power are those that tend towards de-escalating the conflict. Destructive uses tend towards escalation.

Simple disagreements that escalate into conflicts are often really about power. The particular matter at issue may be minor, although the intensity of the conflict may be great. However, since power is something we tend not to talk about explicitly, the focus usually stays on the specific dispute. Until the power conflict is resolved, many other matters between the parties will contain the same power problem.

Power is often associated with aggressive, positional behaviours such as forceful, pointed rhetoric, insults, and raised voices. However, power can be used cooperatively. Aggressive behaviours are usually attempts to gain power in relation to the other person. Aggressive behaviour may also be reflective of a feeling of powerlessness. Unfortunately, these behaviours escalate conflict and create an adversarial atmosphere.

41   M. Deutsch, *The Resolution of Conflict: Constructive and Destructive Processes* (New Haven: Yale University Press, 1973).

42   See C. Anderson, and A. Galinsky, "Power, optimism, and risk-taking," *European Journal of Social Psychology* (Hoboken, NJ: John Wiley and Sons, 2006).

Sources of Power

The bases of power in an organization can be divided into two categories: formal and personal.

Formal power is:

- **Coercive:** Conveyed through fear of losing one's job, being demoted, receiving a poor performance review, having reduced status, or having prime projects taken away, etc.

- **Rewarding:** Conveyed through rewarding individuals for compliance with one's wishes; may be done by giving bonuses, raises, a promotion, extra time off from work, etc.

- **Legitimate:** Comes from having a position of power in an organization, such as being the chief executive or a key member of a leadership team. This power comes when employees in the organization recognize the authority of the individual.

Personal power is:

- **Expert:** Comes from one's experiences, skills, or knowledge. As we gain experience in particular areas, and become thought leaders in those areas, we begin to gather expert power that can be used to get others to help us meet our goals.

- **Referent:** Comes from being trusted and respected. We can gain referent power when others trust what we do and respect us for how we handle situations.

Whether formal or personal, because power is so subjective, it may come from almost any source the parties consider important. The following are some of the many categories from which power can be drawn.

- **People:** Includes numbers, allies, members, supporters, associates, and predominance of same.

- **Personal:** Size, voice, age, gender, personal qualities, skills, knowledge, ethnicity, sexual orientation, abilities and disabilities, and style.

- **Economic:** Accumulated wealth, access to and use of resources.

- **Authority or role:** Organizational, social, or professional status.

- **Status quo:** Law, custom or tradition, societal standards, organizational norms.

- **Social or moral values:** Accepted social/cultural values, religious beliefs, individual values and beliefs.

Each of these power sources can be used in cooperative or adversarial ways. In general, the perceived desirability of these power sources by disputants will determine whether they result in an effective use of power.

Increasing the quantity and quality of power sources can increase one's overall power. Power is rarely, if ever, balanced. It is a dynamic quality that shifts over the course of interactions with each person drawing power from different sources.

Used with permission, The New Yorker Collection/The Cartoon Bank 2017, by Mike Twohy.

Chapter 2: The Five-Stage Conflict Process

Conflict does not appear suddenly and without rational explanation. The Five-Stage Conflict Process[43] is a helpful framework for understanding task-focussed or cognitive conflict.[44]

If you can situate where the group or an individual is in the process, you can predict where it will likely go next and consider ways to best manage the conflict. The five stages are antecedent factors, awareness/emotion, intentions, behaviour, and outcomes.

Figure 12: The Five-Stage Conflict Process

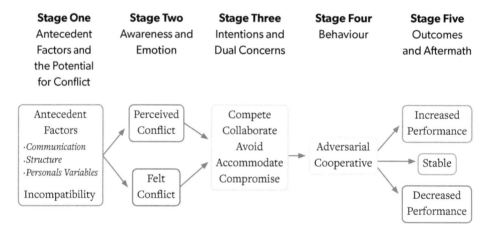

Stage One: Antecedent Factors and the Potential for Conflict

Stage One involves the emergence of potential opposition or incompatibility. It includes the presence of a condition that creates opportunities for conflicts to arise. The conditions that can cause conflict are associated with communication, structure, and personal variables.

---

43   Adapted from Louis R. Pondy, "Reflections on organizational conflict," *Journal of Organizational Behavior* 13, no.3 (1992): 257–261; Louis R. Pondy, "Organization Conflict: Concepts and Models," *Administrative Science Quarterly* 12, no. 2 (1967): 296–320.

44   **Task-focussed or cognitive conflict** is where people focus on the tasks or issues and debate and, through give and take, sort these out and come to creative solutions. The parties might argue and exchange views vigorously yet there is two-way communication and an openness to hearing each other. In contrast, **relationship or affective conflict** is where the differences become personal, where people get into blaming modes and unhelpful behaviours. The mindset moves from "we have a problem" to "you are the problem." Opposition is seen as something to be prevented rather than explored. Negative emotions prevail and the relationship suffers.

- Communication
  - ○ Insufficient exchange of information
  - ○ Semantic difficulties
  - ○ Misunderstandings
- Structure
  - ○ Size and specialization of jobs
  - ○ Jurisdictional, authority clarity
  - ○ Member/goal incompatibility
  - ○ Leadership and working styles
  - ○ Dependence or interdependence of individuals, groups
- Personal variables
  - ○ Differing individual value systems and frames of reference
  - ○ Personality types

Table 3: Origins of Conflict

Conflict Origins	Description
Intrapersonal	Conflict within an individual include ideas, thoughts, emotions, values, predispositions, or drives that conflict with one another
Interpersonal	Between individuals who have difficulty working together and getting along, including: • Relationship conflict—personal feelings and emotions related to the relationship. • Task conflict—disagreements over what is to be done, what is important, and the specific strategies for execution. • Process conflict—disagreements over how it should be done; misalignment of work and tasks. • Status conflict—disagreements over who is in charge, who has the authority to do what and when, and where the ultimate responsibility resides
Intragroup	Within a small group or team such as classes, workgroups, or families.
Intergroup	Between defined groups, such as unions and employers, within community groups, unions, and government authorities.

Stage Two: Awareness and Emotion: Perceived and Felt Conflict

Perception or *sense making* plays a major role in reconciling conflict.[45] Clarity concerning issues, feelings and assumptions is central to reconciling matters at issue.

- Perceived conflict: awareness by one or more parties of the existence of conditions that create opportunities for conflict to arise.

- Felt conflict: emotional involvement in a conflict, creating anxiety, tenseness, frustration, or hostility.

Table 4: Types of Conflict

Conflict Type	Description
Values conflict	Involves incompatibility of preferences, principles, and practices that people believe in, such as religion, ethics, or politics.
Power conflict	Occurs when each party wishes to maintain or maximize the amount of influence it exerts in the relationship and the social setting, such as in a decision-making process.
Economic conflict	Involves the consequences that arise from scarce resources and/or resource allocation, such as monetary or human resources.
Interpersonal conflict	Occurs when two people or more have incompatible needs, goals, or approaches in their relationship, such as different communication or work styles (relationship, task, process, status).
Organizational conflict	Involves perceived inequalities in the organizational chart and how employees report to one another, differences between work groups (intragroup), or between entities such as a union and the employer (intergroup). Includes matters pertaining to both individual and institutional relationships.
Environmental conflict	Results from external pressures outside the organization, such as an economic downturn, a change in government, etc.

Conflicts are situational and occur in many settings, on many scales, and originate on many levels and may be of different types.

---

45   Conflict may be viewed as occurring along cognitive (perception), emotional (feeling), and behavioural (action) dimensions.

Organizations have particular structures and manners of operating and making decisions. They are influenced by and respond to their environment. Consider the potential conflict sources in an organization.[46]

- The matrix structure adopted by many organizations—a structure in which the reporting relationships are set up as a grid, or matrix, rather than in a traditional hierarchy with employees having dual reporting—has resulted in unclear reporting lines, increased competition for resources and attention, and general confusion as managers try to develop an appropriate management style.

- Globalization has caused change and restructuring so that businesses can operate more flexibly. There has been a rapid growth in virtual teams, with people from different backgrounds and cultures working across vast regions and time zones. Email and electronic communication are the most practical ways to connect. While fast and practical they are often one way instead of two way communications, can be anonymous and eliminate the benefit of non-verbal communications evident in person to person interactions. These facts can lead to misunderstanding.

- Additional sources of conflict in the workplace, include:

  o different cultures and assumptions

  o differing values, opinions, and beliefs

  o lack of sensitivity to race, gender, age, class, education, and ability

  o poor people skills, especially communication

  o volatile, fast-changing workplaces

  o limits on resources, both physical and psychological

Stage Three: Intentions and the Dual Concerns Model

Stage Three requires the adoption of a systematic approach grounded in your dual concerns. Managing conflict involves:

- Assessing the situation and developing an approach (plan).

- Understanding the matters at issue, the people involved, and the interests represented.

46   Excerpt from Gill Corkindale, How to Manage Conflict, *Harvard Business Review* (November 15, 2007).

- Being historically alert (understanding the parties' history and how relationships have evolved) and contextually grounded (appreciating the frame in which events occur).

- Adopting a particular approach (performative, distributive, integrative, or transformative as described later) and choosing from alternative conflict strategies.

- Implementing a strategy and learning from results.

Stage Three involves decisions to act in a certain way. Using two dimensions—cooperativeness (the degree to which one party attempts to satisfy the other party's concerns) and assertiveness (the degree to which one party attempts to satisfy his or her own concerns)—how do you proceed? And why, to what end?

Generally, conflict styles are either adversarial or cooperative in nature. The style and approach you use when conflict occurs tends to influence the response you get back. The following are some of the qualities of cooperative and adversarial conflict approaches.

Cooperative

A cooperative conflict style perceives the outcome as better overall than the previous situation. Following *constructive conflict*, parties are satisfied and feel they have gained as a result of reconciling the conflict.

With a cooperative conflict style there is a tendency towards the de-escalation of conflict. This is shown through:

- Demonstrable good faith: willingness to meet and engage in rational discussions with a mind open to persuasion.

- A willingness to listen and understand and an expressed desire to be listened to and understood.

- A friendly and open behaviour, manner, and atmosphere.

- A willingness to recognize and work out differences.

- A motivation to build on commonalities.

- The use of persuasiveness, awareness, and understanding to achieve change.

- Attention to improving relationships.

- A desire to find solutions that work for both parties.

- Using power to benefit both parties.

- Understanding what constitutes a good agreement: fair, efficient, wise, and stable.

Adversarial

This is a conflict approach that seeks to satisfy the interests of one party at the expense of the other; it can result in an overall sense of loss and ill will between the parties and can damage relationships.

With the adversarial style, there is a:

- tendency of conflict to escalate, intensify, and expand (increase in scope and size)

- tendency towards miscommunication and misunderstanding

- guarded, defensive, rigid behaviour, manner, and atmosphere

- the use of positions and positioning

- lack of focus on commonalities

- low concern for the relationship

- close-mindedness and resistance to change

- predominant focus on *what I want* as an outcome and a strong desire to find a settlement that meets own needs

- strong concern for self, with limited or no concern for others

- the use of power to gain advantage for self

It is important to recognize that people approach conflict and workplace interactions from a perspective shaped by their frame of reference. The frame of reference individuals adopts affects their response to the problems they face, and it determines their criteria for making judgements and filters information they receive.

The frame of reference is grounded in beliefs about authority, the role and *inherent* rights of management, and how the workplace should be organized (see Part One: *Employment Preliminaries*).

Comparing Conflict Categories

The following table compares constructive, cooperative approaches with adversarial, positional ones. Consider your dual concerns and what you want to accomplish. Which approach is most appropriate?

Table 5: Constructive, Cooperative Approaches Compared with Adversarial, Positional Approaches

	Constructive, Cooperative	Adversarial, Positional
Atmosphere	Working with the other party; focussed on a problem *we* have	Working against the other party; focussed on *you* are the problem
Stance	Prepared to explore the potential for integration through better understanding of the matters at issue.	Demonstrating that this is more than likely a zero-sum proposition. A gain for you represents a loss for me, both in terms of process and substance.
Strategies	<ul><li>Exploring needs, concerns (interests)</li><li>Using objective criteria</li><li>Building on commonalities</li><li>Influencing with reasoned thinking</li></ul>	<ul><li>Position-taking, positioning</li><li>Accentuating differences; raising doubt</li><li>Coercing with pressure</li><li>Intimidation, threats</li><li>Attacks</li></ul>
Relationship	<ul><li>Goal of building, maintaining and / or strengthening</li><li>Future orientation</li></ul>	<ul><li>Seeking personal gain on the matters at issue</li><li>Potential to damage or destroy</li></ul>
Outcome	<ul><li>Goal of satisfying both parties</li><li>Long-term stability</li></ul>	<ul><li>Goal of satisfying self</li><li>Short-term gain</li></ul>

The Dual Concerns Model

The *dual concerns model*[47] can help us understand conflict responses. Conflict is often best understood by examining the consequences of various behaviours at moments in time. These behaviours can be usefully categorized according to conflict styles.

The dual concerns model[48] provides that categorization. It suggests that conflict requires balancing the concern of meeting one's own goals with concern for other people and maintaining healthy relationships when reconciling[49] matters at issue.

The dual concerns model is a two-dimensional framework that advances the idea that people in conflict have two independent types of concerns:

- **Concern for self:** The degree to which you attempt to satisfy your own interests, which is embodied in the quality of being self-assured and confident without being aggressive (assertiveness).

- **Concern for other(s):** The degree to which you attempt to satisfy the interests of others; embodied in the ability to see the world through the eyes of another person; to share and understand the other's feelings, needs, concerns, and interests (empathy).

---

47   Defined in R. Lewicki, D. Saunders, B. Barry, and K. Tasa, K., *Essentials of Negotiation* (Toronto, ON: McGraw-Hill Ryerson, 2014), 13–14. Based on the dual concerns model (Blake & Mouton, 1964; Pruitt & Rubin, 1986; Rahim, 1986; Thomas-Kilmann, 1976), which propose five styles for handling conflict situations.

48   Based on the dual concerns model (Blake & Mouton, 1964; Pruitt & Rubin, 1986; Rahim, 1986; Thomas-Kilmann, 1976), which proposes five styles for handling conflict situations.

49   Reconciliation: the act of causing two people or groups to become friendly and respectful again after an argument or disagreement and/or the process of finding a way to make two different ideas, facts, etc., exist or be true at the same time.

Figure 13: Dual Concerns Model[50]

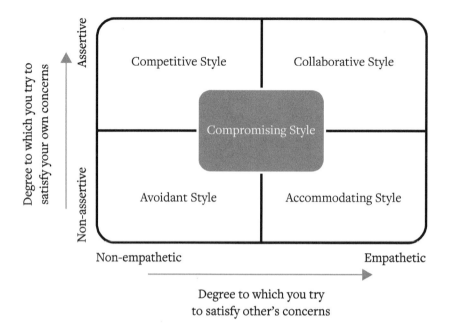

The assertiveness dimension focusses on the degree to which one is concerned with satisfying one's own interests. Conversely, the empathy dimension focusses on the extent to which one is concerned with also satisfying the interests of the other party. The intersection points of these dimensions result in different conflict styles. It is always helpful to not only recognize your own conflict style, but also appreciate the style of the other party.

Empathy is a skill that can be developed and, as with most interpersonal skills, empathizing (at some level) comes naturally to most people. To empathize is to feel how others feel and to see the world as they do.

> There is an important distinction between empathy and sympathy. Empathy is not sympathy. We offer our sympathy when we imagine how a situation or event was difficult or traumatic for another person. We may use phrases like "I am very sorry to hear that" or "If there is anything I can do to help..." and we feel pity or sorry for the other person.

Being empathetic requires effective communication and a strong imagination. Everybody sees the world differently, based on their experiences, culture, religion,

50   This schematic is an adaptation for illustrative purposes of the model presented in Lewicki et al, *Essentials of Negotiation* (Toronto, ON: McGraw-Hill Ryerson, 2014), 14.

opinions, and beliefs. In order to empathize with another person, you need to see the world from their perspective and therefore need to use some imagination as to what their perspective is based on, how they see the world, and why they see it differently from you. Shared experiences can also help you empathize. Many people find it easier to empathize with people who are closer to them and their experiences.

Conflict Styles

Conflicts are situationally specific. Some situations require a considerate or cooperative approach while others benefit from either a competitive or passive approach. The Dual Concerns Model two dimensional framework yields five conflict styles that can be adopted based on what you are seeking to achieve. The adoption of a style should be a considered choice rather than a default to what is comfortable.

Table 6: The Five Conflict Styles

Conflict Style	Description
Competitive Contending, Competing, Forcing, Directing:	Maximizes assertiveness and minimizes empathy; can involve using your formal authority or power to satisfy your concerns, without regard to the other party's concerns.
Accommodation Accommodating, Yielding, Smoothing, Obliging	Maximizes empathy and minimizes assertiveness, allowing the other party to satisfy their concerns while neglecting your own.
Avoidant Avoiding, Withdrawing	Low in assertiveness and low in empathy; not paying attention to the conflict and not taking any action to resolve it.
Compromising	Intermediate on both the assertiveness and empathy dimensions; attempting to resolve the conflict by identifying a solution that is partially satisfactory to both parties but completely satisfactory to neither
Collaborative Collaborating, Integrating, Problem Solving	Highly assertive and highly empathetic at the same time; co-operating with the other party to understand their concerns in an effort to find a mutually satisfying solution.

By understanding each style and its consequences, we may normalize the results of our behaviours in various situations and better appreciate the expected consequences of each approach. Ask yourself what is more important—the substantive outcome or the relational outcome?

Table 7: Conflict Styles and Outcomes

Conflict Style	Outcome
Competitive	We might force others to accept "our" solution, but this acceptance may be accompanied by dissatisfaction and resentment.
Accommodation	The relationship may proceed smoothly in the immediate term, but there may be lingering dissatisfaction and building frustration that our needs are going unmet
Avoiding	Both parties may remain unaware and uninformed about the real underlying issues and concerns, only to be dealing with them in the future.
Compromising	We may feel okay about the outcome, but still have resentments for goals not achieved.
Collaborative	We may not gain a better solution than a compromise might have yielded, but we are more likely to feel better about our chances for future understanding and goodwill.

The Nature of Conflict Styles

Generally, with workplace matters, there are specific circumstances under which each of the conflict styles is most effective. Collaboration is the way to deal with important issues, although forcing can sometimes be appropriate if time is an issue (recognizing the potential consequences of such an approach).[51]

For moderately important issues, compromising can lead to quick solutions, but since it doesn't satisfy either party, or it does not foster innovation, collaboration is preferable.

Accommodating is the best approach for unimportant issues as it leads to a quick resolution without straining the relationship.

From Approaches to Strategies

Engagement strategies[52] can be categorized as:

---

51   Excessive promises, threats, or appeals to authority weaken credibility and defeat their use when a vital issue arises that merits extreme power. Even if successful, excessive power may only buy an expensive, temporary victory, creating resentment and reluctant acceptance. Whatever sanctions, threats, offers, or promises are made, keep them in line with the demand or request; that is, make them consistent with the interests involved. Apply power proportional to the interests at stake, and only as relevant to these interests.

52   See "Characteristics of Different Engagement Strategies" in Lewicki et. Al., *Essentials of Negotiation,* 2nd ed. (Toronto, ON: McGraw-Hill Ryerson, 2014), 91.

- **Active engagement:** Competition, collaboration, accommodation

- **Non-engagement:** Avoidance

Note that compromise is not identified as a viable strategy.

Some Observations on Compromise

In the face of conflict and in response to proposed solutions, some people default to compromise. Compromise is a way of reaching agreement where each person or group gives up something that was wanted (evidenced by the positions they adopt) to end an argument or dispute.

People reduce their demands or change their opinion in order to agree, and to that end they do not balance the concern for meeting their own goals with the concern for others and maintaining healthy relationships.

Some scholars[53] argue that compromise is not a viable conflict management strategy because it results from either lazy problem-solving involving a half-hearted attempt to satisfy the two parties' interests, or simple yielding by both parties.

Lawrence Susskind, a professor at the Massachusetts Institute of Technology and co-founder of the Program on Negotiation at Harvard Law School, answers the question "So, when *should* you compromise?" [54]

> No negotiating party should ever accept an agreement that is worse for them than no agreement. But, a group may be very uncertain about how to predict what no agreement really means. ("If we don't reach agree-ment now, what will happen next and what effects will that have?") So, they might say yes to something that turns out, in retrospect, to be less desirable for them than having said no. But, no negotiator should ever agree to something that knowingly "hurts" their constituency (i.e. is worse than what no agreement held in store for them) just to be liked. Good working relationships (and particularly trust) are not achieved by caving in to pressure. Rather, they are a by-product of all sides acting in what Fisher and Ury would call a "principled way." And, I would argue that one principle of negotiation is that no one should ever "give away" their interests in the hope of "buying" a good relationship. All

53   Including D. Pruitt and J. Rubin, *Social Conflict, Stalemate and Settlement* (New York: Random House, 1986).

54   L. Susskind, "The Consensus Building Approach," August 8, 2011. http://theconsensusbuild-ingapproach.blogspot.ca/

that will do, as Fisher and Ury point out, is teach the other parties that the same behavior be expected in the future.

...and finally Susskind observes:

> The key to win-win negotiation is not compromise, it is getting into the trading zone and creating as much value as possible. If all negotiations involved just two parties and those negotiators didn't have to report to anyone, the process would not be that difficult. But, most of the time, negotiators have someone else (often a diverse and fractious constituency) to whom they must report, and to whom they are accountable. This makes moving into the trading zone more difficult.

When you are tempted to compromise ask yourself what you are trying to achieve and consider the following six observations about compromise:

1. **You end up with watered-down solutions**. *Some deal, even if it isn't perfect, is better than no deal at all!* While it may end the conflict for now, you may well end up with a solution or decision that doesn't make anybody happy and may actually make everyone a little unhappy.

   Compromise may be a good choice for the little day-to-day things that don't ultimately matter in your life, but is likely a poor bargain when relationships and matters of substance matter.

2. **It limits possibility.** When compromise is your primary approach to conflict management, you limit possibilities markedly. That's because when you're stuck in concession-making mode, you fail to see the options that other problem-solving, integrative approaches would illuminate.

3. **It's a poor primary conflict management habit for ongoing relationships and can become something you're *known for.*** Conceding, or giving something up, in order to settle a matter isn't necessarily a bad strategy when negotiating the purchase price of a car—not something generally known for integrative potential—but is a poor basis for any ongoing personal or professional relationship.

   A reasoned exchange of views and the exploration of options reinforces your constructive tendencies in the eyes of others. Apparent conflict avoidance and the push to compromise give others quite a different view of you and what you appear to value.

4. **It puts your fallback approach first.** Sometimes a compromise is the best you can achieve, but that's the fallback—the alternative course of action that may be taken if the original plan fails, not the place you start.

5. **It's collaboration's poor cousin.** While it's common to see compromise and collaboration used interchangeably, they're not the same at all. The problem-solving approach you use should be dependent on the situation and the relationship, not the other way around.

6. **It's lazy.** No effort is made to understand the other party and you are prepared to accept *whatever,* even if that outcome is suboptimal. The *I don't like conflict* people say in their defence that compromise can be faster and helps avoid what *you think* may be a difficult or time-consuming set of interactions. This ignores the reality that conflict can be a constructive force in relationships.

Consider the dual concerns model and the two independent types of concerns—the concern for self and the concern for others—and what you value in a particular circumstance. At its root, compromise means you don't value the relationship enough to become engaged and to use other problem-solving approaches and work together.

Some Observations on *Going Along to Get Along:* Recognize anyone?

Avoidance, a measure of accommodation, and compromise may be employed when individuals experience discomfort with contentious matters. Colleagues and teams sometimes avoid conflict[55] by replacing it with a sense of artificial harmony, defaulting to groupthink, or practicing a measure of *lidism.*[56]

Groupthink: Value *Consensus over* Decision Quality

Groupthink is a phenomenon when a group of people get together and start to think collectively with one mind. When making collective, groups' decisions tend to minimize conflict and reach consensus without sufficiently testing, analyzing, and evaluating their ideas.

> The group is more concerned with maintaining unity than with objectively evaluating their situation, alternatives, and options. Pressures for conformity restrict the thinking of the group, bias its analysis, promote simplistic and stereotyped thinking, and stifle individual creative and independent thought.[57]

55   In the context of teams, author Patrick Lencioni, in "The 5 Dysfunctions of a Team," describes healthy conflict: "Conflict is raising passionate, ideological, unfiltered debate around issues that are important to the team."

56   A termed coined by Paul Rogers, Professor of Peace Studies, University of Bradford, West Yorkshire (2006), to mean measures aimed not to address the underlying issues but to keep the lid on.

57   I.L. Janis, *Groupthink: Psychological Studies of Policy Decisions and Fiascos* (New York: Houghton Mifflin, 1982); McShane, Steven, Steen, S., *Canadian Organizational Behaviour,* 8th ed. (Toronto, ON: McGraw-Hill Ryerson, 2012).

In many cases, people will set aside their own personal beliefs or adopt the opinion of the rest of the group. People who are opposed to the decisions or overriding opinion of the group as a whole frequently remain quiet, preferring to keep the peace rather than disrupt the uniformity of the group. The following symptoms indicate groupthink:

1. **Illusions of invulnerability** lead members of the group to be overly optimistic and engage in risk-taking.

2. **Unquestioned beliefs** lead members to ignore possible moral problems and ignore consequences of individual and group actions.

3. **Rationalizing** prevents members from reconsidering their beliefs and causes them to ignore warning signs.

4. **Stereotyping** leads members of the in-group to ignore or even demonize out-group members who may oppose or challenge the group's ideas.

5. **Self-censorship** causes people who might have doubts to hide their fears or misgivings.

6. **Mind-guards** act as self-appointed censors to hide problematic information from the group.

7. **Illusions of unanimity** lead members to believe everyone is in agreement and feels the same way.

8. **Direct pressure** to conform is often placed on members who pose questions, and those who question the group are often seen as disloyal or traitorous.

Groupthink can have some benefits. When working with a large number of people, it often allows the group to make decisions, complete tasks, and finish projects quickly and efficiently. However, this phenomenon also has costs. The suppression of individual opinions and creative thought can lead to poor decision making and inefficient problem solving.

Artificial Harmony: Valuing *Getting Along* over Decision Quality

Artificial harmony is a process that evolves when a group of people or a team agree on a matter even when they do not believe it to be the best decision for the group. This type of decision is made due to a reluctance to address potentially contentious matters or a fear of conflict. Some people would rather agree than raise issues of disagreement and engage in the stresses of varying opinions.

Artificial harmony leads to artificial agreements or basically false agreements. Signs of artificial agreement syndrome[58] include:

- Lack of broad participation—discussions are dominated by a few voices

- Discussions that always seem to run to the meta-topic instead of the actual problem

- Issues are not resolved and come up over and over

- People are still upset after the meeting because issues have not been resolved

- People have different versions of events and competing stories (narratives)

- Lack of trust for some people to speak for the group

- Outcomes of decision-making meetings are surprises

- Lack of results or missed commitments by the team

Few people are happy when they are engaged in artificial harmony. Progress is slow, if made at all. Goals and objectives may be talked about but if artificial harmony takes root, you should never expect to see anything more than talk taking place. If conflicting thoughts or disagreements are suppressed, the seeds of unhappiness are sown. When there is unhappiness deep in the heart of colleagues, team members the willingness to work together is eroded.

Stage Four: Behaviour

In Stage Four, each party's intentions are implemented. All conflicts manifest in behaviour somewhere along the continuum, ranging from no conflict or minor conflict (such as minor disagreements or misunderstandings, overt questioning, or challenging of others) to efforts to undermine or even destroy the other party (such as threats and ultimatums, aggressive attacks, and the like).

58   Rob Hirschfeld, CEO, co-founder of RackN, physical and hybrid DevOps developer, blog post 2017.

Figure 14: Conflict Continuum

Unmanageable conflict — Efforts to destroy the other party

Aggressive physical attack

Threats

Verbal attacks

Questioning/challenging others

Minor disagreements/misunderstandings

No conflict

At the lower part of the conflict continuum are relatively low-level conflicts. Conflicts in the upper part of the continuum are highly destructive.[59]

Stage Five: Outcomes and Aftermath

The action-reaction between conflicting parties results in two kinds of outcomes. In functional outcomes, conflict results in improved performance of the group. It improves the quality of decisions, brings about creativity and innovations, encourage interests and curiosity among group members. In contrast, dysfunctional outcomes reduce the effectiveness of the group. Dysfunctional outcomes are a result of uncontrolled opposition. These outcomes lead to destruction of the group and reduce group communication and group coordination.

Perspective on Collaboration

Adam Kahane, conflict mediator and peace negotiator, challenges readers to reconsider their notions of collaboration in his book, *Collaborating with the Enemy: How to Work with People You Don't Agree with or Like or Trust.*[60]

Kahane observes that the challenge of collaboration is that to make our way forward, we *must* work with others, and these others include people we do not agree with or

---

59   Adapted from S.P. Robbins, *Managing Organizational Conflict: A Non-traditional Approach* (Upper Saddle River, NJ: Prentice Hall, 1974): 93–97; and F. Glasi, "The Process of Conflict Escalation and the Roles of Third Parties," in G.B.J. Bomers and R. Peterson (eds.), *Conflict Management and Industrial Relations* (Boston: Kluwer-Nijhoff, 1982), 119–40.

60   A. Kahane, Collaborating with the Enemy: How to Work with People You Don't Agree with or Like or Trust, (Oakland, CA: Berrett-Koehler Publishers, 2017).

like or sometimes even trust. And so we are torn, says Kahane: we think we must work with these others and also that we must not or cannot. Collaboration seems both imperative and impossible—but it is neither. It is only one option among four. When we are faced with a situation that is not as we want it to be, we can try:

- forcing it to be the way we want

- adapting to it as it is

- exiting the situation

- collaborating with others to change it

Although the risks and limitations of forcing, adapting, and exiting are well-known, in many contexts, collaborating also seems too daunting, and so we default to one of these other three options—especially forcing.

Kahane posits that the reason such collaborations seem impossible is because we misunderstand collaboration. Our conventional understanding of collaboration is that it requires us all to do what the task demands of us, to be on the same team and headed in the same direction, to agree on what needs to be done and be able to get this done, and to get people—other people—to change what they're doing in order to implement that plan. In other words, we assume that collaboration can and must be under control.

Conventional collaboration:

- tends to be organized around like-minded people trying to find ways to work in harmony

- typically seeks a single and elegant definition of the problem, one *best* solution

- often emphasizes the importance to direct and/or change others This conventional assumption is wrong, and in complex, conflictual, multi-stakeholder contexts, it is always incorrect. In these contexts, conventional collaboration does not and cannot work. When we are working in complex situations with diverse others, collaboration cannot and need not be controlled. The alternative is what Kahane terms *stretch collaboration*.[61]

Unconventional stretch collaboration abandons the assumption of control. He describes that it gives up unrealistic expectations or fantasies of harmony, certainty,

---

61   Stretch collaboration is a variant of conventional collaboration. It abandons the assumption of control, gives up unrealistic expectations of harmony, certainty, and compliance, and instead embraces the realities of discord, trial and error, and co-creation, and emphasizes flexibility and improvisation.

and compliance, and embraces the messy realities of discord, trial and error, and co-creation through flexibility and improvisation.

Such stretch collaboration enables us to get things done even in complex situations with people we don't agree with, like, or trust. This approach involves embracing not only connection but also conflict; experimenting our way forward; and stepping into the game, willing to change oneself. It means embracing plural wholes, plural possibilities, and plural co-creators.

Stretch collaboration requires us to:

- engage with people who see the world differently and embrace—and creatively use—the inevitable conflict of perspectives and power that arise

- "step into the game," participate fully in the work, and be prepared to change ourselves. Making progress on tough issues often requires us to adjust—sometimes radically—our own views and behaviours.

Stretch collaboration requires us to make three fundamental shifts in how we work.

Table 8: Differences Between Conventional and Stretch Collaboration

	Conventional Collaboration	Stretch Collaboration
How we relate with our collaborators	Focus on the *good* and harmony of the team (one dominant whole)	Embrace conflict and connection (multiple diverse wholes)
How we advance our work	Agree on the problem, the solution, and the plan (one best possibility)	Experiment our way forward (multiple emergent possibilities)
How we participate in our situation	Change what other people are doing (one super-creator)	Step into the game (multiple co-creators)

Kahane concedes that collaboration is never straightforward to get things done in complex situations with diverse others. Energies must be mobilized; needs, interests must be balanced; actions must be taken. Stretching does not make this work disappear; it just enables us to do it with less fear and distraction and more connection and awareness.

Stretch collaboration is simple, but it is not easy. It doesn't solve our problems, Kahane says—it just enables us to get unstuck and get moving and find a way forward. It does not guarantee success—it just makes it more likely.

Chapter 3: Orientations and Approaches to Conflict

Conflict takes root, lives, and thrives in the space between our own narrative and theirs—a story or account of events, experiences, or the like, whether evidence-informed, fictitious, or the dance between the lines of fact and fiction. We commit to our own narrative and often reject theirs out of hand. Positioning and position taking characterize the approaches that arise from the stories told.

Consider the following questions. One a scale of 1 to 10, what is the likelihood of each statement being true, with 1 being not very likely and 10 being very likely.

When faced with a potentially contentious interaction, my first instinct is to consider my potential talking points and prepare for an argument.

Reflecting on others with whom I regularly interact, it seems that when dealing with a contentious issue, people easily become argumentative and positional.

How did you score? Remember that when you approach a conversation with someone about something, you have something in mind too—a narrative of sorts, a story, or an account of events and experiences.

Your narrative or story is coloured by your background, experiences, and frame of reference. This narrative has implications for how the matters at issue are identified, understood, and reconciled. As you read this section, keep your scores in mind.

> Involvement in conflict affects all parties in similar ways. No matter what the context, disputes make parties feel fearful, confused, and unsure of what to do. As a result, they feel vulnerable and out of control.

> Moreover, in the heat of conflict, disputing parties typically feel threatened or victimized by the conduct and claims of the other party. As a result, they are defensive, suspicious, and hostile to the other party, and almost incapable of looking beyond their own needs. Thus, across all contexts, conflicts engender in people the experience of relative weakness and relative self-absorption.

> Given such a threatened and self-absorbed profile, it is understandable that people in conflict create, structure, and perform conflict narratives.[62]

During conflict, we tend to turn our attention to managing the other person or getting them to behave differently. Realistically, though, the only person we can truly control or manage in a contentious situation is ourselves. And in managing our own reactions, in seeking more constructive responses from ourselves, we inevitably change the interaction with the other person. When we change, and improve the quality of the whole interaction, then we may increase everyone's capacity to act differently or "better."

Concerns, Choices, and Consequences

The concerns, choices, and consequences framework builds on the five-stage conflict process and the dual concerns model and illustrates the concepts introduced in Chapters 3 and 4.

This framework proposes an approach to advance understanding characterized by systematic analysis, conscious choices concerning courses of action, and finally an assessment of the consequences resulting from those choices.

The *concerns, choices, and consequences framework* has eight interrelated components:

1. **Incident and circumstance:** The issue, event, or circumstance central to the conflict. As identified earlier in the five-stage conflict process, there can be perceived conflict—awareness by one or more parties of the existence of conditions that create opportunities for conflict to arise—and felt conflict, which is emotional involvement in a conflict, creating anxiety, tenseness, frustration, or hostility.

2. **Narrative:** Stories people tell. A way people in conflict organize the events and characters involved in an incident or circumstance. Contained in a narrative is the initial value or starting point adopted by the narrator to best describe the issue, circumstances and concerns. This starting point represents an anchor of sorts and one with implications for proceedings. It is the first value assigned, or position taken and tends to, for the narrator, anchor the discussions that follow.

---

62   Robert A. Baruch Bush and Joseph P. Folger, *The Promise of Mediation: Responding to Conflict Through Empowerment and Recognition,* (San Francisco, CA: Jossey-Bass Publishers, 1994), 191.

3. **Nature of possible interactions:** There are four different kinds of possible interactions or combinations of interactions: performative, distributive, integrative, and transformative.

4. **Type of discourse:** A specific type of *discourse* is associated with each of the four possible interactions.

5. **Reconciling dual concerns:** Conflict requires balancing the concern of meeting one's own goals with concern for other people and maintaining healthy relationships when reconciling matters at issue. Apply the dual concerns model and ask yourself this question: what do you value?

6. **Orientation:** We are influenced by our frames of reference and how we see the world, our view of power, authority, and what we believe specific interactions to be about. Taken together, a general orientation emerges that informs our approach to potentially contentious discourse, as well as the approach we adopt to reconcile matters at issue. Orientations can be placed in one of three general frames—maximalist positioning, equitable positioning or the integrative approach.

7. **Approach:** The three orientations give rise to one of two approaches to reconciling matters at issue: distributive—dividing up a resource or array of resources that parties have identified—or integrative, integrating across multiple issues to create new sources of value.[63] Often, what looks distributive is in fact integrative, as there may be additional issues that can be added to the discussion.

8. **Results and consequences:** The final component relates to the enactment of the decision resulting from the interactions and the consequences that flow from that decision.

Depending on the matters at issue and the nature of the reconciliation of conflicts, a workplace restoration process may be necessary. This process re-establishes positive working relationships so that members of an organization can move on after a stressful event.

The workplace restoration process is necessary after any significant disruption in workplace relations resulting from prolonged conflict, an accusation of bullying or harassment, an investigation, employee terminations, and other organizational changes.

---

63   Note: Consider the matter at issue and remember that the reconciliation of interests involves creating value to facilitate problem-solving, creating packages of matters to maximize value, and finally claiming value to conclude the matters at issue. A one-dimensional money issue is generally a distributive exercise while multi-dimensional people matters necessitate an integrative approach.

Figure 15: Concerns, Choices, and Consequences Framework—Discourse Flow

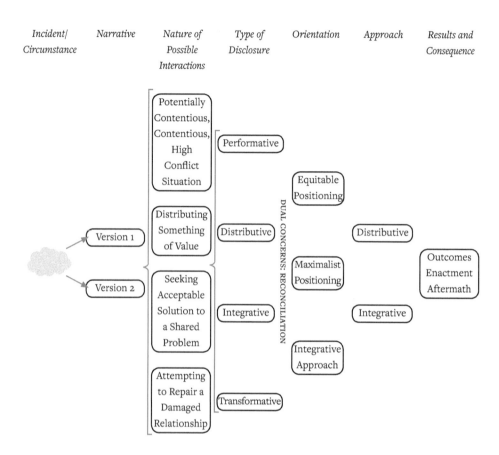

Narratives and Conflict–Problem Narratives

You tell a colleague about an encounter you recently had with a senior colleague and project leader, explaining how unreasonable the person was and the treatment you experienced. You have just created a narrative—a conflict-problem narrative, to be more precise.

Deconstructing a Narrative

A narrative is a story that connects and explains a carefully selected set of supposedly true events, experiences, or the like, and which is intended to support a particular viewpoint or thesis. To further understanding and address matters at issue, it is necessary to deconstruct a narrative, *tracing the contradictions to their fractured source.*[64]

64   Observations of Russell Jacoby, *Social Amnesia,* (London, U.K., Transactional Press, 1975), 60.

Considerate following: What am I being told? Why did this person go to the trouble of telling me this? The following is a schematic representation of a narrative.

Figure 16: Narrative Deconstruction Details

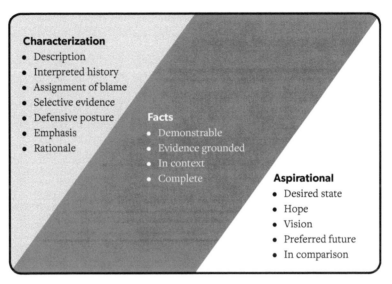

To make sense of what you are being told you need to have an inquiry/question-ing strategy (see Chapter 20 for a discussion of question types and questioning approaches). Further, you must be an active listener, suspend judgement, and attempt to deconstruct the narrative with a focus on understanding the what (the issues and perspectives) and the why (the concerns and needs). With the what and why comes the what to do now.

Keep in mind the following as you pursue understanding through this deconstruction:

- People's interests and priorities are embedded in their stories. Determination of interests and their relative priority is the route to reconciling matters at issue.

- Make sense of the circumstance by building a chronology of events. Differentiate between facts and opinions.

- People are entitled to their own opinions, not their own facts.[65] Facts are provable.

65   Sentiments attributed to Daniel Patrick "Pat" Moynihan, an American politician and sociolo-gist (1927–2003).

○ Narratives are stories and may contain what the narrator sees as a set of *alternative facts.*[66] This needs to be an evidence-informed exercise, which focusses on evidence that is complete and in context. People's narratives will contain both facts and manipulations and characterizations of those facts. The goal is to move beyond this framing.

- Always certain, *seldom right:* be aware of *assumed knowledge* or the illusion of knowledge regardless of how strongly or confidently the story is told.

○ Test the proposition: Just because someone with authority (standing, position, role, perceived knowledge) or credentials asserts a matter doesn't necessarily make it so. Don't be reluctant to test assertions.

- It's not what you think (or what the narrator thinks), it's what can be proven. Be cognizant of known unknowns and speculation.

○ *Reports that say that something hasn't happened are always interesting to me, because as we know, there are known knowns; there are things we know we know. We also know there are known unknowns; that is to say we know there are some things we do not know. But there are also unknown unknowns—the ones we don't know we don't know... it is the latter category that tend to be the difficult ones.*[67]

The Narrative Examined

People narrate incompatible stories arising from particular circumstances. In a work-place context, individuals' particular frames of reference and how they believe the organization really works form the backdrop against which their story is set. It affects their response to the problems they face—it determines their criteria for making judgements and filters information they receive.

Telling a story is a common way to make a point, describe a situation, or vent. Individuals who are in a contentious situation incorporate the most difficult and enduring aspects of events into the narratives (stories) that they tell. When a narrative is created, we use our story as a frame, as a way to organize the events and characters involved in the matter.

66   A phrase used by US Counselor to the President Kelly-Anne Conway during a Meet the Press interview on January 22, 2017, in which she defended White House Press Secretary Sean Spicer's false statement about the attendance numbers of Donald Trump's inauguration as President of the United States.

67   Response United States Secretary of Defense Donald Rumsfeld gave to a question at a U.S. Department of Defense news briefing on February 12, 2002.

People in conflict create and perform conflict-problem stories. These stories may be incompatible, arising from circumstances that are contentious, high-conflict, or potentially high-conflict. Conflict-problem narratives:

- Are "true" expressions of the narrator's reality. They are not intended to be a fair, balanced, accurate, or complete description of the conflict.
- Conceal and reveal facts which in some way threaten the 'face' or self-esteem of another are feelings and/or identity issues.
- Involve actual or imagined interpersonal confrontation and are often coloured with strong emotions.
- Cast the narrator as victim (or hero) and the other person as the wrongdoer.
- Deny any wrongdoing by the narrator and cast all blame (and power) on the other person.
- Conceal and reveal the narrator's contribution to the conflict and justify and condemn his/her behaviour in the conflict.
- Focus on the past (blaming), not on the present (problem-solving) or the future (desiring).
- Explain why the narrator had "no choice" but to act in just one way.
- Identify why the narrator does not want to listen to, acknowledge or affirm the other person's conflict-problem narrative.
- Tend to speak of *we* instead of *I*, and use generalizations to speculate on the other's motives.
- Reportedly speak for others (people say; it's not me but others tell me that...) when the narrator can only speak for themselves. A variant of this approach is the use of what can be termed as borrowed courage. If it were up top me I would.....but I can't because my boss won't let me.
- Seek understanding from an "audience:" are they seeking to appeal to others through their stories? Seeking vindication, support, or sympathy?
- Can be an opportunity to ventilate or let off steam.

Conflict-problem narratives can be very limited in scope and very limiting. They create a frame for the narrator and in many cases an anchor. Positions and position taking common to narratives establish limits and what can be perceived as barriers. Other features of narratives include:

- Those who are involved in the narrative are often portrayed using hero, victim, and villain characteristics,[68] which restricts the range of motives and actions that individuals might have.

68   See the drama triangle or "Karpman's triangle," a social model conceived by Stephen Karpman (1968); used in structural analysis (defining the conflict roles of persecutor, victim, and rescuer) and transactional analysis (diagramming how participants switch roles in conflict).

- In some instances narrators enemyfy[69] one or more parties in their story. Polarizing in nature, individuals or groups are not simply *people I disagree with*, but rather the derisive *other people* is used to describe them. *They are people who I can't work with and what I really want more than anything is for them to just go away, for them to be excluded or eliminated.*

- The focus within the narrative is on *what we can get* from a person or circumstance, a view that can only conceive of benefits for one side not the other.

- Are position-focussed. The position(s) we take and argue for during interactions is motivated by and purportedly represents our interests. These positions create an anchor of sorts around which the narrator's thinking revolves.

Why Do People Create Conflict-Problem Narratives?

Holbrook and Cook, in *Advanced Negotiation and Mediation: Concepts, Skills and Exercises,* identify seven underlying reasons people create conflict-problem narratives. Note that more than one of the reasons may be involved in a specific conflict. Also, one may trigger another or increase its intensity in a conflict-problem narrative.

Unresolved Fears and Related Unfilled Needs

People create conflict-problem narratives in part because of unresolved fears and related unfulfilled needs, which include the following (see figure 17).

Figure 17: Unresolved Fears and Unfulfilled Needs

Unresolved Fears	Related Unfulfilled Needs
Helplessness	→ Control
Hopelessness	→ Agency (Choice)
Rejection	→ Intimacy
Humiliation	→ Respect
Abandonment	→ Inclusion
Speechlessness	→ Speaking Truth to Power
Being Wrong	→ Being Right
Losing	→ Winning
Injustice	→ Fairness
Discrimination	→ Equality
Being Ignored	→ Being Acknowledged
Being Invisible	→ Being Understood

These unresolved fears and related unfulfilled needs are also incentives to engage in dialogue about the conflict or problem.

---

69   A. Kahane, *Collaborating with the Enemy: How to Work with People You Don't Agree with or Like or Trust,* (Oakland, CA: Berrett-Koehler Publishers, 2017).

Unworkable information, expectations, assumptions, and conclusions

The nature of one's work, the perception of it, and their reaction to it are common sources and subjects of narratives generally and conflict-problem narratives specifically.

Overly Intense Emotions

Roger Fisher and Daniel Shapiro, in *Beyond Reason: Using Reason as You Negotiate*, contend that strong emotions narrow the parties' focus of attention and create tunnel vision. This creates vulnerability such that the parties' emotions take control of their behaviour, making them unable to see the consequences of their choices.

To compound the issue, emotions feed off one another, so one person's anger can stimulate the other person's anger.

Threatened Identity

People have many different identities rooted in their gender, sexual orientation, national or ethnic origin, cultural norms, languages, religious affiliations, economic class or status, personal values, self-interests, etc.

Different conditions (e.g., actual or perceived abuse of asymmetric power,[70] betrayal, disrespect, humiliation, misallocation of resources, violation of rights, etc.) can create conflicts in which identities are "miniaturized" and people are classified as belonging to a single group ("not us") or having a single dimension or characteristic ("not me"). In addition to these many different existential identities, conflict-problem narratives may implicate a person's threatened sense of personal identity for:

- competence
- integrity
- self-worth

Threatened "Core Concerns"

The following relationship identities can animate a conflict-problem narrative, either as part of the presenting conflict or as part of a back-story for one or both of the narrators.

---

70   A state in which differences in status exist between individuals and groups of individuals within an organizational hierarchy, and these differences result in differential ability to take action or cause action to be taken.

Appreciation

Appreciation can take two forms. A person's feeling of valued recognition and from an understanding of someone's point of view, finding merit in that person's thinking, feeling, or actions and communicating that understanding to the other person.

Affiliation

Affiliation is a person's sense of connectedness with another person or group; these connections can be structural, personal, or both.

Autonomy

Autonomy is a person's freedom to affect or make decisions without impositions from others.

Status

Status is a person's standing in comparison to the standing of others; social status is a person's standing in a social hierarchy. Status may also refer to a person's standing in some defined substantive field (e.g., a person's professional status).

Role

Role is a person's job title or label and the corresponding set of activities that is expected or required of that person in a specific situation.

Unmourned Trauma

Trauma is a type of damage to the psyche that occurs as a result of a severely distressing event. When we are traumatized, our world shrinks, our vision narrows, and we look inward, not out. We are hyper-vigilant,[71] and subject to startle responses (largely unconscious defensive responses to sudden or threatening stimuli), hair-trigger defensiveness, irritability, hyper-ventilation, and flashbacks.

We cannot relax, rest, or sleep soundly. We do not trust that anyone else will relate to or understand our situation. We have not grieved traumatic loss. The trauma affects who we are, what we feel, and what we are capable of doing. Our experience of earlier trauma shapes and colours the way we process subsequent, unrelated traumatic experiences.

The change curve, originally based on a model developed in the 1960s by psychiatrist Elisabeth Kubler-Ross to explain the grieving process, is a helpful tool. It has since been widely utilized as a method of helping people understand their reactions to trauma, significant change or upheaval.

Kubler-Ross proposed that a terminally ill patient would progress through five stages of grief when informed of their illness. The original five stages of grief—denial, anger,

---

71   A state of heightened alertness, accompanied by behaviour that aims to prevent danger.

bargaining, depression, and acceptance—have been adapted over the years. There are many variants of the curve in existence. However, the majority of them are consistent in their use of the following basic emotions, which are often grouped into three distinct transitional stages: shock and denial; anger and depression; acceptance and integration.

Each of us moves towards acceptance at our own pace. Unfortunately, that progress isn't a straight line. The change curve is a useful resource when considering the notion of unmourned trauma and individuals' conflict-problem narratives. Knowing where an individual is on the curve will help when deciding on how and when to communicate information and will assist in better managing the matters at issue.

Figure 18: The Change Curve

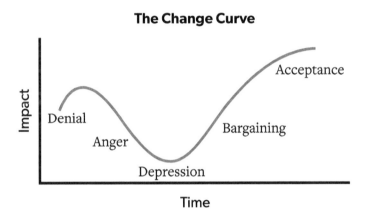

Source: http://www.slideshare.net/peoplewizconsulting/change-management-models-a-comparison

Anxiety about Scarcity

When parties are in conflict, power often is manifested in their struggle for control over the distribution of resources that are assumed to be in short supply. Those resources can be anything considered of value to the parties, ranging from emotional and relational support to material commodities, including money.

Often there are actually or potentially more than adequate resources available to the parties but, because of their unresolved fears and unfulfilled needs, they may experience unacceptable scarcity. Sometimes the conflict is over how to distribute resources in a way the parties will perceive to be fair and satisfactory.

Childhood Experiences of Conflict and Conflict Communication

We are influenced by our past and what we have come to know. Read and reflect on the following questions. What conclusions do you draw?

When you were a child, how did your family handle conflicts?

If you had a conflict with a parent or a sibling, how did family members communicate about the conflict and how were you required to act and speak about it?

Do you see any similarities with how you handle conflict and speak about it now?

Approaches to Understanding

The narrative we use to describe a circumstance and consequent interactions can influence its course. When the conflict-problem narrative is rigid or accusatory with strict roles and potential outcomes, the interaction between the disputants can be rigid, unaccommodating, and increasingly positional.

The following approaches can help expand the scope of the conflict-problem narrative:

- Build a chronology of events to better understand the story. What happened when, who was involved. Differentiate fact from opinion in creating your picture of the circumstance.

- Suspend judgement and the temptation to characterize the actors in a situation as the victim, villain, or hero. Everyone, from time to time, has a part of each of those associated traits.

- Recognize that every individual is unique and is defined by his or her environment, personal experiences, and particular frame of reference.

- Instead of focussing on what you can get from the conflict, engage a perspective that seeks to understand the matters at issue and looks for mutual gains for all parties involved by identifying interests. Try to focus on concerns.

- Be aware of the reality that the parties have external factors (social, cultural, systemic) and internal factors (individual personality, frames of reference, values) that they must work with.

- Adopt a hopeful perspective, as opposed to a fatalistic one, with a mind open to persuasion. This allows for more options to be meaningfully explored and better allows for opportunities to emerge that moves you towards the satisfaction of interests.

Remember your objective is to transform the narration of stories into genuine conversation and dialogue72 that can open each party to the possibility of another point of view through mutual willingness to listen and speak. Dialogue—that is, conversation rather than narration—allows the parties to listen and talk to one another, which can make it possible for their competing positions to become clear and, ultimately and more importantly, their interests to emerge.

Author and co-founder of the consultancy Viewpoint Learning, Steven Rosell[73] provides instructive observations about dialogue that can inform the transformation from narration:

Three distinctive features separate dialogue from simple discussion and most other forms of talk. For true dialogue to take place, it is essential that the participants:

- suspend status differences and treat one another as peers;

- listen to one another with empathy; and

- bring assumptions to the surface in a non-judgemental way.

Rosell goes on to suggest when dialogue should and should not be used:

Dialogue should not be used when simpler forms of communication will suffice. Dialogue is needed, in particular, when people with different viewpoints, beliefs, problem-definitions, backgrounds, professions, interests, values, or traditions must find common ground, must build a shared framework within which they can work together. These circumstances are becoming more common in the face of globalization and the growing diversity of organizations, societies, and cultures.

Dialogue does not replace debate, negotiation, or decision making. It precedes them and creates the shared framework, language, and set of expectations within which they are more likely to lead to a productive outcome.

72   Dialogue stems from the Greek words *dia* for "through" and *logos* for "words." Dialogue is a synergistic activity through which the exchange of ideas yields knowledge not previously held by participants.

73   S.A. Rosell, "Changing Frames: Leadership and Governance in the Information Age," *Report of the Roundtable on Renewing Governance,* www.viewpointlearning.com, October 2000.

In Summary: Four D's

- **Dialogue** for understanding. What is the problem we are trying to solve or situation we are trying to understand?

- **Dialectic for integration:** A discourse between two or more people holding different points of view but wishing to establish a way forward through reasoned arguments. Consider the concepts of analytic frame, integrative potential and creating value.

- **Debate for distribution:** There will always come a time for the distribution of value (resident in a resource or array of resources identified) to conclude the matters at issue. The challenge is to create value though integration before seeking to claim it through distribution.

- **Decision and enactment:** Having identified and clarified the matters at issue, created and claimed value, now is the point of decision. What now, what next and so what?

Nature of Possible Interactions: Conflict Discourse and Dialogue

As mentioned previously, conflicts between parties can involve four possible interactions or combinations of interactions—performative, distributive, integrative, and transformative discourse.[74]

> The noun *discourse* comes from the Latin *discursus*, meaning "an argument." The argument in *discourse* refers to an exchange of ideas that often follows a kind of order and give-and-take between the participants.
>
> It is an extended communication, often interactive, dealing with some particular topic, as well as the activity of communicating and conveying information. The discourse may transition to a form of negotiation—the back and forth communication designed to reach an agreement when you and the other party have some interests that are shared and others that are opposed.
>
> Contrast negotiation and dialogue. The aim of negotiation—back and forth communication—is to reach agreement among parties where some interests are shared, and others are opposed. The intention of dialogue is to reach new understanding and, in so doing, to form a new basis from which to think and act.

---

74   Adapted from James R. Holbrook and Benjamin J. Cook, *Advanced Negotiation and Mediation: Concepts, Skills and Exercises* (St. Paul, MN: West Academic Publishing, 2013).

Table 9: Types of Discourse and Possible Interactions

Type of Discourse	Nature of Possible Interaction
Performative Discourse[1]	What happened, why did it happen, and what should I do about it; potentially contentious, contentious, and/or high-conflict situation; improving communication and advancing understanding are the issues
Distributive Discourse	Identifying, distributing something of value; exchange of value is the issue
Integrative Discourse	Seeking a mutually acceptable solution to what is recognized as a shared problem; creative problem solving is the goal
Transformative Discourse	Attempting to repair a damaged, conflicted relationship; improving a relationship is the goal

1   J.R. Holbrook developed performative negotiation principles with Dr. Leonard C. Hawes, Professor of Communication, at the University of Utah.

Types of Discourse

Different styles of communication are associated with each type of the four types of discourse.

Performative Discourse

The language we use and the narratives we perform create our reality.

For example, during a workplace conversation, harsh feelings may emerge and can lead to responses that bring different perceptions about the issue into play. As new information gets incorporated into the situation, the result is a new view of the original feelings and the situation.

The objective of a performative discourse is to transform the:

- telling of stories into genuine conversations, and through understanding, work towards a meeting of the minds on next steps

- repetition of positions or conflict-problem stories into a conversation that can lead to problem solving

Effective performative interactions forego blame. Seeking answers to questions about the truth of what actually happened in the past is often not relevant to the resolution of conflicts. Determining who started it or where or when it all began or who is right and who is wrong are questions for which the answers have little or no problem-solving value. Asking such questions may even protract or exacerbate the conflict by provoking defensiveness and reciprocal blaming.

Paul Falcone, in the introduction to his book *101 Tough Conversations To Have With Employees,* suggests that there are a few key rules to follow for what we have termed performative discourse:

1. It's **not what you say but how you say it** that counts. In the world of work, people tend to respond in kind. If you demonstrate respect and compassion, you're likely to receive a similar response, even when dealing with the most uncomfortable and confrontational workplace situations.

2. Your **greatest asset when dealing with others is *guilt*, not anger.**[75] Anger is an external response. When people are mad at another person, they look outward to voice their frustration. Guilt, on the other hand, is internal. When people feel guilty, they look inward and tend to assume responsibility for the problem at hand.

   Allow people to assume responsibility for their actions, and you'll "pierce their heart" and get them to want to change for themselves.

   Try to force them to do something by making them mad or by challenging or embarrassing them, and they'll resist the change that's being forced on them.

3. ***Whatever you want for yourself, give to another.*** So many times, people demand respect, open communication, and other forms of social acceptance without realizing that they don't give those things to others.

Distributive Discourse

A distributive discourse is positional in nature and focussed on the distribution of something of value. Distributive approaches are often about who should pay, how much, to whom, and why. Simply stated, it is a situation in which parties are seeking to obtain rewards from some limited pool—anything not going to A will go to B and vice versa.

75   Adapted from Paul Falcone, "Golden Rules of Effective Communication" in *2600 Phrases for Setting Effective Performance Goals* (New York: American Management Association (AMA), 2017).

Integrative Discourse

Integrative discourse seeks to find a mutually acceptable solution to what emerges and is recognized as a shared problem. An integrative approach is an alternative to pure positional discourse and is a distinct subset of cooperative approaches.

Where typical cooperative approaches tend to focus on positions and in varying degrees, employ accommodation and compromise conflict styles to find common ground, integrative approaches focus on interests and promote a high degree of informational exchange, aimed at mutual problem-solving, with objective criteria or standards as a point of comparison. Participants work to advance understanding, find alternatives, and enhance chances for reaching agreements by discovering innovative approaches that reflect the underlying interests of the parties, and then seeking to arrange the alternatives in packages that yield maximum benefit to both.

Transformative Discourse

Transformative discourse is interactions that centre on the parties' relationship and explore how the parties can interact more constructively with each other.

In some conflicts, the relationship between the parties is more important than any particular solution to the problem that faces them.[76] Because neither party wants to admit to being the one at fault, the parties in a conflict relationship often do not notice their own contribution to the problem.

As a result, they rarely look in a productive place (i.e., at their own contribution) to help themselves change.

When something happens, the parties may feel anger, blame, injustice, guilt, regret, shame, helplessness, resignation, etc. Each response avoids accepting or acknowledging their own responsibility. As in performative discourse, the parties tend to have conflicting stories about who is responsible for their circumstance. They tend to get stuck in the past and in blaming each other.

In a transformative discourse, the parties must attempt to meld their competing individual stories into a working draft of sorts, a *third story*. A third story is one an impartial or neutral observer, such as a mediator, would tell; it's a version of events both sides can agree on. The key is learning to describe the gap—or difference—between the narratives, your story and the other person's story.

76   Adapted from James R. Holbrook, "Using Performative, Distributive, Integrative, and Transformative Principles in Negotiation," *Loyola Law Review* 56 (2010).

With a third story, whatever else you may think and feel, you can at least agree that you and the other person see things differently. You each recognize your own contribution to the relationship problem and the polarizing patterns of communication that underlie it. Participants are drawn to the need to focus on the present and disclose how they feel.

The parties also need to begin to talk about the future and about the possibilities of relating to each other in a different way. To set the stage for a productive dialogue, opening a difficult conversation with a third story can be a powerful tool.

Within a transformative discourse, those involved must understand the nature of their conflict. To do this, they must have the capacity for self-awareness and critical observation, subsequent reflection, and correction, honesty, and especially empathy.

Transformative Discourse Tips

People need to feel they have been heard and understood, which results in a need for them to tell their story. Meeting that need can markedly shift the tone of a conflict. This involves an accurate, non-judgemental understanding of the other person's needs, concerns, and perspectives without necessarily agreeing with them. The key to better transformative discourse is better listening. Listening is a commitment implemented by four kinds of behaviours—attending, inviting, confirming, and summarizing.

Attending Behaviours

Maintain appropriate posture and proximity to the other person.

Make eye contact

Use encouraging nonverbal expressions (e.g., head nodding).

Inviting Behaviours

Seek to understand. Listen without interrupting, judging, or preparing to talk.

Use encouraging verbal expressions (e.g., "uh huh," "I see").

Encourage the other person to keep talking (e.g., "Tell me more about X . . .").

Confirming Behaviours

- Ask follow-up questions with sincere curiosity to get additional information.

- Show you understand the other person's feelings using reflective empathy.

- Acknowledge that you find something of merit in what you have heard.

Summarizing Behaviours

- Briefly summarize what you heard, using the other's key words and feelings.

- Ask whether your summary is complete and accurate.

- If necessary, revise your summary and re-ask whether it's correct and complete.

And, finally, test the validity of your assumptions. Refer to Part 5: *Interactions with Purpose* for listening skills and techniques.

Reconciling Your Dual Concerns

Review and apply the dual concerns model—the concern for self and the concern for others—and what you value in a particular circumstance. In this circumstance, what do you value?

Chapter 4: Orientations Emerge

We are influenced by our frames of reference and how we see the world, our view of power, our authority, and what we believe specific interactions to be about. Taken together, a general orientation[77] emerges that informs our approach to potentially contentious discourse, as well as the approach we adopt to reconcile matters at issue.

Orientations can be placed in one of three general frames.[78] Two of the orientations can be characterized as focussing on positions and positioning (maximalist positioning and equitable positioning) and the third focussing on interests and options (integrative approach). This general orientation, or stance, then becomes our reality and we live within it, subject to imprisoning assumptions and the reinforcing influence of confirmation bias.[79]

- **Maximalist positioning** is characteristically competitive and position-based. This approach assumes a zero-sum game (any gain for one party is offset by an equal or opposite loss by the other). From the maximalist position, participants assume they maximize their outcomes by making extreme initial demands.

- **Equitable positioning** is characteristically position-based, yet through interactions there is a potential to be more cooperative. The central concerns are equity and fairness through compromise. From the equitable position, participants assume they can best respond to one another's needs by making equal concessions on their positional demands and accepting lesser than proposed outcomes.

- **The integrative approach**, characteristically cooperative and interest-based, is driven by its interest-based aspects, seeking to reconcile the underlying needs, concerns, and problems to achieve an efficient solution.

---

77   *Negotiator orientation* generally refers to the negotiator's inclination towards either a competitive or cooperative approach. In this chapter, it may also indicate the inclinations to use either interest-based or position-based negotiation.

78   Adapted from C. Craver, *The Impact of Negotiator Styles on Bargaining Interactions* (Washington, DC: George Washington University Law School, 2010) and C. Craver, American *Journal of Trial Advocacy* 35, no. 1 (2011); J. Folberg, et al, *Resolving Disputes: Theory and Practice,* 2nd ed. (New York, Aspen Publishers, 2010).

79   Once we have formed a view, we embrace information that confirms that view while ignoring or rejecting information that casts doubt on it. Confirmation bias suggests that we don't perceive circumstances objectively. We focus on selected facts, data, and opinions that make us feel good because they confirm our prejudices. The result is that we may become prisoners of our assumptions.

Maximalist positioners, equitable positioners, or those who adopt an integrative approach all seek to solve problems. The first two start from set, established positions and the third starts with the identification of interests, generation of options, and the selection of an option based on objective criteria or standards.

Figure 19: Interrelationship of Orientations

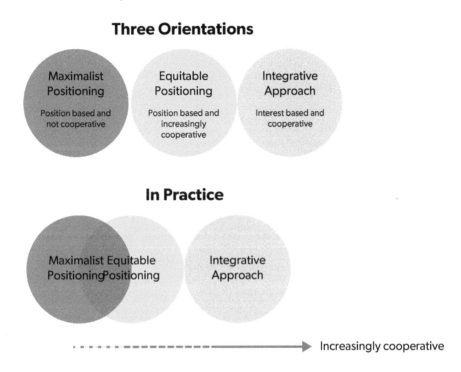

An Attitude as Much as an Approach

One might argue that at a practical level, these orientations represent a continuum of strategies. In other words, you could start out positional and see how the other party responds, with the goal of becoming generally integrative.

On the journey to reconciling the matters at issue, you can employ various forms of equitable positioning, increasingly introducing your integrative action.

Figure 19, above, represents the three orientations that one has or adopts at the outset of a situation, maximalist position, an equitable position, or an integrative approach. The maximalist position is characteristically competitive and position-based, and it makes extreme initial demands.

The equitable position is characteristically position-based, yet increasingly cooperative as positions are revealed. The integrative approach is cooperative and interest-based. It seeks to resolve the underlying concerns and problems to reconcile the matters at issue.

Note that there is a measure of overlap between the position-based approaches and the cooperative approach because some negotiations (the equitable position) can be characterized as both position-based and cooperative. The part of the position-based sphere outside the cooperative sphere represents the most competitive region (the maximalist position), where cooperation is low and differences in positions are seen as fixed. Conversely, the part of the cooperative sphere outside the position-based sphere represents the most integrative region (the integrative approach), where cooperation is high and differences are not seen as fixed to positions.

In answering the question as to whether this is a continuum, one argument is that negotiations can take on hybrid forms. Negotiations are not either/or propositions and they are not interest-based or position-based. Rather, negotiations are characterized by certain qualities that can be shown along a continuum, generally reflecting purely position-based approaches on one end versus purely interest-based approaches on the other.

Another argument is that the integrative approach has principles and associated strategies, and that it focusses on the long relationship—one of acknowledged interdependence. The back and forth of negotiations serves to better define that interdependence.

However, starting from a position—whether from a maximalist or an equitable position—and moving to an integrative approach has its limitations, including:

- Your motivations can't be seen only your actions. What you intend to do is only known to you.

- What message do your actions send to the other party, their constituents and to your constituents?

- Actions are subject to interpretation. What's to stop you from cycling in and out of approaches, and then are you really seeking to be interest-based and cooperative?

- It is difficult to avoid the anchoring effect.

- You can't control the other party's responses or their reactions in the face of your actions.

- It is inefficient; the so-called hybrid is really equitable positioning labelled as an integrative approach.

- You are more likely than not to become hostage to the norm. It is easier to retreat to the position-based status quo approach.

- It relieves you from being prepared: you go with what you've done before and what you've come to know. The emphasis is on positioning and reaction rather than a process of engagement and information exchange to identify interests.

- How the negotiation process is framed will influence whether a positioning/distributive or integrative approach is pursued. The stereotype of negotiation is a contentious win-lose process, not the exercise of collaborative problem-solving. Simply labelling the task at hand as a negotiation or bargaining can drive the assumption of a fixed-pie, distributive, positional approach.[80]

- It is questionable what you are seeking, whether in terms of process or substance, long term versus short term.

As you read the next sections, bear this discussion in mind. How is your approach informed by what you learn?

Positions and Positioning

The position-framed, positioning approach views negotiation as an adversarial, zero-sum[81] exercise focussed on claiming rather than creating value. Typically, one party will stake out a high (or low) opening position (demand or offer) and the other a correspondingly low (or high) one. Then a series of, usually reciprocal, concessions are made until an agreement is reached somewhere in the middle of the opening positions, or no agreement is reached at all.

Positioners believe that when approaching a negotiation, the starting position should be more ambitious than where one is willing to settle. But when the starting bid is so far outside the realm of possibility, it doesn't help that side's negotiating position. In fact, it could have the opposite effect.

Maximalist positioning and equitable positioning are the primary forms of positional negotiations. In position-based negotiations, parties typically focus on some plan of action or objective to fulfil their sets of needs. Positioners craft a set of positions that are advanced and argued for during negotiations. These positions are motivated by

80   C.C. Smith, *Moving from Distributive to Integrative Negotiation* (Garland, TX: Amberton University, 2012).

81   A zero-sum exercise is a situation in which each participant's gain or loss of utility is balanced by the losses or gains of the utility of the other participants. If the total gains of the participants are added up and the total losses are subtracted, they will sum to zero.

and purportedly represent the proposer's interests—positions being something that you decide upon, and interests what caused you to so decide.

The effort to secure an agreement focusses on these objectives, or positions, and not on the parties' overall concerns or interests. Position-based negotiators typically view differences as fixed; they see the agreement as the conclusion of a zero-sum contest and focus on obtaining some desired portion of gains. In position-based negotiations, parties can work either cooperatively or competitively.

Positioners adopt the main tenets of distributive bargaining to varying degrees and employ tactics that include[82]:

- Adversarial and advocacy stance: You do your job, I'll do mine. You give me your proposals and I'll give you mine, and out of the clash of these positions will come the reconciliation of what we both want (and possibly a clearer definition of the problem).

- Not making the first offer and requiring the other person to make the first offer.

- Starting with an extremely aggressive position (if adopting a maximalist strategy) to anchor the other person's expectations.

  The concept of "anchoring" refers to the tendency to attach (or "anchor") our thoughts to a reference point—even though it may have no logical relevance to the decision at hand. It is a cognitive bias that describes the common human tendency to rely too heavily on the first piece of information offered (the "anchor") when making decisions and is considered a bias because it distorts our judgement, especially when matters are unclear or otherwise unexplored.

  The tactic of anchoring is the attempt to establish a reference point (anchor) around which a[83] negotiation will revolve and use this reference point to make subsequent adjustments. The initial value, or starting point, may be suggested by the formulation of the problem, or it may be made as the result pf a partial computation. In either case, different starting points yield different estimates, which are biased toward the initial values.

  Anchoring is inevitable because one of the parties must open discussions, negotiations first. Opening offers are anchors whether you intend them as a tactical move or not because the opening offer often has the psychological effect of

82   Adapted from R. Lewicki et al., *Essentials of Negotiation* (Toronto, ON: McGraw-Hill Ryerson. 2014), 31–43.

83   Katherine Shonk, *"What is Anchoring in Negotiation?"* Program on Negotiation Negotiation Briefings Newsletter May 15, 2018, www.pon.harvard.edu/daily/negotiation-skills-daily/what-is-anchoring-in-negotiation.

framing what each side will view as the possible outcomes in the ensuing negotiation. The best way to avoid anchoring in negotiations is to engage in rigorous critical thinking.

When you believe the other party likely knows more than you do about the size of the zone of potential agreement (ZOPA), you will have difficulty anchoring effectively. Before dropping an anchor in such situations, arm yourself with as much information as possible.

- Not disclosing their underlying interests, related information, or that they have limited alternatives.

- Concealing or misrepresenting relevant settlement information.

- Repeating their initial position again and again.

- Not acknowledging the other person's perspective.

- Not engaging in problem solving that requires them to change their position and move away from the anchor they have dropped.

- Making very small moves and taking a long time between moves.

- Making **take-it-or-leave-it** demands, stating that that no additional movement is possible.

- Engaging in **doubt-creation** behaviours such as theatrics, threats, exaggerations, distortions, or bluffs.

- Getting up and walking out or **threatening** to walk out, if demands are not met.

The positional approach—whether maximalist or equitable positioning—has its limitations. Disadvantages of positional bargaining:

- locks participants into positions that make movements difficult

- can lead to a polarizing kind of impasse on specific issues or on an agreement generally

- conceals the parties' underlying concerns, needs, and interests

- can result in parties becoming angry or entrenched in their positions

- encourages continued positioning and positional bargaining

- interferes with reaching an agreement efficiently

- tests, if not potentially endangers, relationships

Maximalist Positioning

Maximalist positioning begins with the assumption that the opening position is a bargaining stance, and that no matter how long the proposers may deny it, they expect to come down from these positions to find agreements.

A maximalist anchors aggressively and adopts what can be characterized as an extreme opening position, leaving the impression that the proposer will not or is unlikely to make substantive adjustments to their initial positions.

Maximalist position statements:

- effectively hide the proponent's real or minimum expectations and they eliminate the danger of committing to an overly modest objective

- provide covers while they seek to learn the other party's real positions

- will very likely induce the other party to reduce their expectations (begin to negotiate with themselves to present another offer in the hope the maximalist will move)

- provide proponents with something to give up, with concessions they can make, to come to terms with the other party.

  This may be especially important when the other party also opens high and negotiators are required to trade concessions as they move towards mutually agreeable terms.

The maximalist approach may lead to the belief that those who make high opening demands, have high expectations, make relatively small and infrequent concessions, and are perceptive and unyielding fare better overall than their opponents. The potential benefits of the maximalist position need to be weighed against its potential disadvantages, which are those associated with competitive/adversarial strategies. The disadvantages of using this approach include:

- Increased risk of situational stalemates. Competent opponents will prefer their non-settlement alternatives to the unreasonable demands and supporting tactics of the maximalist negotiators, unless the opponents themselves can devise effective strategies to counter such maximalist behaviours.

- Some demands may lack credibility by their inappropriateness and lack of congruity in the context in which they are made; proposals, positions don't appear to be conceivably achievable.

- The approach does not consistently bring high returns for those who use it— only for those who employ it effectively. A more typical maximalist approach is to start with initial positions that are seen as somewhat unreasonable, but not seen as absurd. After protracted negotiations and a series of modest concessions, the truly important matters are revealed.

The effectiveness of high demands will depend on the party against whom the high demands are made. In cases where the other party is unsure of the actual value(s) of the matters at issue, high opening demands by a maximalist have the desired effect. A party, unsure of values, uses the maximalist's high opening demands as standards against which to set their own goals. In other words, they begin to bargain with themselves to come up with something that moves them towards the maximalist's stated positions.

However, when the other party has evaluated their circumstance and arrived at an appropriate value, the reaction may be that the high opening demands are evidence of unreasonableness. This causes credibility to be diminished, increasing the likelihood of process breakdowns.

Equitable Positioning

Equitable positioners craft positions that are designed, calculated and framed to be viewed as *fair or reasonable* to both sides. Notions of *fair or reasonable* are subjective, situational and—so to speak—in the eye of the beholder.

For many people, equitable positioning represents the bargaining norm—and they believe that's just the way bargaining works, whether engaged in party-to-party interactions or collective bargaining.

This approach is considered to be the most economical and efficient method of resolving matters at issue. It minimizes the risk of deadlock and avoids the costs of delay occasioned by extreme bargaining positions.

Like maximalist positioning, equitable positioning involves positioning and position taking but differs from the maximalist approach. Equitable positioning requires that:

- Demonstrable evidence exists of sustained trust in words, actions, and undertakings; adoption of a good faith orientation.

- Negotiators avoid the temptation to take advantage of situationally naïve and/or trusting opponents.

- Trust tempered with realism. Parties trust, and they verify. It is out of trust that negotiators make concessions, but if their trust is not rewarded or returned in what they consider a fair fashion, further concessions will likely be withheld until the other party reciprocates.

- Proposals be conceivably achievable. Equitable positioners cannot be perceived as maximalists.

Equitable positioners do not always open discussions with statements specifying their desires to achieve mutually beneficial solutions. Rather, they open with positions that show they are serious about finding an agreement, and they trustingly work towards mid-points between what they characterize as their reasonable opening positions. Unless both sides come forward with what is seen as reasonable opening positions, it will be difficult for one side to compel the other to move towards an agreement.

The principal disadvantage of the equitable positioning approach is the focus on stated positions and to a much lesser degree on why one party takes the positions they do. The challenge in this approach becomes how you create the value to be used to create options and ultimately come an agreement beyond the stated positions that represent pre-established targets.

Integrative Approach

The integrative school of thought emerged from the research and publications of the Program on Negotiation at Harvard Law School—an intra-university consortium dedicated to developing the theory and practice of negotiation and dispute resolution.

The concept, also referred to as interest-based or principled negotiation, represents a departure from the game theorists' view[84] and the popular negotiation literature that focusses on the strategy and tactics of negotiation primarily as variants of position-based, distributive approaches.

In the 1981 book *Getting to Yes*,[85] Roger Fisher and William Ury, co-founders of Program on Negotiation, set out the basic approach:

- separating the people from the problem

- focussing on interests, not positions

- inventing options for mutual gain

---

84   The game theory paradigm proposes negotiator orientation as competitive versus cooperative and is position-based versus interest-based. Integrative negotiation is an approach to interactions that focuses on the basic need or underlying concern that is addressed by a proposal. In contrast, position-based negotiation focuses on a "position, proposal, or chosen solution to a particular problem, or goal.

85   The second edition was published in 1991 with Program on Negotiation colleague Bruce Patton: Fisher, Roger, William Ury and Bruce Patton, *Getting to Yes: Negotiating Agreement without Giving in*, 2nd ed. (New York: Penguin Books).

- insisting on using objective criteria.

The integrative approach is a means of decision making that conceptualizes the actions and contingencies of all possible outcomes, options, and scenarios with the intention of incorporating the goals and aims of the parties to create maximum value through collaboration.

It can be seen as problem-solving dialogue where parties co-operate by pooling efforts to uncover information, develop alternatives independent of the degree to which outcomes serve self-interests, and then agree on the alternatives that is best for each party and for the relationship as a whole. This approach is characteristically cooperative, but is also distinguished by aspects that are not essential to a cooperative negotiation.

The integrative approach:
- Observes the principles of the dual concerns model: the concern for self and the concern for others balance.

- Seeks to identify, understand, and focus on underlying interests.

- Directly examines sets of needs and concerns (position-based seeks need fulfilment by achieving certain stated desired positions).

- Exhibits mutual problem-solving behaviour.

- Reframes the problem in non-positional terms and avoids specific outcome engendering words.

- Does not advocate positions/outcomes to serve self-interest in early stages (distinguishes creating value from claiming value; see below for a detailed discussion).

- Stresses seeking, assembling, and sharing information.

- Adopts an analytic frame to examine the matters at issue.

- Establishes points of comparison (objective criteria).

- Places emphasis on developing new alternatives/use of dialogue.

- Acts assertively in selecting favourable alternatives; good for self and relationship.

- Proceeds independent of trust.

- Takes a long-term view: As Fisher and Brown advise in *Getting Together, Building Relationships as We Negotiate, we either look out for both parties, or we don't proceed; we won't risk an adversarial future.*

An integrative approach seeks the potential for parties' interests to be combined, or elements incorporated, in a way that creates joint value. If both parties can independently satisfy their interests, there is no need for an integrative approach, but if they are interdependent, then there is no other way to find a fair, effective, wise, and sustainable (stable) path forward.

An integrative approach is based on good faith. While it is as much an attitude as an approach, it also requires particular skills such as:

- active listening

- suspending judgement in order to achieve an understanding of all parties' interests

- constructively managing the tension of opposing ideas and, instead of choosing one at the expense of the other, generating a creative resolution of the tension in the form of a new idea that contains elements of each of the opposing ideas but is superior to either alone.[86]

The approach is more than opening demands, offers, and counter offers. It describes an attitude and approach that carries through to the other stages of the interaction, and is an alternative to pure positional discourse (maximalist positioning and equitable positioning).

All those involved should be explicitly committed to the search for integrative potential and willing to hone the personal skills necessary for it to succeed. The following factors indicate the potential for integration:

- The parties cannot achieve what they need to achieve independent of one another.
- More than one issue is involved.
- It is possible to add more issues to the mix.
- The parties' interactions will recur over time.
- The parties have varying preferences across issues

---

86   Concept of integrative thinking introduced in *The Opposable Mind: How Successful Leaders Win Through Integrative Thinking* by Roger Martin, 2007.

Integrative solutions are based on a shared understanding of an evidentiary base that includes relevant facts and research, as well as an appreciation of the contested aspects of an issue and the beliefs and desires of each party that are the root cause of the disagreement. Therefore, the use of an analytic frame to develop those shared understandings is an important preparation.

As the analytic frame is developed, factual foundations, areas of agreement, and areas of difference become clarified. The original problem statement often shifts as a result and to increase the integrative potential, it is useful to develop a shared statement of the challenge or opportunity using neutral, non-positional language. The analytic frame can begin the process of assembling objective criteria that will serve as a point of comparison to inform any final agreement.

Integrative potential is also increased by standing back from the specific issue to view it in a broad systemic way. Nothing exists in isolation and action on any matter both affects and is affected by other matters. Considering an issue from a systemic point of view complicates it, of course, but that very complexity also adds variables that can be used to create value. A narrow focus on an issue, particularly when it is defined as a problem to be solved, limits possible action and thus limits creative response.

In addition to having a sound foundation of facts and understandings, and a statement of the issue that creates potential for constructive responses, it is equally important to have the right people present. Consider: who do they represent, what influence do they have, and do they have the skill and the will to meaningfully participate? Do they have the authority to reach agreement?

Both procedural and behavioural ground rules are critically important to a successful search for integrative potential. Mutual understanding should be developed around matters critical to process success, such as the following.

- **Nature of the discussions:**

  - An environment where people focus their discussion on the issue while maintaining respect for people having other points of view encourages people to present their divergent viewpoints so that ideas and recommendations can be clarified, redesigned, and tested for logical soundness. Discussions should be not only congenial and cooperative but also collaborative. Creativity should be encouraged; compromise avoided.

- **Time table:**

  - A timetable includes commencement and frequency of meetings, dovetailing any committee work with the main discussions and so on. The discipline of a timetable discourages perseveration on issues. If you are stuck, agree to set an issue aside for the time being and move on to something where more progress can be made.

- **Ground rules such as:**

  O The process for information-sharing to encourage free disclosure of information;

  O How to encourage active participation by all and avoid funnelling communication through spokespersons;

  O The definition of consensus and an individual participant's obligations when the group has achieved consensus about an issue;

  O The process for communicating with, and reporting progress to, constituents and others (if this is done at all during the process, when, how, and in what form); and,

  O How matters are concluded and the processes for ratification of any agreement.

Ideally, an integrative approach will lead to constructive reconciliation of all aspects of an issue and a mutually agreed course of action, but often some aspects remain unresolved. However, even these matters benefit from a deeper appreciation by each party for the reason for their differences—not just the difference in their initial positions but also the difference in their underlying interests.

To engage in this type of problem-solving, the parties must minimize interpersonal conflict so that they can work together. Some who adopt the integrative approach incorporate simple form or format changes to offer a difference in attitude and process.

Examples include:

1. A different working structure. Use the meeting space in a way that is different from typical meetings. Try a side-by-side process, sit at a round table, or even place the negotiators on the same side of the table as opposed to the traditional across from each other construct.

2. Breaking the problem down into more easily managed component parts. This constructs a multi-issue negotiation out of what at first may appear to be a single-issue negotiation, allowing both parties to make decisions based their differing priorities.

   To engender a creative and collaborative environment conducive to integrative negotiations, ask many questions and listen intently to the answers given, with an eye towards using this information to reconcile your respective differences during the course of the discussions. Additionally, opening up the table to multiple proposals acts as a social cue, which indicates you are flexible and open to suggestions, inviting similar behaviour from your counterpart.

3.   Brainstorming. Writing mutual interests and possible options identified on a white board or flip chart to heighten the sense of working together. Brainstorming rules include:

- Criticism is not allowed and judgement is to be suspended. No other member can say whether an idea is good or bad.

- Questions can be asked only to clarify an idea.

- A long list of suggestions and ideas is encouraged even if outside the norm. They can be generated by looking from new perspectives and suspending assumptions. These new ways of thinking might give you better solutions.

- Go for quantity. Quantity breeds quality. The more ideas you can surface, the better the process will be.

- Combine and improve ideas, and build on others' contributions.

4.   Use word associations in a process such as mind mapping to create diagrams of relationships between concepts, ideas, or other pieces of information to engender creative non-positional thinking. Mind mapping allows you to record your ideas in any order, as soon as they come to you. You are not constrained by thinking in order. You can order and prioritize them later, having identified all of the ideas, concepts, etc. A general outline of mind mapping:

- think of your general main theme and write that down in the centre of the page. The main idea, subject, or focus is crystallized in a central image

- identify sub-themes of your main concept and radiate them from the central image as branches. Make sure to use very short phrases or even single words.

- try to think of at least two main points for each sub-theme you created and create

  o   branches out to those

  o   branches comprise a key image or key word, drawn or printed on its associated line

  o   topics of lesser importance are represented as twigs on the relevant branch

  o   branches form a connected nodal structure

5. Using facilitation[87] to explore matters at issue: Facilitation is a bundle of meeting-management skills that includes coordinating the flow of conversation, ensuring that participants observe time limits, cooling tempers when talks get overheated and periodically summarizing the essence of working agreements.

6. Focussing on the three Ps: purpose, people, and process. Meditation Works Incorporated (MWI), a Boston area consulting firm that specializes in dispute resolution services, defines an effective meeting as "a collaborative process involving a defined group of people reaching their stated purpose."

   - Purpose: Before arranging a meeting, determine why you are calling one in the first place. Complete the sentence, "If our meeting is successful, we will have accomplished our goal of..." Don't have the meeting if you're having a hard time naming the objective.

   - People: Determine who needs to attend the meeting and the roles they will be asked to play. Ask for input about who should be at the meeting. It's important to have the right people in order to provide perspective, share expertise, and make and implement decisions.

     o Who will facilitate? The facilitator should be able to remain objective and guide the group in a constructive way.

     o Logistics and operations: Who will keep time, take notes, and provide feedback to the facilitator after the meeting?

     o Meeting rules and roles: Inform participants of the basic meeting guidelines and their role. Let them know why they have been asked to attend the meeting and inform them of the expectation that they will come prepared to participate fully and add value to the discussion.

   Ask what resources will be available and if technology be allowed at the meeting. Review the advantages and disadvantages carefully—allowing laptops, phones, tablets, and the like will mean some participants might ignore the content of the meeting.

---

87   The terms *facilitation* and *mediation* are often used interchangeably, yet important distinctions exist between the two processes. A facilitator helps groups to understand their common objectives and assists them to plan to achieve those objectives. A mediator is of assistance when a negotiation has already reached a standoff or when communication is entirely blocked. Mediators are generally expected to be strictly neutral and to bring a substantive knowledge of the issues under discussion to the table. Mediators often also focus on getting the right people to the table and implementing the final deal.

- Process: The process breaks down into three parts: preparation, meeting facilitation, and follow up.

Preparation

- Work with the group to structure the agenda. Send the agenda to all participants prior to the meeting and ask for feedback from the group in advance of the meeting.

- Develop an agenda that reflects the objective(s) you wish to achieve. What activities or discussions will allow you to have the desired outcome? Each of the discussion points should have a time estimate.

- Remain fluid with the agenda if it looks like participants are making progress outside the time parameters.

- Be deliberate when choosing the time, date, and location of the meeting. When is your team most focussed and cohesive?

- Ensure that the meeting rules and expectations are known before starting.

Facilitation

- Be prepared to welcome all participants and decide whether an icebreaker will be necessary.

- Define the objectives at the beginning of the meeting with the group. Allow the participants to visualize success and ask them what they need to do to get there. This step reassures participants that time will not be wasted and that there is a tangible goal in mind.

- Review the agenda and acknowledge any changes that may have been made. By respecting the agenda and its time recommendations, you are respecting the group.

- Set and enforce consensus-building[88] ground rules. Prepare a short list of ground rules that the group can quickly endorse.

---

88   Consensus decision making: a group decision-making process in which group members develop, and agree to support, a decision in the best interest of the whole. Consensus may be broadly defined as an acceptable resolution, one that can be supported, even if not the favourite of each individual; majority opinion; general agreement.

These can include processes to encourage equal participation, such as the use of a talking stick that is passed to each person when they have a contribution to make and the three popsicles allocation, where each person in a group is provided with three popsicle sticks. Place one on the table each time the person speaks. When all three are used, the person is unable to speak until all other participants have spoken their allocation of three popsicle sticks.

- Prepare a draft summary of all discussions and decisions, and distribute them within 24 hours of each meeting. Each member has an opportunity to make corrections to the summaries before they become final.

Codifying these ground rules can allow the process to move forward with the group's full support.

- Make sure to ask for input from all participants and also ensure that one participant does not dominate the conversation.

- Ask participants to follow the "Step Up or Step Back" guideline.[89] If they tend to let others do the talking during a meeting, perhaps they will consider stepping up; or, if they recognize that they dominate the conversation, hopefully they will step back and let others be heard.

Follow up

- Reserve 10 to 15 minutes at the end of each session to check-in with participants. Were the objectives achieved? If not, why not? What are the next steps?

- Record in writing a fair and accurate summary of negotiated outcomes. Produce a single text—a written proposal incorporating everyone's suggestions for a package that would satisfy them all.

89   Participants should be aware of how much they are speaking. If they feel they are speaking a lot, they should let others speak, and if they find themselves not talking, they should try to contribute some comments, ideas, or suggestions.

The integrative approach and communications

Communications in an integrative approach are more inviting and cooperative. Participants tend to present overlapping stories and focus on satisfaction of their individual interests, which may require them to fashion alternatives.

A party's opening statement can strongly suggest the type of solution he or she is seeking. Opening remarks can communicate interest in the outcome of the process, the way to achieve it, and the relationship with the other party.

This signals a desire for a more integrative solution, as opposed to opening remarks that demonstrate interest only in the outcome or only in the relationship used in other approaches.

With an integrative approach, there must be a free flow of information so that the parties' respective interests can be revealed. Each party must be able to hear and understand the interests of the other, as well as disclose their own interests.

- Interests may also relate to third parties, such as co-workers, a board of directors, and, sometimes, important third-party interests that must be disclosed and satisfied if there is to be an agreement.

- A party who perceives and understands the other party's perspective and important interests is better able to frame the integrative potential productively and more effectively identify potential options and measures of legitimacy that might satisfy both parties.

  To support your communication, you will need to clarify the priority of interests into needs and wants. Needs are more important and usually must be satisfied before an agreement can be reached, whereas wants may be traded or given away.

Caveats and Common Process Concerns

An Integrative approach is not the current norm. Many professionals and those labelled as experts are invested in the status quo of positioning, advocacy, and the like and are quick to say that the complexity of issues, relationships, and the desires of the other side does not lend itself to what they view as a softer, untested approach—it may be good in theory but not in practice.

The integrative approach skeptics or *bargaining traditionalists* go on to observe that if the other side is competitive and positional, you must meet that approach with an equally hard approach, fight fire with fire if you will. This oft-practiced approach has limitations that we are all very familiar with both in the short-term wisdom of decisions and the success in the actual implementation of those decisions—not to mention the spillover effect on relationships, culture, and system health.

The other party's approach does not prevent you from adopting a constructive stance. Planning, persistence, and objective clarity are the path to a new normal. We can either work to establish that new normal or reinforce a default pattern of conflict and confrontation. That is not to say that the integrative approach is either easy or a panacea, simply that it is an alternative well worth trying.

Other than a general skepticism about its efficacy, some common concerns with the integrative approach include:

Fear of Revealing Interests

A concern frequently expressed by traditional negotiators is whether they should reveal their bottom line. An integrative approach neither requires nor encourages disclosing one's bottom line. There is, however, a requirement to reveal one's interests. The articulation of interests on a particular issue is an expression of the issue's importance. Interests must be articulated and data shared, but neither party should be expected to prematurely reveal the minimum level for satisfying its interests on an issue.

Alleged Unsuitability for Economic Issues

A closely related concern is the applicability of interest-based discussions to issues that are seen as predominantly economic ones. If it is not possible to increase the available budget, how creative can you be? Applying an integrative approach to these issues can be difficult, but still helpful. With an agreement on appropriate data (through the analytic frame), the parties can frequently find ways to use the available resources most effectively because an integrative approach is helpful in focussing them away from extreme, staked-out positions towards substantive discussion on the value associated with the various aspects of the matter at hand.

Lack of Time

A final concern regarding this approach is the amount of time required. There is no magical solution to this ever-present challenge. However, creating an analytic frame, developing a neutral non-positional statement of the issue, ensuring that each party's interests have been clearly articulated and are understood, and establishing a clear timeline expedites the flow of discussions and makes the best use of the time we have.

As the parties become more experienced with an integrative approach, process efficiencies are realized. An abbreviated process may be used to resolve an issue where little is in dispute and using subcommittees to explore particularly complex sub-issues in advance of more extensive discussions can help to use available time well. In the end, however, haste makes waste in decision making just as it does in other endeavours. Sometimes you just have to take the time to do something well.

Point of Clarification: Integrative and Cooperative

Integrative discourse or negotiation is often confused with cooperative approaches. While both can be cooperative in nature, the point of comparison is better focussed on the foundation of the particular approach—one approach focusses on *interests* while the other focusses on *positions,* statements that purportedly represent interests.

> Some writers and those practitioners who advocate and adopt what are considered traditional strategies characterize both approaches—integrative and cooperative—as soft and vulnerable to the tactics of the competitive, adversarial negotiator who feigns cooperation.

The two approaches, often generalized and rarely analyzed, can be distinguished from one another and positional approaches and, in so doing, reveal an antidote:

- Use of Roger Fisher and Scott Brown's guidelines of unconditionally constructive behaviour (later in this section).[90]

- Are evidence-informed: development of a factual foundation, identification of areas of agreement and clarification of areas of difference; beyond the narratives and positions

- Alternatives are considered: In most negotiations, parties are influenced consciously or unconsciously by their assessment of their alternatives to a negotiated agreement. The better their alternatives, the more they may push for a more favorable agreement. The worse their alternatives, the more accommodating they may be in the negotiations. Unfortunately, parties frequently fail to undertake an accurate and comprehensive analysis of their alternatives and, therefore, negotiate poorly based on unrealistic and uninformed ideas of what they might obtain in the absence of a negotiated agreement. In any negotiation, it is important to make sure that you establish your best alternative, but also your worst so you can assess your options with greater accuracy, and, hopefully, better results.

90   Adapted from R. Fisher and S. Brown's *Getting Together Building Relationships as We Negotiate* (New York: Penguin Books, 1988), 38.

Develop the best alternative to a negotiated agreement (BATNA)[91] and worst alternatives to a negotiated agreement (WATNA) before beginning discussions. The BATNA and WATNA are the negotiator's walk-away alternative (i.e., it represents what you will do if you cannot achieve a better agreement through the negotiation). Before entering into a negotiation, it is advisable to improve the BATNA to the greatest extent possible having full appreciation for your WATNA.

When you consider BATNA and WATNA, you can't forget about the context of the situation. If you are trying to surmise what is going to happen if you walk away, and if you don't have any good alternatives, you're really looking at your worst case, or your WATNA.

- Alternatives and options are differentiated: An alternative is a choice limited to one or more possibilities, propositions, or courses of action. A selection of one alternative precludes any other possibility.

  Options are ideas that the parties may generate within the context of a negotiation for possible resolution. The parties evaluate these options, formally or informally, to see how well they satisfy their interests. The parties may consider some ideas to be favorable options and others to be less so, but all are theoretically possible bases for resolution between the parties to the dispute even though some are not realistic or would never be acceptable to both parties. The options analysis remains within the context of the negotiation with the other party and is not the same as the best, worse alternatives analysis.

- Objective criteria is developed and used as standards to inform the substance of the matters at issue, to inform the process to identify interests, and as a point of comparison, to inform any final agreement.

- Proposal accreditation is considered: Consider how you will legitimize a proposal, your ideas, and yourself. Enhancing a proposal by basing it on a prevailing standard or objective criterion: logic, precedents, relevant research, scientific standards, and market value of the agreement or your personal and organizational credibility. An accreditation of sorts.

  O How best to accredit your proposal depends on your objectives, the personalities of the proponents, and the importance of the outcome and the relationship.

91   How do you determine your best alternatives to a negotiated agreement? First, you have to dissect both your position and your negotiation interests. Then, look at the sum of these parts relative to all the alternative options available. Pick the best option. Finally, do the reverse from your counterpart's perspective.

○ If someone objects to the prevailing standard you propose, invite the other party to work with you to advance understanding. What are the appropriate measures and standards? What more do we need to know to inform our deliberations? Brainstorm ideas and alternatives.

> The integrative approach underscores the importance of long-term relationships. But a constructive relationship is a collective effort.
>
> As Roger Fisher observes, "we either look out for both parties, or we refuse to deal. To do otherwise is to undermine the long-term relationship and establish an adversarial future." In other words, you won't go along to get along—employ accommodation, comprise conflict styles, and other like approaches to satisfy an adversarial, positional bargainer and keep them at the table.

Integrative discourse or negotiation is a distinct subset of cooperative discourse or negotiation. It involves a high degree of informational exchange aimed at mutual problem-solving and uses objective criteria as points of comparison. It is characterized by interactions that facilitate relatively higher levels of trust than would be found in other negotiations. Trust is not a requirement of integrative negotiations; however, those actions typical in integrative negotiations generally promote trust.

Cooperative discourse or negotiations, in contrast, entail a broad set of negotiations where parties accommodate their counterparts' efforts to explore their own needs rooted in the positions advanced. In cooperative discourse or negotiations, the parties are more open to persuasion. In distributive negotiations (which by structure and practice are position-based), parties typically focus on an objective or plan of action to fulfil their needs.

In position-based negotiations, parties can work either cooperatively or competitively. Cooperative position-based negotiators typically view differences as fixed: they focus on securing objectives to meet end goals, allow for their counterparts' efforts to pursue their own objectives, and expect that fair agreements can be achieved through compromise.

Competitive position-based negotiators' focus and view of differences is the same as that of cooperative negotiators. However, competitive position-based negotiators see the agreement as on dimensional, the conclusion of a zero-sum contest.

Fisher and Brown's Guidelines of Unconditionally Constructive Behaviour

Fisher and Brown, in *Getting Together Building Relationships as We Negotiate,* set out the imperatives for developing a constructive working relationship through being unconditionally constructive. The guidelines have as a foundation the notion of good faith.

Table 10: Advantages of Unconditionally Constructive Behaviour

Unconditionally Constructive Elements	Advantages for the Relationship	Advantages for Me
1. **Rationality: Suspend judgement, balance emotion with reason.**	An irrational response and the consequence battle are less likely.	I model a reasoned posture and make fewer mistakes.
2. **Understanding: Even if the other party appears not to understand you, try to understand them. Understand the history and appreciate the context.**	The better I understand you, the fewer collisions we will have, and the fewer ill-conceived conclusions I will make.	The better informed I am, the better solutions I can invent and the better able I am to influence you.
3. **Communication: Inquire, consult, and listen. Seek to understand before seeking to be understood. Use neutral language; provocative language is a positional trigger.**	We both participate in making decisions; better communication improves them.	I reduce the risk of making a mistake without giving up the ability to decide.
4. **Reliability: Even if the other party is trying to deceive you, neither trust nor deceive them. Practice *alert watchfulness*.**	It tends to build trust and confidence.	My words will have more impact.
5. **Non-coercive approaches to influence: Be open to persuasion; try to persuade.**	If people are persuaded rather than coerced, both the outcome and compliance are better.	By being open, I keep learning; it is easier to resist coercion if one is open to persuasion.
6. **Acceptance: Accept and respect the other party's legitimacy. Accept the other party as worth dealing with and be open to learning from them**	To deal will with our differences, I have to be prepared to learn from you.	By dealing with you and your circumstance, I remove obstacles to learning the facts and to persuading you on the merits.

Positional-Distributive, Integrative Approaches and the Concept of Value

At the outset of negotiations, negotiators adopt an approach that supports one of three orientations[92]: a maximalist position, an equitable position, or the adoption of an integrative approach.

All three orientations focus on identifying, creating, and claiming value to achieve a purpose. Maximalists and equitable positioners focus on claiming value resident in the parties' positions and adopt what can be characterized as a more traditional negotiation stance and approach. Typically, they adopt the tenets of distributive bargaining from the outset.

Figure 20: Traditional, Positional Negotiations

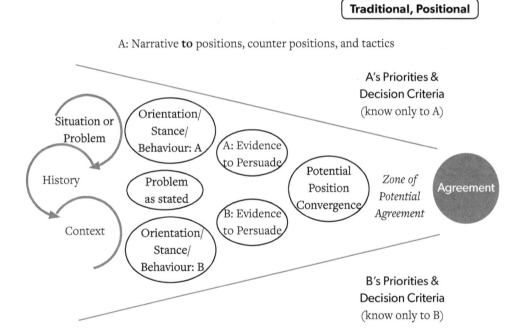

In contrast, the integrative approach proposes that:

- Interactions should focus on the identification of interests, not on the advocacy of positions that are claimed to represent interests. Parties should first seek to

---

92   G.R. Williams, *Legal Negotiation and Settlement* (St. Paul, MN: West Publishing Co., 1983).

create value by identifying interests, and those processes should precede those to claim value.

- Every negotiation has the potential to require distributive skills when at the claiming value stage.

- Processes to create value are effective when done collaboratively and without a focus on who gets what.

- Claiming value involves distributive bargaining processes that must be introduced carefully so as not to harm the relationship and derail the progress made to date.

- Most negotiations take place in a space where there are some standards or objective information available as points of comparison and reference when evaluating options.

- Collaborating and competing both look for ways to increase the value for all parties, often by identifying differences across issues and making trade-offs. And they also rely on distributive bargaining to try to claim as much value as the greater number of options afford them.

Figure 21: Integrative Negotiations

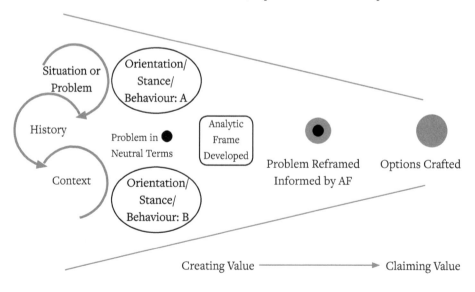

The Concept of Value

Creating and claiming value are two of the most fundamental aspects of a negotiation strategy that exist in tension with one another. In any negotiation, the parties must decide whether to be competitive, cooperative, or some aspect of both.

Negotiation scholars[93] call this the negotiator's dilemma because the best outcome for one person is not necessarily the best for both, but if both pursue their best option, they will often both get the worst outcome.

A pie analogy best illustrates the creation of value—each party collaborates with the other to try to create a bigger, mutually beneficial pie (or the pie is enlarged) to share in negotiations through a cooperative, integrative process. This means that the parties in the circumstance have managed to find ways to increase the amount of beneficial goods (things they want or that will make their situation better than before) that will be divided between them. This may also be called joint value or joint gains, meaning that new developments are considered improvements by both sides.

The primary way to create value is to focus on the underlying interests of the parties involved—what are their concerns and why do they want what they want? By sharing information openly and communicating with one another, the parties work to find shared interests and create joint value. Creating value makes it more likely that both sides will get something they want out of the negotiation.

The competitive process is one in which parties are negotiating to obtain rewards from some limited pool, with the pool framed by their respective positions. Anything not going to A will go to B, and vice versa. Any gain by one party is offset by an equal and opposite loss by the other. In this scenario, claiming value involves dividing up a fixed pie, or the total amount of value available to the disputing parties. This process is most closely associated with distributive bargaining, in which each side tries to get as much of the pie as possible.

The more one side claims, the less the other side gets. To claim value in a negotiation, you use competitive tactics to try to convince the other side that they want what you have to offer much more than you want what they have. Some tactics for winning at distributive negotiation include: starting high; conceding slowly; exaggerating the value of your concessions; minimizing the value of the other's concessions; concealing information; arguing forcefully for principles that imply favourable settlements; making commitments to accept only highly favourable agreements; and, being willing to out-wait your opponent.

---

93   D. Lax and J. Sebenius, *The Manager as Negotiator: The Negotiator's Dilemma, Creating and Claiming Value* (Boston: Little Brown and Co., 1992), 49-62.

The Link between Creating and Claiming Value

Creating value and claiming value are linked activities.[94] Creating new value improves both parties' outcomes. However, having created new value, negotiators must still divide the resulting pie.

Unfortunately, the cooperative strategies needed to create value tend to undermine the competitive strategies used to claim value (and vice versa). The exaggeration and concealment needed for effective competition is directly opposed to the open sharing of information needed to find mutual benefits.

In contrast, taking an open cooperative approach makes one vulnerable to the hard-bargaining tactics of a competitive negotiator. Therefore, if both parties co-operate, the result is usually good, whereas if one co-operates and the other competes, the competitor usually does better.

However, if both compete, they usually come out worse than they would if both co-operated. The assumption, however, is that claiming value in integrative (i.e., situations with integrative potential) situations is more likely to be balanced. This is because the parties have created sufficient value that satisfies their interests acceptably. And further, they are expected to develop cooperative relationships and communicate freely, which is not generally allowed in competitive situations.

And Finally, Results and Consequences

In the end, when it comes to effective bargaining strategies, the difference between distributive and integrative negotiation is not great. Both aspects of negotiation require you to engage in significant reflection and research in preparation. The more you know about the issues at stake, your counterpart's interests and constraints, and your own preferences and limitations, the better positioned you will be to successfully deploy distributive bargaining strategies and claim value in your next negotiation. The question for you is whether you adopt a positional stance or an integrative one.

Based on your assessment of the situation, what you said you valued, and the approaches you adopted, is this the optimal result (process, substance, and relationships)? Results are for learning. What about next time?

94   Ibid.

Chapter 5: Bargaining Zone Model

One way to view the negotiation process is one where each party moves along a continuum in opposite directions to an area of potential overlap called the bargaining zone.[95] The bargaining zone model[96]—described as a distributive goal-setting model—assumes that tangible (measurable) goals are easier to understand and deal with. Maximalist and equitable positioning are examples of distributive goal setting.

Typically, each team meets before engaging with the other side to identify their common objectives or objectives crafted as particular positions. They then set three positions:

- an *initial position* (in the case of the maximalist, usually extreme) that is the opening offer to the other party,

- a *target* (the desired outcome) that is the realistic goal or expectation for a final agreement, and

- a *resistance point,* which is the bottom line the party is extremely reluctant to go beyond, based on resource constraints, other available options, and personal preferences. No further concessions will be made beyond this point.

Negative Settlement Range

Resistance points indicate potential common ground and the basis for negotiation. When the resistance points of the two parties do not overlap, a negative bargaining zone is said to exist.

Figure 22: Negative Settlement Range

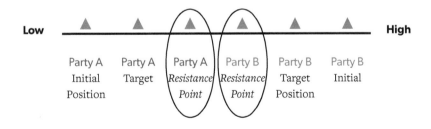

95   Described in S. McShane and S. Steen, *Canadian Organizational Behaviour* (Toronto, ON: McGraw-Hill Ryerson, 2012), 314-316.

96   R. Walton and R. McKersie described this as a distributive goal-setting model in *The Behavioral Theory of Labor Negotiations* (New York, ILR Press, 1965, 1991). Defined in R. Lewicki et al., *Essentials of Negotiation* (Toronto, ON: McGraw-Hill Ryerson, 2014), 19-22.

Positive Settlement Range

When the resistance points and/or the targets overlap, a positive bargaining zone exists.

Figure 23: Positive Settlement Range

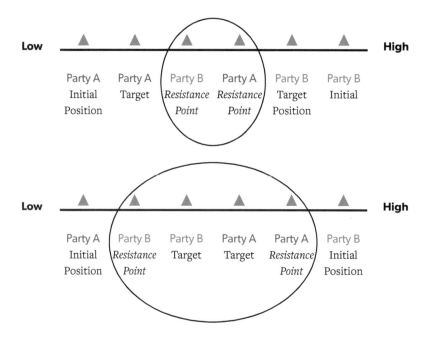

This bargaining model implies that the parties compete[97] against each other to reach their target point. At some point, the negotiator will have to claim value that represents the best that can be done.

The challenge in this model is one of determining how you create the value to be claimed beyond the stated positions that represent the targets.

A measure of cooperation through discussions, exchange of information, sound relationships, and trust is required to meet that goal. In this model, the notion of cooperative discussions is a secondary exercise after establishing the target/resistance points and the positions that support them. Cooperation involves accommodation and concession conflict styles (review the dual concerns model in this section).

97   Review the dual concerns model (concern for self-vs. concern for others), specifically the competitive style (contending, competing, forcing, directing): maximizes assertiveness and minimizes empathy).

This model has advantages and limitations:

1. Operates within a position-based framework. Positions tend to be strenuously advocated for and obscure true interests and their relative priority. Generally suitable for one-dimensional issues but not complex, multifaceted matters.

2. Shows there are instances where no agreement can be reached (at least not unless one or both parties move their resistance points).

3. Is realistic in the sense that people really do think in terms of opening positions and bottom lines.

4. Helps exhibit the potential to lose with openness. You could go all the way to your resistance point, when a settlement in the middle of a positive bargaining zone might have been viewed as fairer.

5. Presents the necessary, but not sufficient conditions, for a settlement to be reached. One can see the potential for a settlement, but one cannot guarantee the parties will settle or predict where that settlement might be. The parties might not settle, even if they have a positive bargaining zone due to factors such as:

   • a bad past relationship that inhibits conversation and concession making

   • pressure from constituents or those with influence who believe a better deal is possible

   • people are too ambitious and fail to get momentum started that would result in settlement

   • the interactions that take place may offend one or both parties, so they lose interest in tangible matters

6. Shows the implications of establishing positions. It assumes a limited or finite amount to be divided or distributed with a focus on convincing and claiming. Positions can have the potential of locking you in to one course of action and forestalling an exploration of interests.

7. Demonstrates that distributive bargaining can be influenced by the audience effect and is seen by some as traditional bargaining, or the way bargaining is normally done. The audience effect refers to how people who are representing others react/act when their constituents are present. Specifically, this may result in parties being tougher to deal with, tending to dig in, and becoming more distributive.

The constituent-lead negotiator dynamic poses further challenges:

- There are social costs involved when the leader fears losing face. He/she will also receive pressure when unpopular trades, exchanges, or position changes are made, or even offered. When people are allowed to watch, the audience (while informed in real time) will also form judgements about the other side and the efficacy of their own side's strategy. Depending on the audience, this can be helpful for the negotiator or it can be distracting as individual members muse about they would have done.

- One can also anticipate more negotiator distractions. When the constituents are present, they will see the resistance the other side is mounting as framing the constituent's expectations. As a result, the negotiator must beware of appearing soft as they try to work out a deal.

In general, one would expect that the greater the area of overlap, the greater the chances for settlement. On occasion, though, when people perceive the other side as being far more agreeable than expected, they may raise their goals. We assume that people will have carefully set their points and simply follow these guides in the ensuing discussions, but this is not always the case. In some negotiations, fellow team members recognize some of their team's objectives are unrealistic, and instead of taking action themselves, they let the other side take the flack, and try to get their teammates to come around later, behind the scenes.

Distributive Bargaining Checklist

Katherine Shonk, the editor of the *Negotiation Briefings* newsletter, a monthly source of negotiation advice for professionals published by the Program on Negotiation at Harvard Law School, proposes the following considerations when competing for scarce resources through distributive strategies[98]:

1. *Estimate the other party's bottom line. Most negotiators understand the value of evaluating their own bottom line—the least amount they would accept before walking away from the bargaining table. But we often overlook the importance of estimating our counterpart's bottom line. To do so, research the other party's bargaining strength and interests, which may include examining the outcomes of her past negotiations and her likely best alternative to a negotiated agreement (BATNA). Once at the table, ask lots of questions to determine her interests and constraints as well.*

2. *Set high aspirations. Another important part of your negotiation preparation is to set an ambitious yet realistic aspiration level, or goal. That doesn't mean*

98   *Negotiation Briefings*, November 20, 2017.

making outrageous demands; rather, prepare arguments that will make your ambitious aspirations seem reasonable.

3.   Anchor aggressively. The negotiator who makes the opening offer in a price negotiation typically gets the better deal, considerable negotiation research shows. Why? Because the first figure named in a negotiation "anchors" the discussion that follows. If you are well informed about the value of the commodity you're negotiating, prepare to drop an ambitious first anchor.

4.   Identify a strong BATNA. When you have a strong BATNA, you will be in a good position to reject a mediocre agreement. As a result, a strong BATNA is typically your best source of power in a negotiation. After identifying your BATNA, you should take steps to improve it, when possible, by conducting negotiations on multiple fronts.

"I sure hope the negotiations go well."

Chapter 6: Integrative Negotiation Model

This chapter builds on the ideas and concepts introduced in Chapter 4: *Orientations Emerge*. In *Essentials of Negotiation* by Lewicki et al., the key steps in the integrative negotiation process are describe in detail. The authors also contrast integrative and distributive negotiations. In simple terms, the integrative approach can be summarized as follows.[99]

Attitude, approach, and interdependence

- Recognize the negotiation cultural norm ("it's the way we bargain" or "it's the way it's done") and people's default strategy, which tends to be positional and, to a large degree, distributive. It takes you to lead the constructive change ... we will eventually get there!

- Appreciate interdependence. Recognize the power manifest in joining forces, which allows the achievement of something in concert that would not be possible to do separately. The focus here should be on creation, prior to claiming value.

- Emphasize collaboration, as is best illustrated by the dual concerns model introduced earlier in this section.

- Reframe the matter(s) at issue in non-positional, specific outcome engendering words. Use neutral language.

Separate people from the problem

- Avoid the ego battles that can emerge in positional, distributive situations.

- Be soft on people. When you manage the emotional level of the talks, the matter at issue is depersonalized.

Focus on interests, not positions

- Do not look at the other side's stated position and strive to split the difference (compromise). Don't be distracted by positional anchors. Try to determine what they really want to accomplish and what underlies their positions and stance.

99   Adapted from Roger Fisher et al., *Getting to Yes: Negotiating Agreement without Giving In*, 2nd ed. (New York: Penguin Books, 1991).

- Be tough on interests, not positions. Seek clarity and determine the relative importance of the interests and what the components of a good agreement are from the other party's perspective.

- What are the concerns? It is not solely a question of getting the facts straight and sorting out what is evidence-supported from what is just rhetoric and positioning. There are many opinions but few facts, evidence, or analysis. Facts and data are the foundation of an evidence-informed approach. Exploring concerns begins to lead you to why, and why takes you to interests.

Generate alternatives without judging them

- Brainstorm: Get people to identify their ideas, even seemingly crazy ones, and record them on a flip chart.

- Combine or modify the ideas that were generated. "If" questions can be used to explore possibilities. Eventually, you will prioritize them in order of potential.

Seek objective criteria and standards as the basis for your ultimate judgements

- What type of statistics and data can everyone agree are relevant?

- Do the parties accept some people as experts who are worthy of being consulted?

- Promote evidence-informed, fact-based decision making.

- Research and agree on objective standards before negotiations. Other matters can be added later, but an initial foundation sets a constructive tone.

- When one side is more powerful, keep inquiring about the reasons they have taken certain positions, and suggest the proper criteria to judge the equity/efficacy of the proposal.

Develop the best alternative to a negotiated agreement (BATNA) and consider the worst alternatives (WATNA)

- How do you determine your best and worst alternatives to a negotiated agreement? First, you have to identify your interests and differentiate them from your positions. Then, look at the sum of these parts relative to all the alternative options available. Pick the best option. Finally, do the reverse from your counterpart's perspective.

- Consider the elements, propositions, or courses of action that meet your test of the BATNA with the other party.

- If you are able to walk away from the talks and still meet your objectives, the talks will go more smoothly.

- As a result, you should vigorously pursue all of your options.

Some of the most crucial factors to consider when establishing a BATNA include:

- **Cost:** How much it will cost to make the deal relative to the cost of your best alternative? Cost estimation may entail both the short term and the long term. It boils down to figuring out which of your options is the most affordable.

- **Feasibility:** Which option is the most feasible? Which one can you realistically apply over all the rest of your available options?

- **Impact:** Which of your options will have the most immediate positive influence on your current state of affairs?

- **Consequences:** What do you think or estimate will happen as you consider each option as a possible solution?

When creating a BATNA:

- brainstorm a list of all available alternatives that might be considered should the negotiation fail to render a favourable agreement

- choose the most promising alternatives and expand them into practical and attainable alternatives

- identify the best of the alternatives and keep it in reserve as a fallback during the negotiation

- keep your WATNA in mind as a measure of potential options

And finally ...

- Be creative. Simply ask yourself what other options you might employ that could enhance your circumstance. Brainstorm the situation with all the key players in your organization. Your planning must also factor in your counterpart's interests and options.

- Improve your alternatives, your BATNA keeping in mind your WATNA. Endeavour to expand your options. One possibility is to consider bringing other interested third-party partners into the mix. A third-party's interests may coincide with key components of your interests, or of your counterpart's. For example, this might entail creative financing or assigning different responsibilities with the associated accountabilities (which presents a more attractive option to your counterpart). If you weaken the other side's best alternative by injecting another element into the mix, the situation takes on a whole new dynamic.

- Use experts. Neutral parties and acknowledged subject matter specialists with their own relevant expertise might be able to deconstruct your problem and offer another perspective. If one or both parties lack some area of expertise, other experts can deepen understanding and provide an avenue to potential options.

- Don't focus exclusively on your BATNA. Understanding the other party's BATNA gives you a better understanding of their priorities. Also, consider both parties' WATNA.

- Focus on facts and evidence-informed resources/information rather than assumed common knowledge, posturing, and biases. Take the view that if you can't prove an assertion or contention, it doesn't matter. Most overestimate their BATNA and often grossly over or underestimate the other side's BATNA.

Practicalities in Practice: Is This Easy to Accomplish?

The answer to this question? It depends.

1. Given the cultural norms of negotiations, people's default strategy and experiences, it takes focus, persistence, and clarity of approach to chart a path forward to a constructive continuing working relationship.

2. In some instances, you will be challenged to suspend judgement and separate people from the problem. People can add complexity. Characterizations of people, actions, or events and snap judgements can lead people away from carefully studying those involved and their history, which inhibits the examination and understanding underlying interests.

3. Identifying the other person's interests is sound. Yet many people go to great lengths to hide or distort this information. Further, in the case of intangibles, they may be at least partially unaware of what they want, or they may be unable to fully articulate their interests. It requires considerable and authentic discussion-seeking to understand the other party's interests.

4. Some people will have great difficulty identifying and assessing the feasibility of alternatives. They may question spending valuable time on ideas that seem unrealistic. Other people feel it is being evasive not to have "the answer" or become frustrated having to run cost figures on

numerous scenarios, and then possibly have to do many more "what-if" scenarios.

5.   Identifying objective criteria can help, but the problem is there may be no universally accepted criteria. If the parties can agree on a body of knowledge or an expert, objective criteria can be said to exist. Anticipate potential disagreements in advance and develop or agree to a common data/information set that will be used to evaluate or inform matters.

6.   People are influenced by their frames of reference, view of power, authority, and what they believe negotiations to be about. If you hear *I've been doing this for 30 years. That's just how the game of negotiation is played. It's a no-holds-barred game where each side just tries to get the best deal they can.* Return to the first observation.

> **Actions speak louder than words. Being unconditionally constructive and not responding to positional, distributive tactics with positional, distributive tactics can begin to reframe the circumstance and the negotiation.**

An Integrative Approach: Summary

- The notion of good faith: a willingness to meet, to engage in rational discussions with a mind open to persuasion (unconditionally constructive orientation).

- In pursuit of what and the reason to engage: satisfaction of interests. You want to satisfy:

  O   your interests well: that's why you're negotiating in the first place

  O   theirs acceptably, because their interests must be satisfied also

  O   others tolerably, because as interested parties or constituents, they influence their negotiators.

- To decide based on what? Evidence-informed decisions.

- Measured against: Objective criteria and standards.

- Alternative: If an agreement is not possible, the walk-away alternative is a considered BATNA appreciating the WATNA.

- In search of a good agreement that is fair, efficient, wise, and stable (described below).

In Search of Integrative Potential: How to Start

The integrative approach requires specific skills including active listening, brainstorming, and consensus decision making.[100]

The first place to start is with the development of a plan (refer to Part Five: *Interactions with Purpose* and Chapter 4: *Negotiation Planning and Strategy of Essentials of Negotiation*, Lewicki et al 2017).

> Traditional approaches thrive on the perception of zealous advocacy and typically default to a form of positioning—utilizing the procedure of stated positions followed by proposal, caucus, counterproposal, caucus, and so on—all proposals are carefully reviewed up and down the organizational hierarchy.
>
> In contrast, the integrative approach represents an attitudinal shift from positions, positioning, and advocacy to inquiry, active listening, and co-creation. It is a more free-flowing, dynamic, and spontaneous process.
>
> Where traditional bargaining emphasizes control, the integrative approach accents creativity with the belief that those who know how to gain valuable information perform better than those who solely focus on what they know; they have an inquiring, investigative mindset. Through the synergy resulting from the problem-solving process, unimaginable options are often generated.

The integrative approach starts with the assessment of integrative potential and revisiting the concept of interests in the context of the matters at hand. As it is an evidenced-informed endeavour an agreement on an analytic frame is necessary to inform the process. The work of the framework allows the parties to properly frame the matters at issue in non-positional, specific outcome generating language. With the stage set, working meetings can begin.

100   As a preparatory matter, participants should engage in skill-building practice to deepen their understanding of the integrative approach, and hone their skills through a series of increasingly complex and challenging simulations, accompanied by critical feedback from a skilled practitioner. Following the training, both parties can make an informed decision whether or not to utilize this approach. If yes, their preparatory work must begin immediately with the constituents of each party. All constituents should be given an explanation of the process to include how it works, why it is being proposed.

Is there integrative potential?

Integrative potential is the potential for the parties' interests to be combined or elements incorporated in ways that create joint value. In other words, join forces to achieve something together that cannot be achieved independently though joining several elements or parts into a whole, focussed on creating value before claiming value.

The following factors indicate the potential for integration:

- The parties cannot achieve what they need to achieve independent of one another.

- More than one issue is involved.

- It is possible to add more issues to the mix.

- The parties' interactions will recur over time.

- The parties have varying preferences across issues

When a situation contains integrative potential, one should adopt a cooperative orientation, seek and exchange information, attempt to understand the other parties' interests, and search for solutions that reconcile the interests of all parties.

The integrative approach arising from the recognition of integrative potential is based on the notion of good faith.

Integrative Potential and the Analytic Frame

What do we know and what do we need to know: as a preliminary matter, agree on an analytic frame that can be used to inform the exercise of inquiry. The framework also helps illustrate the potential for integration.

- How is the problem articulated?

- What is the situation?

- What are the concerns with the situation?

- Reframe: Using neutral language, what is really the matter at issue?

- Detail factors that influence the situation

- Assemble and examine the record:

- policies, processes, systems that have bearing on the situation

- statistics, demographics, and other like data

- studies, literature re current like situations and best practices

In the Beginning

With the analytic frame as a foundation resource, in advance of initiating formal meetings on the matters at issue, frame the issues in neutral language and non-positional, specific outcome engendering terms in a similar fashion to the initial problem description.

Brainstorming is a useful tool to collect ideas. For complex issues, however, it may not be an adequate one. For complex issues, facilitation can be used, joint task forces or subcommittees can be specifically chartered—well in advance of discussions—to assemble the most relevant data, and/or benchmark best practices.

If having the right data is important to expedite the process, having the right people present is equally important. The decision to utilize the integrative approach requires that careful attention be paid to the composition of the working, negotiation committees.

Consider: who do they represent, what influence do they have, and do they have the ability, skill, and willingness to meaningfully participate?

In Simple Terms

Reconciling the matters at issue to solve the problem requires the satisfaction of interests. You want to satisfy your interests well, theirs acceptably, and others tolerably. Remember, the other party has the same needs to satisfy.

The process of meeting the interests is informed by the evidence revealed through the analysis of the analytic frame.

The Integrative Approach: Process

The integrative approach requires an understanding of the concept of integrative potential and of creating and claiming value. These concepts represent a shift in attitude and process from traditional approaches to negotiations. With this foundation consider the processes in this section.

Setting the Ground Rules

Set procedural and behavioural ground rules, including a mutual understanding of the nature of the discussions, a time table, information sharing, the role of spokespersons, among other mentioned previously.

Getting Started

The first session should be used to set the tone for the process and establish ground rules. Begin the first session with statements of commitment to the values supporting an integrative approach.

Set the stage by preliminarily framing the matters at issue. The third story technique is particularly helpful.

Now that you have set the stage, consider the kind of information you will share and how you will share it. The parties should next examine the issues and determine the relative importance of each to establish a time budget for the discussions. Against the backdrop of the information gathered through the analytic frame, knowing which issue to tackle first can have a strong bearing on the success of the discussions and set the tone.

There is an advantage in picking an easy, yet meaningful, issue first. It is important that the parties see that the time and energy they have applied to their first issue resulted in a satisfactory solution, one that has brought about meaningful gains for both parties.

Both parties should be encouraged to take risks and to let go of the desire to control the outcome. Exhibiting behaviours aimed at helping the other benefit goes a long way towards creating the positive climate that encourages both parties to find creative solutions.

Finally, alternating between each party's issues may minimize the perception that all the focus and attention (and possibly the gain) is being given to one party.

Tackling the Issues

Take each issue and work through the seven-step integrative process.

1. Describe and define the issue.

An issue is an important topic or problem under consideration. There can be central issues and secondary or sub-issues that comprise a topic or problem. An issue is not a position. While positions can be limiting, issues can more readily lead to a discussion

Properly framing the issue is critically important. Issues can be defined too narrowly or too broadly. If defined too narrowly, the issue may allow little opportunity to develop an adequate option pool. However, issues that are defined too broadly invariably lead to frustration or exasperation. The general rule is to be as specific as possible in defining the issue, without becoming so specific that only part of the described problem can be resolved.

The challenge is to use neutral language and avoid positional or specific outcome engendering language. Use terms that invite inquiry rather than those that point you in a particular direction.

The mind mapping technique identified earlier is a useful and creative tool to describe and identify the issues.

2. Identify and explore interests.

This is an interest-based process and well-developed and clearly articulated interests are essential. Remember powerful interests are basic human needs

The parties must exhibit a genuine desire to understand the other's point of view. Interests, by their very nature, must be accepted as legitimate and not-to-be-debated. Asking clarifying questions and confirming understanding of the interests is desirable.

3. Determine which of the interests are mutual.

This is not a matching process requiring each interest to appear on both lists. It is simply a means of quickly surfacing common or shared interests, which in turn, reveals fertile opportunities for developing viable options. Interests not shared by both parties are referred to as separate interests and remain because they may be required to be satisfied in the final solution.

4. Create options.

The key to success in this step is to go for quantity. A technique to encourage brainstorming is to focus on the list of interests. Multiple options should be generated to cover every interest.

5. Agree on criteria.

Criteria are the gauges by which we measure, compare, and judge options. There are few objective criteria. One of the best gauges for evaluating options is the respective interests of the parties. Generally, there are a few interests that must be satisfied for the solution to be viable or acceptable. In effect, these are criteria and should be treated as such. Coming to agreement on these and any other appropriate criteria determines the outcome of step four. The work generated by the analytic frame provides the basis for evaluative criterion.

6. Test the options against the criteria.

Evaluating each option in light of the agreed-upon criteria can inhibit dialogue and become overly mechanical and cumbersome, especially when there is a long list of options and a number of criteria. Techniques are required to avoid getting bogged down and people checking out.

Review the list of options and focus on those that present broad approaches to solving the problem. Each broad approach should be thoroughly discussed and evaluated for its ability to satisfy the interests of the parties.

Idea 1: Testing Preferences. Give each participant a marker and ask them to place a checkmark next to the five or six options that they believe best meet the criteria. One must make clear that this is not a voting process, but a way of testing for initial preferences. The heavily favoured options then become the primary focal points. The remaining options are examined to see if they meet the criteria and can be incorporated into the favoured options to enhance their utility. Frequently, many ideas are woven together in ways that meet as many interests as possible.

Idea 2: Fishbowl Activity. One approach that is particularly helpful with larger committees is the fishbowl activity.[101] The fishbowl is a tool for facilitating dialogue between experts in a way that exposes others to their knowledge while expanding the collective understanding of a subject.

- Knowledgeable people (the fish) sit in circle to discuss a series of directional questions, surrounded by a larger group of observers in an outer circle (the bowl).

- The inner circle is the stage for speaking and contributing. Those in the outer circle must listen actively and move into the role of fish when they wish to participate in the conversation.

The fishbowl is a table placed within the larger U-shaped table. Those with the role of lead spokespersons are each asked to designate two or three people who are particularly knowledgeable about the issue being discussed. The designees are seated at

---

101   The fishbowl activity is used to manage group discussion. The general idea is that rather than a large group having an open discussion about something, which can be difficult to handle and often only benefits a few active participants, a smaller group (ideally 3 – 6 people) is isolated to discuss while the rest of the participants (maximum of 50 people) sit around the outside and observe without interrupting. Facilitation is focussed on the core group discussion. Less people = easier to facilitate. Fishbowls are useful for ventilating hot topics or sharing ideas or information from a variety of perspectives.

the small table (fishbowl) and are tasked with weaving together the promising options identified by the full committees. Two empty chairs are placed at the small table. At any time, other participants observing the deliberations may occupy an empty chair to offer suggestions or make comments. Once made, they must return to the outer table, thus making the seat available for others to do likewise.

Process difficulties are not the only obstacles that can arise at this stage. Substantive concerns can also surface. Groups frequently discover that the ultimate solution to the issue being worked is dependent upon what is being done on some closely related issue. When this situation is encountered, parking the unfinished solution and working on the related issues is the best course of action. Once the solutions to these related issues are more clearly focussed, the parties can resume work on the parked issue.

The integrative approach, however, does not utilize a tit-for-tat procedure. No one must give up something on one issue to realize a gain on another. Horse trading (unofficial discussions in which people make agreements that provide both sides with advantages) is discouraged. Each issue must be viewed as a joint problem to be solved.

7. Commit agreements to writing.

The final step can be done by a drafting committee. In drafting, confusion or gaps may appear, requiring clarification from the full committee. The final written solution comes back to the group to ensure the group's consensus approval.

At this stage, the parties should consider the process for ratification beyond the committees and the technicalities around communication.

Preliminary Considerations

Consider the power dynamic. If you believe you have more power:

- Consider working through the conflict in a location that is the most comfortable for the other person.

- Share the resources you have (e.g., information, expertise).

- Seek to understand before seeking to be understood. Be willing to listen to the other person first.

- Do not use your power base to intimidate or retaliate against the other person. Seek to create a way in which you and the other party have an equal chance to succeed and develop a level playing field.

- Look for indications that may suggest the other person perceives you as having more power, and find out what you can do to correct it.

- Respond to challenges non-defensively.

If you believe you have less power:

- Find ways to increase your own power sources.

- Describe the consequences of a competitive use of power and the benefits to the other person of a collaborative use of power.

- Assert yourself and continue to keep your interests on the table while continuing to listen and acknowledge the other person's interests.

- If asserting yourself results in the other person exerting his or her power over you, shift temporarily from a focus on your interests to a focus on the other person's interests.

- Think about ways to lessen your dependence on the other person's source of power.

Information: What, When, and How to Share

Consider setting the stage with the third story, the impartial and neutral story. Having set the stage, consider what information you will share and how. Where do you start? What do you reveal initially, if anything? What if the other party is a positional, distributive bargainer?

The prospect of sharing information with a negotiating counterpart can give you pause[102]:

- Say something specific and it can fix your counterpart into a position at the negotiation table you didn't intend (an example of the anchoring effect[103]). The party who moves first typically benefits by anchoring the discussion that follows on the offer—even if the anchor is arbitrary. The anchoring bias, or anchoring effect, is considered a bias because it distorts our judgement, especially when the bargaining zone is unclear. This knowledge of the anchoring bias in negotiation can help make and respond to first offers more effectively.

102   Adapted from the Program on Negotiation Daily Blog, https://www.pon.harvard.edu/blog, April 6, 2017.

103   The observation that people who make decisions under certain conditions are influenced by initial starting numbers (Lewicki et al, *Negotiation Essentials,* 3rd Cdn ed. (Toronto, ON: McGraw Hill-Ryerson, 2017), 38.

- Share too much, and the other side might conclude that you're desperate to make a deal, any deal. There's also the risk of giving away privileged information that your counterpart could use against you.

- Share too little and risk being perceived as evasive, not worthy of trust, and trying to get your counterpart to guess what's important so you can limit what you reveal and when.

A careful analysis of the advantages and disadvantages of sharing information in a negotiation will help you approach negotiation scenarios with a greater sense of confidence and security.

- Don't wait for the other side to open up to you first. A negotiation is not one-sided, and if we expect to receive information, we must also be willing to share it.

- Reciprocity is the key to successful fact finding, as this is the only way we will be able to find creative solutions that benefit both parties. Thanks to the power of reciprocity, your counterpart is likely to match any information you share with valuable information of their own. By going first, you can set the stage and provide a framework of sorts to assist the process.

- Ask and answer questions. Neither side can proceed effectively until each begins to fully understand the other, and the only way to begin this process is to ask intelligent questions.

We will already have determined the questions we want to ask in our preparatory stage, which should be analytical and problem-solving in nature. One or both parties are likely to have a problem or challenge, and we want to find the best means of addressing this through a mutually attractive solution.

Likewise, we are anticipating the questions they will be asking us. The more information each party can glean about the other, the more readily they will be able to develop creative solutions addressing the needs and objectives of both.

In general, you should feel comfortable revealing information about your interests in the negotiation, as well as your priorities across different issues. That doesn't mean that if there are five issues on the table, you should reveal that you care about only two of them. Rather, stress that all the issues are important to you, but you'd have a hard time budging on two of them. You may also want to describe the situation that gives rise to this discussion and some of your general priorities. Further discussions can provide the necessary detail.

Other types of information to share include:

- **Information required by law.** Don't risk creating a problem (including the erosion of trust) by concealing information you're legally or ethically required to disclose. If such matters are part of the context, ensure that they are raised. Research relevant laws and professional standards before you negotiate.

- **Information that requires damage control.** Remember, if it's going to come out eventually, it's much better to have it come out immediately. Just as a defence counsel questions their client in court about incriminating information before the prosecution can raise the issue, the best way to handle troubling facts may be to come clean to your counterpart.

- **Readily available information.** Given the state of technology and statutory disclosure requirements, information—including financial statements, legal documents, and news reports—may be accessed simply through a Google search, for example. When deciding whether to share sensitive information that's widely available, assess what would happen if your counterpart discovered such information on their own.

Some Value Creation Ideas

Creating value is the essence of negotiation. Value is the importance, worth or usefulness of something. In creating value consider the nature of the matters at issue and *what that value is* in this particular circumstance. What is of value to me and to the other party, and why?

Multiple Negotiation Issues and Multi-Package Offers/Proposals

Few negotiations revolve around a single issue. One error is to present or propose a single offer, which can act as an anchor where everything revolves around it because it has such a narrow scope. Talks can easily be affected because there is a limiting attitude in working with a single offer. However, if a package is presented that simultaneously contains multiple offers or proposals simultaneously, we are much more able to creatively discuss trade-offs in addressing the issues we face.

A multiple negotiation package will enable parties to add more value to an agreement because they will be able to compare and distinguish issues when trade-offs are discussed. When more issues are put onto the table, more flexibility results to negotiate trade-offs such as time preferences, valuations, forecasts, and capabilities.

Resist the temptation to compromise, as this does not yield value and will diminish the resources to be negotiated. Instead, negotiate trade-offs that are of greater relative value to you, or at the very least of equal relative value. Anything less will reduce the value of the agreement.

The process of creating value in negotiations can only occur once both parties adopt the mindset of creative problem solving.

Contingent Agreements: Use Your Differences as Strengths

Contingent agreements are a good way of creating value in a negotiation. In virtually any negotiation, parties must make forecasts and assumptions about the future.[104] Contingent agreements are "if this happens, then we do this or that" promises that parties add to their negotiated agreement to reduce their risk in the face of uncertainty about the future. A contingency agreement addresses differences and expectations, as a contingency itself is premised on an if-then tier-type design and considers changes in circumstances. An agreement is crafted to address the different viewpoints by saying that:

1.   If circumstance A happens, we agree to the following process.

2.   If things change and circumstance B occurs, we agree to this next step.

This type of agreement does allow for greater latitude and flexibility in keeping negotiations moving forward and is a viable means of addressing the differences in negotiation expectations. Contingent agreements offer benefits that include:

- Eliminating the need to come to agreement; by allowing parties to bet on their predictions, a contingent agreement enables parties to live with their differences.

- Making commitments self-enforcing by eliminating the need to reconvene or renegotiate when a surprise crops up.

- Heading off disputes by reducing the likelihood that conflict will arise over surprising events and by spelling out exactly what will happen if a conflict emerges.

Use Risk and Time Differences to Create Value

Many people are averse to risk. One party will signal their aversion to risk by stating that they are adamant about a certain issue. This should not be viewed as an obstacle but rather an opportunity to make a trade-off and gain something in return. Different attitudes about their perceptions of risk offer alternatives to enhance value.

---

104   See Lawrence Susskind, *Good for You, Great for Me: Finding the Trading Zone* (New York: PublicAffairs, 2014).

This concept also applies to differences in time expectations. For example, one party may insist on guaranteed delivery on a specific date, and this can be agreed to by rearranging a payment schedule that is more suitable to us in return.

Cost-Cutting, Resource Reallocation, and Adding Resources Strategy to Add Value

Another effective strategy to employ in adding value is cost-cutting, resource reallocation, re-purposing certain assets, and the like. This occurs when one party achieves an objective while the other has specified costs that are affiliated to their concession either lowered or eliminated. A second means of strategically gaining value is to consider ways to add necessary resources when the problem of scarce resources is creating conflict. This could include finding another supplier or suggesting a subcontract arrangement with a mutually agreed-upon party.

From Creating to Claiming Value

Regardless of how cooperative the parties may choose to be in creating value, they must at some point engage in the distribution of the value they created. The process of claiming value re-introduces the competitive aspects of negotiation that have been de-emphasized in the mutual gains or principled approach.

Lawrence Susskind urges negotiators to enter the frame of mind he calls "the trading zone," where gains for both parties can be discussed. He defines the trading zone as a point in the negotiation when both parties have reason to be optimistic there is an agreement to be made.

In *Good for You, Great for Me,* one of Susskind's key concepts is that negotiations should be handled with the idea of "back tables" in mind—that is, negotiators represent larger organizations (constituencies) and are limited in their power.

Remember you and the other person may be acting on behalf of someone else, not for yourselves. In other words, you are acting as agents, not principals—with the result that your constituents' interests become critically important. Who are your and the other parties' constituents and what influence do they have?

There are always challenges when deciding who to consider: some choices may be obvious and others less so. A main area for discussion is selection of those who are considered key or primary.

To a large degree, the criteria for this selection depend on the goals and desired outcomes of the negotiation or conflict management process. It also includes decision-making authority and influence. Who has the greatest influence over the acceptance of what you achieve and its successful implementation? Who do you need as an advocate for the agreement?

Primary constituents are those who are most affected or influential. They usually have the greatest dependency on the matter in question and/or are the most affected by the outcomes (conflict affects their basic interests).

Important but secondary constituents are those who are more indirectly or less affected by the outcome of the conflict. For example, the conflict does not affect their basic interests, but they may influence or be influenced by the conflict management process.

Others are those who have a connection with the primary and secondary groups but have limited influence.

With the concept of constituents in mind, the challenge it is to create a solution that satisfies both those present and those at the back table (boards of directors, the board executive, members, public constituents, and family members) by creating sometimes-unlikely coalitions and mapping that crucial territory at the outset. Remember, you are seeking to satisfy your interest well, your primary constituents' interests acceptably, and your secondary and constituents' interests tolerably.

Better negotiating means studying the other party's interests closely—whether that produces small gains for one side or new ideas about expanding mutual gain scenarios. Negotiators should think about everyone's strategic interests, grasp how much licence to manoeuvre their counterparts have, seek flexible agreements with logical contingencies, and consider what constitutes an acceptable outcome for each party. Susskind observes:

So, in actuality, a win-win outcome is one that gets all parties more than what no agreement would have guaranteed them. But, that doesn't mean that all parties "gain the same amount." I might like an agreement because it gets me well above my BATNA. You might grudgingly accept my proposed agreement because it gets you more than what you are likely to get if we reach no agreement at all. Win-win agreements do not promise all sides equal or similar gains. They only promise that all sides—because they enter into the trading zone, engage in joint problem-solving, and agree to be realistic, even honest, about their highest priority interests—get an outcome that is better than their most realistic estimate of what they would have ended up with had they walked away with no agreement.

Thus, the way to "win" at "win-win" negotiation is to make sure you come up with a proposed agreement that is "good" for other side(s) and "great" for you. You can only do this by working hard to uncover and respond to the most important interests of the other parties. Whatever "opening" stand you take (to ensure your "people" that you are fighting hard on their behalf), you have to be able to move from there into the trading zone and function effectively in that "what-iffing" environment. Then, you must have the right mandate from your "side." That is, you need to have worked out ahead of time a clear understanding of your group's priority interests. And, you need to know who you can call for authorization to enter into an anticipated agreement at the last minute as long as the package exceeds your group's realistic estimate of what no agreement means to them.

And finally, Susskind thinks that before negotiators sit down at the table, they should "write the victory speech for the other side." Is the deal obtained by the other party in a negotiation good enough for them to advocate as well?

"I have to put myself in your shoes in a really empathetic way, to try to sell you on why the version of the deal I want is one you can take home," Susskind explains.

At a minimum, Susskind notes, he would like people to realize that negotiating practices are an essential part of an organization's larger strategic vision, and can be studied with scholarly rigour.[105]

---

105   Source: MIT News Thursday, July 3, 2014. *The* MIT *News is the Massachusetts Institute of Technology's (MIT) central hub for news about MIT research, initiatives and events. It reports MIT news directly and works with journalists around the world to help showcase the achievements of its students, faculty, and staff.*

THE ART OF THE DEAL

by Uncle Sidney

CHAPTER 7: THE BUSINESS LUNCH

Step One:
Admire something the other guy is wearing.

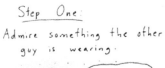

Step Two:
Share a funny story about yourself.

Step Three:
Look for something in common.

Step Four:
Make observations about somebody else's business acumen with materials at hand.

Step Five:
Suddenly, get deep.

Step Six:
Go in for the kill.

Used with permission, The New Yorker Collection/Cartoon Bank, by Roz Chast, 2017.

Chapter 7: When Competitive/Positional, Distributive Approaches and Integrative Potential Meet

By default, or with intent, some view conflict, collective bargaining, or the general back and forth of employer-employee relations as essentially a series of predominantly distributive exercises—competitive, positional in nature, and taking the form of a maximalist or an equitable positioner using particular positional strategies and approaches. Consider your alternatives.

The Competitive/Positional Approach: What to Watch Out For

The competitive/positional approach uses a variety of identifiable tactics. An individual with a competitive/positional orientation may use some or all the following strategies:

1. Lead with a compelling narrative. Take control of establishing the ground rules for the negotiation, such as timing and location.

2. Anchor early and treat the matters at issue as essentially a distributive exercise.

3. Use surprise and make changes at the last minute so as to throw the other party off balance when negotiations begin.

4. Bring more people to the meeting than originally advised.

5. Keep what they believe to be non-negotiables invisible. Don't bring them up or put them on the agenda for discussion; thus, they appear to arise by happenstance.

6. Make sure the agenda is ordered so that your least important issues come before your most important ones. Take extreme positions on your less important issues, and give a concession that they characterize as large, to build up points for your most important issues.

7. Give as few concessions as possible and makes them as small as possible (while making them seem large), and every time you give one, takes the position that they are entitled to one that's bigger.

8. Establish positions far in excess of what they really expect to get. Every item is reported as being of equal importance.

9. Attempt to make you think they have the ability to walk away, and let you know they are willing to do so whenever they hold out.

10.	Stress that you are getting a great deal that results from their difficult choices and concessions.

Examples of competitive strategies include:

- **Artificial deadlines:** Used to create pressure on you when, in fact, there is no real reason for the deadline.

- **Bluffing:** Also known as lying, this strategy is aimed at having you believe something that would get you to agree to the other negotiator's terms.

- **Bottom lining:** Making you think they will not negotiate beyond a certain point.

- **Delay:** Finding excuses to put off negotiations to test if you are desperate, and/or to make you think they are not very interested so you will accept anything.

- **Downward pressure:** Exerting continual pressure to extract the maximum from you. Mirror image of escalating demands. Also known as grinding or nickel and diming.

- **Escalating demands:** Every time you concede or agree to something, they ask for more. This is to get you to agree quickly and under pressure in order to avoid more demands.

- **False issues:** Using a non-issue or minor concession framed as a major concession, in order to appear fair in seeking a major concession from you.

- **Good guy and bad guy:** Attempt to make you think the good guy is on your side against the bad guy, to get you to accept the good guy's deal.

- **Insults:** Undermining you personally in an attempt to make you feel intimidated, or to trigger you so you are less confident and more emotional.

- **Overreacting:** Behaviours aimed at making you feel like you are being unreasonable, so you will back down.

- **Swarming:** Creating confusion so you will agree before you can think, by overwhelming you with information at high speed, often manipulating facts and numbers in a way that makes the deal look reasonable at first glance, when it actually isn't.

- **Tantrums:** Behaving badly in the hope that you will give up and give in.

In assessing and responding to these strategies, remember that they are designed to put you in a defensive mode. Respond in a way that limits the effectiveness of the strategy, and which provides avenues for the competitive negotiator to take a more collaborative/integrative approach.

Responding to Competitive Strategies[106]

When negotiating with a competitive negotiator (whether a maximalist or equitable positioner), there are specific constructive-collaborative actions you can take to change the game and encourage them to negotiate collaboratively. The following categories outline some collaborative moves for responding to competitive strategies.

General

- Review and fully understand the fundamentals of an integrative approach.

- Consider if you should seek agreement on meeting protocols.

- Set the stage, use the *third story* technique to open. Without being argumentative, deconstruct the narrative that frames the matters at issue.

- Check facts, figures, and other information.

- Avoid anchoring in discussions by engaging in rigorous, evidence informed critical thinking.

- Be well prepared.

- Ask open questions, requiring more than simple yes/no answers.

- Focus on issues rather than personalities.

- Seek a shared information base and encourage verification of information.

- Provide a rationale for your perspective.

- Describe why their idea doesn't meet your needs and concerns.

- Describe what might meet your needs and concerns.

- Remain open to hearing disagreement with your point of view; ask questions rather than go on the defensive. Don't take things personally.

Testing Assumptions

- Test the validity of your assumptions. In being well prepared, think through your assumptions and verify your perceptions against demonstrable evidence.

106   See Chapter 11: Responding When the Other Side is Being Difficult in Lewicki et al., *Negotiation Essentials,* 2nd ed. (Toronto, ON: McGraw Hill-Ryerson, 2014), 216.

- What are your assumptions? Are they important enough that you need to clarify what you have assumed with the other party? What key phrases from the other party should you listen for that might lead you to question your assumptions?

Responding to Position-Taking

- Ask questions about the competitive negotiator's needs and concerns.

- Express your willingness to meet their needs and concerns.

- Reframe: State their needs and concerns, as you understand them, and ask if you are correct.

- Neither accept nor reject their position and treat it as one possible option.

- Ask how their position meets your needs and concerns.

- Point out the consequences of the negotiation breaking down.

- Point out the benefits of negotiating; show what they stand to gain by negotiating.

- Don't respond at all; they may reconsider their statement.

- Ignore the position and refocus on the issues; this is only effective if the position-taking occurs within a general willingness to negotiate.

Responding to Manipulation, Pressure, and Attacks

- Shift the focus from discussing the issues to identifying the tactic (describe the competitive negotiator's behaviour) and the negative effect it is having on negotiations.

- Show them how to be more effective in gaining your cooperation and describe what you are willing to do with their cooperation.

- Don't trust prematurely; don't take all statements at face value.

- Describe what you expect in order to continue negotiations (set limits).

- Give choices. Describe the negative consequences of not negotiating or competitive negotiating, and the positive consequences of negotiating collaboratively.

- Give yourself time to respond; break if necessary.

- Reframe, refocus, ignore tactics, and focus back on the issues.

Examples: Responding to Competitive Strategies

- "What are your major concerns? I'm interested in finding ways to meet those concerns."

- "That would be one way to resolve it. Let's see if there are others."

- "I'm concerned that if you insist on finalizing this before I can check my numbers, we won't have a deal at all, and I don't think either of us wants that. Am I right?"

- "I think if we both outline what we're trying to achieve here, we could come up with an agreement that will benefit both of us."

- "I want to respond to your request, but I need to do it in a way that is reasonable for me."

- "I'd like to suggest we sit down and look at some ways to resolve this."

- "I agree that continuing to do something just because it's been done that way for years is not a good enough reason. Help me understand the benefits of changing."

Climate Interventions

The following interventions may be helpful to maintain or facilitate a productive environment. Individual judgement is required as to appropriateness of the intervention.

- **Ignore:** The event may not require intervention, particularly if it is minimal or not having an impact on you.

- **Body language:** For example, use body orientation, gesture, and facial expression to demonstrate the seriousness of the situation.

- **Acknowledge:** "You're very angry about how the contract has developed to date."

- **Normalize:** "I understand how difficult it is for us both not to just jump in and contradict each other when we see things so differently. If we can try to hold back our comments until the other is finished talking, maybe we'll understand each other better."

- **Educate:** "I'm trying very hard to listen to your perspective on this issue. When you use language or phrases like, 'I can't believe someone like you really believes all that,' I stop listening and want to defend myself. Could we focus on the shortfalls of the report in more neutral terms, and create a report we both agree on?"

- **Consequence:** "We've argued like this in the past, and what usually happens when we do is that one of us gets angry and walks out before we get the issues resolved. I'm hoping for a more positive outcome this time."

- **Emphasize agreement to negotiate:** "I know it's hard not to argue, and I don't believe either of us wants to since we've decided to try to work this out. What do we need to do differently in order to avoid the arguments?"

- **Encourage rational vs. emotional discussion:** For example, "*Name,* a few minutes ago you wanted to say something, and I think that was because what I was saying really upset you. Perhaps you can tell me what you were reacting to."

- **Confront:** To help the other negotiator gain insight into how their behaviour is preventing them from moving ahead to the attainment of the goal (a viable agreement). For example, "You say you agree with this approach, but the tasks you've agreed to remain undone ..."

- **Ask them to give you suggestions:** "Can you think of some ways that we could adjust the process so that you'll be more comfortable moving forward?"

- **Move to a less contentious issue.**

- **Point out negotiation will break down:** "My fear is if this continues, this session will break down."

- **Call for a break:** "Perhaps it would be useful for us to take a 15-minute break in order for both of us to rethink our approach."

- **Recognize difficulty of the issue and point out progress:** "This hasn't been easy for either of us, yet we are near completion on three of the major issues."

- **Point out understanding is not necessarily agreeing:** "I understand that ... is your perspective (paraphrasing their points accurately), and I still see things differently."

Setting Limits

When the other person acts in a way that impedes balanced and respectful interaction, you can use assertion to simply and directly ask for what you need from them.

Though the following elements are set out as a framework, it's important to be flexible. You may find it more natural and appropriate to use the elements in a different order.

In some cases, you may choose to only use a few of the elements below.

Acknowledge

Acknowledge the speaker's:

Positive intent

Emotions

Describe

Describe the situation objectively and specifically—avoid judgements, assumptions, and generalizations

Express

Use "I" messages to let the other person know the effect their actions or the situation is having on you.

Specify

Assert your needs (not your position) and ask for what you want.

Consequences

State the positive consequences of creating a change in behaviour

Refocus

Redirect to the matter at hand

Stalemate?

If the other party is unwilling to share, use good inquiry methods to get at interests. The bottom line is that you need to figure out *why* people feel the way they do and *why* they are demanding what they are demanding. Be sure to make it clear that you are asking these questions so you can understand their interests (concerns, needs, hopes, fears, or desires) better, not because you are challenging them or trying to figure out how to beat them.

Further Thoughts on Interests

Interests are the things that people want to achieve in a conflict situation. Unlike people's positions—which are simple statements that purportedly represent their interests, the interests underlying a position answer the question "*Why* do you want that?" or "*Why* do you feel that way?"

It is important to appreciate that each party is probably trying to satisfy multiple interests. Not only will a single person have multiple interests, but if you are negotiating with a group, you must remember that each individual in the group may have differing interests, previously referred to as back table interests.

Also important is the fact that the most powerful interests are basic human needs. If you can address the basic needs of both sides, agreement will be easier. Make a list of each side's interests as they become apparent. This way you will be able to remember them and also to evaluate their relative importance.

Consider the following further observations about interests identified by Lewicki et al in *Negotiations Essentials:*[107]

There is almost always more than one type of interest underlying a negotiation. Parties can have more than substantive interests about the issue—they can also care deeply about process, the relationship, or the principles at stake. Note that ' interests as principles' effectively cuts across substantive, procedural, and relationship interests as well, so that the categories are not necessarily exclusive.

Parties can differ on the type of interests at stake. One party may care deeply about the specific issues under discussion, whereas the other cares about how the issues are resolved—questions of principle or process. Bringing these different interests to the surface may enable the parties to see that in fact they care about very different things and thus they can invent a solution that addresses the interests of both sides.

Interests can change. Like positions on issues, interests can change over time. What was important to the parties last week—or even 20 minutes ago—may not be important now. Interaction between the parties can put some interests to rest, but it may raise others. Thus, the parties must continually be attentive to changes in their own interests and the interests of the other side. As we will point out, when parties begin to talk about things in a different way—when the language or emphasis changes — it may indicate a change in interests.

Surfacing interests. There are numerous ways to get at interests. Sometimes we are not even sure of our own interests. In these cases, we should be asking ourselves not only 'What do I want (from this negotiation)?' but also 'What do I really want?' 'Why is that important to me?' 'What will achieving that help me do?' 'What will happen if I don't achieve my objective?' Listening to your own inner voices fears, aspirations, hopes, desires—is important to bring your own interests to the surface.

The same dialogue is essential in clarifying the other party's interests. Asking probing questions and paying careful attention to the other party's language, emotions, and

107   Adapted from R. Lewicki et al., *Essentials of Negotiation* (Toronto, ON: McGraw-Hill Ryerson, 2017), 64.

nonverbal behaviour are essential keys to the process. You might also want to distinguish between intrinsic interests- that need to be satisfied as ends in themselves- and instrumental interests- which help us get other outcomes. In both cases, once these interests are understood, it may be possible to invent a variety of ways to address them. The result is a mutually satisfactory solution.

Surfacing interests is not always easy and to your best advantage. *Critics to the "interest approach' to negotiation have identified the difficulty of defining interests and taking them into consideration. Provis108 suggests that it is often difficult to define interests and that trying to focus on interests alone often oversimplifies or conceals the real dynamics of conflict. In some cases parties do not pursue their own best objective interests but focus on one or more subjective interests, which may mislead the other party.*

Focussing on interest can be harmful. *There are situations where focussing on interests can impede negotiations. For instance, with a group of negotiators whose consensus on a particular issue is built around a unified position rather than a more generalized set of interests, a focus on interests may not help achieve a solution. If a coalition is held together by a commitment to pursue a specific objective in negotiation, then encouraging the chief negotiator to discuss interests rather than push for the specific objective is clearly encouraging him or her to deviate from the coalition's purpose.*

Interests and a *Good* Agreement or Settlement?

What are you trying to achieve? What you're seeking informs your strategy and approach. If you seek to satisfy solely your own interests you will adopt a positional, distributive approach. It is a question of winning or losing. If you seek to satisfy your interests and those of others, you will adopt an integrative approach. It is a question of what constitutes a *good* agreement.

Win-Win = Good?

Approaches to negotiations, conflict management, and the like have been the subject of many popular books. Challenging readers to find a better way, many of these books extol the virtues of what they characterize as win-win bargaining. A good agreement is a win for me and a win for you, or so the story goes.

In *Conflict Resolved? A Critical Assessment of Conflict Resolution,* Alan Tidwell takes issue with such simplified prescriptions. He finds that these publications tend to:

- trivialize or generalize conflict and provide simplistic solutions

108   C. Provis, *Interests vs. positions: A critique of the distinction.* Negotiation Journal, 12 (Boston, Mass: Program on Negotiation, 1996), 305-323.

- routinize methods of handling it

- undervalue the role that situations, circumstances and context play in handling matters at issue

At page 27, Tidwell comments on what he describes as the win-win discourse:

> Generalized across all conflict contexts, the win-win discourse is not genuine conflict resolution, but rather a mechanism for persuading others that they have what they want, without giving anything away. It is clever, but not very productive towards long-term conflict resolution.

Professor Lawrence Susskind[109] of MIT made instructive comments in his 2011 blog report about the oft-used, little understood expression.

> I hear the phrase "win-win" all the time. I'm not sure that very many people who use it know what they are talking about. I have a hunch they mistakenly assume that if everyone would just cooperate, then all parties would get what they want. That, of course, is ridiculous. There are almost no negotiations in which everyone can get everything they want. And cooperation or even compromise isn't the issue.

Susskind went on to encourage *Thinking Clearly About Win-Win:*

> *No one should agree to anything in a negotiation that is worse for them than what they are likely to get if no deal is reached. Roger Fisher and Bill Ury made this point thirty years ago in Getting To Yes.*
>
> *First, figure out what no agreement is most likely going to leave you with, try to generate something (a walk-away) that's better than that, but when you are in an actual negotiation don't reject something that's better than your realistic walk-away, even if it won't get you everything you'd like to have. Fisher and Ury called this point of comparison, your Best Alternative to the Negotiated Agreement (BATNA).*
>
> *A win-win negotiation is something that gets all sides an outcome better than their BATNA. It doesn't necessarily get anyone everything that they might want.*

Tidwell and Susskind's observations are instructive. The back and forth communication designed to reach an agreement when you and the other party have some interests that are shared and others that are opposed is better described as making the best decisions to maximize your interests. The parties involved—their roles, motivations,

---

109   Lawrence Susskind, Ford Professor of Urban and Environmental Planning at MIT and Vice-Chair of the Program on Negotiation at Harvard Law School, *The Consensus Building Approach* blog post August 8, 2011. http://theconsensusbuildingapproach.blogspot.

and interests—present an added level of complexity to this form of negotiation that doesn't lend itself to simplistic prescriptions or approaches.

Elements of Good

Something is considered good when it is "... suitable to a purpose, effective, efficient."[110]

In their book, *Breaking the Impasse: Consensual Approaches to Resolving Public Disputes*, dispute resolution experts Lawrence Susskind and Jeffrey Cruikshank identify four characteristics of what can be termed a *good* negotiated settlement or agreement: fairness, efficiency, wisdom, and stability.

Figure 24: Elements of a Good Agreement

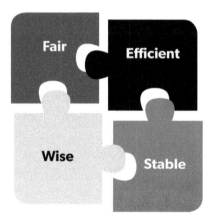

Fairness

Fairness is a general concept that implies treating both sides alike, without reference to one's own feelings or interests.

Susskind and Cruikshank say that the perceptions of the participants are most important in evaluating the fairness of a negotiated outcome. The key question is: "Were the people who managed the process responsive to the concerns of those affected by the final decision or outcome?" Unfortunately, the issue of fairness is situational and subjective. What one party perceives as a fair settlement may be seen quite differently by the other.

On page 25 of their book, Susskind and Cruikshank observe, "In our view, it is more important that an agreement be perceived as fair by the parties involved than by an

110   *Webster's New World Dictionary*, 2nd ed. (1986): 602.

independent analyst who applies an abstract decision rule. If the involved parties think a given process has been fair, they are more likely to abide by its outcome; if they do not, they will seek to undermine it."

Efficiency

The second way to judge an agreement is by testing its efficiency. Something is efficient if it directly produces the desired result with a minimum of effort, expense, or waste. Efficiency is established by asking two questions:

- Could one or all of the parties to the agreement be made better off without making the others worse off? If the answer is "Yes," then the agreement is efficient.

- Did it take an inordinately long time and a great deal of effort to reach the agreement? If so, do the benefits of the agreement outweigh the costs associated with achieving the agreement? If the answer to this subsequent question is "No," the agreement cannot be considered a good one.

Wisdom

Something is considered wise if it is informed, sound, and prompted by a considered judgement of the relevant aspects and circumstances concerning the matter or matters at issue. In a sense, wisdom is only obvious in hindsight. Negotiations involve forecasts or predictions on areas of settlement and potential consequences of particular courses of action.

It is virtually impossible to have complete confidence in a forecast and have that forecast come to pass or stand up to the test of time. Agreements are concluded at a particular time and under particular circumstances, and they govern the relations between the parties over a considerable period. During this time, substantial changes may take place—changes not contemplated when the agreement was reached. It may also take an indeterminate amount of time for the forecast to be tested. We only realize that what we have done was an incorrect approach when it is too late.

Key to a wise agreement is what Susskind and Cruikshank term "prospective hindsight"—an assessment and forecast based on past experiences and knowledge. Unfortunately, in some areas even our past experiences tell us very little, because the result of previous actions has not yet been realized. It is also extremely difficult to remain constantly objective when assessing a problem.

A wise agreement contains all the relevant information to minimize the risk of being wrong. The search for a wise solution requires a collaborative inquiry into the problem. This inquiry breaks down a complex problem into a series of mutually agreed-on pieces that can be examined individually.

By looking at the smaller pieces, we can reach a wise solution that satisfies all the underlying interests, without having to rely solely on our predictions of future consequences. Remember, we are free to choose a course of action, the interests we seek to satisfy, and strategies to employ, but we are not free to choose the results or consequences, intended or otherwise, of our choices.

The concept of wisdom and the consequences of our choices are closely linked to the fourth characteristic—stability.

Stability

Stability is the final element of a good agreement. Something is stable if it cannot be easily moved or thrown off balance, or is not likely to break down, fall apart, or give way. A settlement that is perceived by all parties as fair, that was reached efficiently, and that seems technically wise is unsatisfactory if it does not endure.

A good agreement will endure over time and remain unchallenged by the parties and/ or their respective constituents. That is, none of the parties to the agreement will have any motivation to break the agreement before it expires naturally.

Instability can be caused in several ways:

Is the overall agreement feasible? A negotiator may reach an agreement in a labour dispute, but if it cannot be sold to the negotiator's constituents, the efficiency, wisdom, and fairness of the agreement become irrelevant.

Can the agreement be implemented by both parties? If the agreement contains provisions that are not realistic, the agreement will not be stable. It is not helpful to extract unrealistic commitments that cannot be relied on, even if such promises seem like victories at the time they are achieved.

Is the agreement based on mistaken assumptions? In framing the agreement, negotiators should make a commitment that if the agreement has been based on a mistaken assumption, the parties will reconvene and correct that mistake. Remember that one side may grant a large concession, not realizing the potential impact. Once that impact is known, however, it may be used in an attempt to destroy the entire agreement, or used as a weapon in future negotiations. As a result, the agreement, as well as the relationship, is now unstable.

Is the agreement legal? It is of little use to enter an agreement that is not enforceable. Knowledge of the limitations on all parties is necessary. Further, you must know to what both you and the other party are legally able to commit.

The authors conclude that outcomes—whether substantive or relationship—generated by positional bargaining, coercion, and situational compromise often fail to meet these four tests and as a consequence set the stage for further conflict.

The following table summarizes the characteristics of a good negotiation or settlement.

Table 11: Characteristics of a Good Negotiation or Settlement

A good negotiation →	Fair	Efficient	Wise	Stable
Produces better technical solutions		✓	✓	
Increases the likelihood of compliance by constituents			✓	✓
Improves the relationship between the parties	✓			✓
Is most efficient (less costly—time, money, stress)		✓		

Chapter 8: Analyzing Workplace Conflict

Consider Conflict and Work from Another Perspective

Earlier, we described workplace conflict, a form of interpersonal conflict as an expressed struggle between at least two interdependent parties who perceive incompatible goals, scarce resources, and interference from the other party in achieving their goals.

To narrow the definition of conflict and work, consider the following two general categories. The first is what we call the *something happened* category, Conflicts – Circumstance, and the second, Conflicts – Approach, which focusses on how one deals with power and authority in the workplace and the conflict that flows from the approach adopted.

These two categorizations are not mutually exclusive but are presented in this way to focus discussion and further exploration.

Conflicts – Circumstance

Conflicts – circumstance focusses on the substance of a conflict—what each party perceives got them to this point. It is an inquiry about details and circumstances and the impact of the decisions made and actions taken. It should be aimed at separating impact from intention. We often jump to false conclusions about others' intentions.

This category often encompasses interpersonal conflict and the difficulty of working together and getting along, and can include:

- Relationship conflict: personal feelings and emotions related to the circumstances.

- Task conflict: disagreements over what is to be done, what is important, and the specific strategies for execution.

- Process conflict: disagreements over how something should be done; misalignment of work and tasks.

- Status conflict: disagreements over who is in charge; who has the authority to do what, when; where the ultimate responsibility resides.

A conflict – circumstance is best reconciled through a performative discourse; where relationships are concerned, restorative discourse may prove useful. This approach has implications for the reconciliation of particular circumstances.

Conflicts – Approach

Conflicts – approach can take a variety of forms, including how institutional structures are administered and incongruities between one's words and action.

A case of incongruity: Conflict often emerges from a misalignment between a person's perceived way of acting and authority (their theory-in-use) and their espoused theory (the world view and values on which people believe their behaviour is based[111]).

In light of the earlier section on *Power, Authority, and Rules,* consider the following example:

> If you ask a manager how she handles conflict, she may say that she gets the relevant people to work together and sort the problem out. This is her espoused theory. However, you may observe that in practice, she resolves conflict by intervening and drawing on formal authority. This shows her theory-in-use. The manager is not being deceitful when she says she encourages people to get together to talk, but she is unaware of her actual behaviour.
>
> Since espoused theory is often different from theory-in-use, when people are asked why they do things, we may not get the correct answer. We may be able to change people's espoused theories while leaving their theories-in-use untouched. Managers will say all the right things, but continue to do the wrong things. When asked, even honest interviewees may not accurately describe how they behave—which is why "how did you ..." questions are better than "how would you ..." ones. Does this sound familiar?

The key to managing this phenomenon is to uncover the theories-in-use so that managers can better understand their own behaviour. You can better understand theories-in-use by observing actual behaviour and inferring the underlying theory. Once identified, we can draw lessons from the effective theories-in-use and work to change the ineffective ones.

A case of an institutionalized norm. In unionized workplaces, collective agreements are periodically negotiated periodically to define and redefine the rewards employees receive for their services, and the conditions under which these services are rendered. In these workplaces, the conflicts—approach can take two forms: the negotiation or

---

111   C. Argyris, D.A. Schon, *Theory in Practice: Increasing professional effectiveness* (San Francisco, CA: Jossey Bass, 1974); and *Organizational Learning: A theory in practice perspective* (Reading, MA: Addison Wesley, 1978).

re-negotiation of the collective agreement, and the interpretation and administration of the agreement.

Whether the negotiations can be characterized as adversarial and highly conflictual, or as more cooperative and positive, can affect the level of cooperation and harmony between the parties during the organization's day-to-day operations. This has implications for how disagreements are approached over the application and administration of the agreement during its term (see Part Four: *Disputes and the Collective Agreement* for a comprehensive analysis of grievances and the grievance process).

Ideally Conflicts—Approach are reconciled through integrative discourse and, where appropriate, performative and transformative discourse. Unfortunately, individual, group, and institutional norms and default approaches may lead one or both parties to adopt a positioning and positional orientation that emphasizes distributive discourse.

Conflict Analysis Template

The conflict analysis template[112] includes two assessment tools. The first is an assessment of the levels of conflict and the second is a detailed process to analyze conflict.

The conflict analysis template provides a process to:

- analyze a conflict situation

- help you make a decision whether to adopt either an active-engagement strategy—competition, collaboration, accommodation, or a non-engagement strategy—avoidance

- learn from the results of your efforts

It's a puzzle of sorts ... only when you understand the context, have assembled all the pieces and organized them in the right order, do you see the picture ... and can make a make a reasoned, informed decision.

112   Adapted from the global organizational development consultancy Transnational Management Associates (TMA World), 2002.

Figure 25: Levels of Conflict

Level 3 Conflict to Dispute (High Intensity)	Minimizing Adverse Consequences and Refocusing Strategies: Adjudicative vs. Consensual Processes

- Mandated formal processes: fact finding with recommendations, mediation, med-arb., arbitration
- Establish a "cooling off" period
- Provide the parties with a clear sense of direction

Level 2 Disagreement/Discord (Moderate Intensity)	People Management Strategies

- Issue, examination/analysis
- Create a safe environment
- Be hard on facts and positions, but soft on people
- Share responsibility for finding solutions
- Focus on points of agreement; mediative mindset
- Allow time for the conflict to work itself out
- Integrative problem solving; challenge either/ or thinking

Level 1 *Nuisances* (Low Intensity)	Coping Strategies

- Avoidance
- Accommodation
- Creative, integrative problem-solving
- Developing mutual awareness
- Identifying points of agreement

Figure 26: Conflict Analysis Process[113]

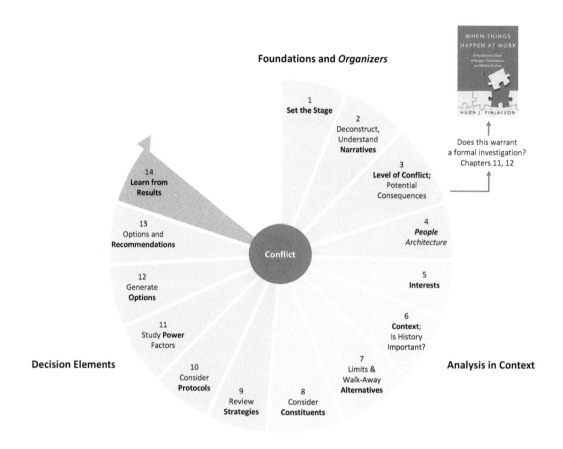

Foundations and *Organizers*

Does this warrant
a formal investigation?
Chapters 11, 12

1
Set the Stage

2
Deconstruct,
Understand
Narratives

3
Level of Conflict;
Potential
Consequences

4
People
Architecture

5
Interests

6
Context;
Is History
Important?

7
Limits &
Walk-Away
Alternatives

8
Consider
Constituents

9
Review
Strategies

10
Consider
Protocols

11
Study **Power**
Factors

12
Generate
Options

13
Options and
Recommendations

14
**Learn from
Results**

Conflict

Decision Elements

Analysis in Context

113   The two foundations of this process are the global organizational development consultancy TMA World concept and the planning guide articulated in Lewicki et al., *Essentials of Negotiation* (Toronto, ON: McGraw-Hill Ryerson, 2014), 71–92.

1. Set the stage: plan and then inquire in a manner that encourages open, candid, and focussed dialogue. Start to build a detailed chronology of events.

2. Understand the conflict-problem narratives with a goal of transforming the narration of stories into a genuine conversation and dialogue. What are the issues? Which issues are connected to other issues? Distinguish between source and symptoms. What is the source of the conflict (values, beliefs, and perceptions of self-interest, conflicting goals and priorities, different methodologies, different interpretation of events, different expectations)?

3. What is the level of conflict? What are the potential consequences of the conflict? Does this warrant a formal investigation?

> Caution: **Does your preliminary inquiry lead you to conclude that a more formal investigation is required?** If maybe, potentially, or yes, initiate the processes and strategies in Part Three: *Investigating Workplace Incidents.*

4. **People Architecture:** Who is directly and indirectly involved, who reports to whom, who represents whom, who has influence, who observes, and who is a decision-maker or adviser to a decision-maker? Brainstorm a list and assemble the people architecture.

5. What are the underlying interests of the participants? Distinguish between positions, issues, and interests. Are there common interests? What stated position(s) is each side taking on the matters at issue?

6. What do you know about the context in which the conflict is occurring (history, cultural, and organizational factors,[114] resources that could be useful, and constraints)?

7. What are the limits of the participants? If they are not successful, what is their walk-away alternative?

8. Who are the constituents and what do they want done? What do you know about them? How do both sides perceive the issues involved in the conflict?

9. What do you want to achieve? What overall strategy do you want to select? What are the strategic options? When do you act? Is timing an issue? Do you want an active or non-active engagement strategy? What are the advantages and disadvantages of the different available strategies?

114   Does a union represent the employer's employees necessitating their involvement?

10. Where applicable, what protocol needs to be followed in conducting these discussions?

11. What is the balance of power in the conflict? Relevant factors could include authority, financial resources, legitimacy, information, expertise, and time.

12. Given the interests, what and how many options can be generated? Do these options accurately address the issues, the real source of conflict, and the needs of the organization (if applicable)?

13. Frame options and recommendations to the parties involved. Identify the parties who will be presented with the options, how the options may affect them, and in what ways can they be presented professionally, concisely, and while preserving working relationships.

    Consider, is a workplace restoration process necessary to re-establish positive working relationships so that members of an organization can move on after a stressful event? The workplace restoration process is necessary after any significant disruption in workplace relations resulting from prolonged conflict, an accusation of bullying or harassment, an investigation, employee terminations, and other organizational changes.

14. **Learn from results:** Examine your plan, conflict analysis, process adopted and how the matters at issue were reconciled. What could we have done better? (e.g., a better understanding of the context and people involved; explored interests further)

Chapter 9: Some Final Thoughts

In today's diverse and demanding workplace, misunderstandings are bound to arise between employees at all levels in an organization. To foster a more cooperative and productive environment, you must be able to defuse workplace stress, promote civil discourse, and help others channel emotionally charged conversations in a constructive direction.

For the human resources professional, it is important to be able to identify conflict in the workplace and know how to resolve the underlying issues in a positive way, quickly and effectively. Managing conflict in a positive, constructive manner can lead to much-improved professional and personal relationships.

When dealing with a disagreement between co-workers, a deliberate process that considers the different conflict resolution styles of each participant is a recommended best practice. Done well, conflict management can save relationships, time, and resources, while improving productivity and helping move projects forward towards completion.

Workplace conflict is one of the greatest causes of employee stress. Taking simple steps to address conflict immediately can prevent many workplace conflicts from escalating. Employee stress, and many related health complaints, as well as workers' compensation and bullying claims, can be prevented by acting quickly to resolve issues between co-workers.

One Approach to Workplace Conflict Management: Act, Meet, Decide

This section assumes that you have used the process for analyzing conflict—the conflict analysis template—to inform your approach and have incorporated the principles of the constructive interactions framework in Part Five: *Interactions with Purpose*. Consider the following additional points when finalizing your approach. Missing or glossing over steps in that process can lead to entirely avoidable problems.

1. **Act immediately, decide on your course of action, develop a plan, and act**. There are generally three ways of dealing with conflict.

    - **Do nothing.** Assume matters will work themselves out. This can work for some Level 1 conflicts.

    - **Address the matters indirectly.** Adopt an informal inquiry approach through passive communications and talking about peripheral issues to inform a potential way forward.

- **Address the matters directly.** Assume time is of the essence and that a direct intervention is the first step in reconciling apparent matters at issue.

With these three general ways in mind, remember that conflicts do not go away. Choosing to do nothing is a choice, but it can be a risky one. Unresolved conflicts can lie dormant for days, weeks, or months, only to explode on another occasion. Avoiding conflict is one of the main causes of claims being made against an organization. Employees who make claims often feel that no one has listened or done anything to resolve a matter of concern to them. They feel they have no choice but to seek the help of professionals.

Unresolved workplace conflicts can quickly impact workplace climate or culture. Whole teams are affected as conflict spreads and other employees become involved. Productivity, performance, and workplace relationships are impacted quickly when conflict takes hold.

2. **Meet** separately with people involved in the conflict. Get a clear under-standing of the issues before you try to intervene. People often have very different perceptions of what has occurred. Remember the power of the narrative and the goal of transforming the narration of stories into a basis for dialogue. Understanding their perceptions will help you focus on what is important to each person and finding common ground.

3. **Perception is reality.** Focus on what the people involved need and what's important to them, not on trying to judge who is right or wrong. Often both people have contributed something to the situation. Judging who is right and wrong, and particularly commenting on these judgements, can quickly escalate conflict.

4. **Decide** whether to mediate or to call in others to help. Once you have discussed the issues with those involved, decide whether you will be able to manage the matter to conclusion yourself or if you will need the help of other management colleagues or external mediators.

Managers often successfully resolve simple disputes involving two people that have only been an issue for a few hours, days, or weeks. Generally, it is best to leave complex and long-standing issues involving a number of people to individuals with experience in resolving such matters. These workplace conflicts are often sensitive and require high-level skill to bring them to a conclusion.

5. **Arrange** the next steps as soon as possible. While it can be difficult to arrange meetings in busy workplaces, ensure resolving the conflict is a

top priority. Generally, the longer the conflict goes on for, the harder it is to resolve.

The Future

You can't do anything about the past but you can learn from it with a goal of positively influencing the future. Consider your own work environment:

- What are some key sources of conflict in your workplace?

- Is there congruence between what is said and done, between the stated rules and expectations and those that are unwritten and seen as organizational norms?

- When do conflicts tend to occur?

- How do people respond to these conflicts as they arise?

- When your workplace solves problems, does it do so for the moment, or do you put in place practices, processes, and systems for addressing these types of concerns in the future?

- Do the transactional and psychological contracts that define the employment relationship lead to or limit workplace conflict? Why?

Normal, healthy organizations will experience their share of conflict, both constructive (leading to improved engagement and decision making) and dysfunctional (with the consequent implications for relationships, productivity, and the like). Anticipating conflicts is necessary in either circumstance for transforming these situations into opportunities for growth and learning.

Organizations have formal and informal structures (written and unwritten rules). What is the difference between the organization's hierarchy (as it appears on paper in an organization chart) and the organization's networks (the informal way things get done)? Who has influence over what? Where does the real power lie to get things done in a particular way?

There is a discernible ebb and flow to organizational life. Are there seasonal peaks in the workload that tend to occur annually? Chart the occurrence of such challenges, and consider whether they can be managed as a normal period of stress and transition.

Change is an inevitable part of organizational life. How does the organization seek input concerning changes that impact employment and how are organizational changes communicated, to whom and for what purpose?

An organization's environment—both physical and psychological—can contribute to conflict. Are there certain environmental factors that make problems worse, especially at times of conflict?

When problems and concerns occur, is the organization proactive? Are there avenues for identifying problems and expressing concerns in a predictable, reliable manner?

Examine the systems for managing problems, including conflict management processes and formal dispute resolution systems, and use times of relative harmony to identify process improvements that can be implemented in times of stress. Review and codify processes for managing during stressful times.

Part Three: Investigating Workplace Incidents

When an incident happens in a workplace, you will seek to learn more about what happened through a process of inquiry—asking questions and testing propositions. This initial inquiry may reveal that a formal investigation is necessary.

Compared to an inquiry, an investigation is a more formal and organized process of examining a problem through inspection and assessment. In a workplace setting, investigations are usually undertaken in response to reports of an employee's misconduct, which could range from simple misunderstandings and inappropriate remarks to allegations of theft, sexual touching, or abuse.

When an allegation is brought against an employee, it is important for both the *complainant* and the employee that a comprehensive investigation establish to what extent, if any, the alleged behaviour occurred, and to determine the appropriate consequence. The investigation must be systematic and thorough, so that it can provide a sound foundation from which to decide on reasonable consequences.

If you are overseeing an investigation into employee misconduct, you will need a firm understanding of:

- the rights and obligations contained in workplace contracts and employment statutes

- how to elicit information during an investigative interview

- the process for initiating, conducting, and successfully concluding an investigation

Although this section focusses on strategies and guidelines for investigating workplace misconduct, the principles and procedures described here apply equally to other situations, which could include investigating workplace health and safety matters, harassment complaints, Workers' Compensation Board claims, and accidents. Keep in mind that each issue presents its own unique characteristic due to the nature of the employment relationship (union, non-union), and in unionized workplaces, the terms of the collective agreement or applicable legislation or protocols.

This section begins by defining misconduct and conduct (including culpable and non-culpable conduct). It then outlines a process for conducting an investigation, from how to collect evidence to best practices in planning and conducting it, including how to conduct investigative interviews. We then turn to post-investigation considerations, including the use of non-disciplinary and disciplinary responses. For additional investigation resources, see Appendix A and Appendix B.

Chapter 10: Conduct and Misconduct in the Workplace

What is Misconduct?

The employment relationship or employment contract is based on a set of mutual expectations and responsibilities. The employer agrees to compensate an employee with the expectation that the employee will attend work regularly, perform their job duties satisfactorily, and not engage in conduct contrary to the best interests of the employer.

Misconduct is a transgression of some established and definite rule of action, a forbidden act, a dereliction from duty, unlawful behaviour, improper or wrong behaviour, delinquency, impropriety, mismanagement, or offence. Misconduct is not negligence or carelessness.[115]

As described below, misconduct can typically be divided into four general areas:

- wilful misconduct
- wilful neglect of duty
- insubordination
- off-duty behaviour that is prejudicial to the employer

Wilful Misconduct

The misconduct must have been behaviour on the part of an employee. In other words, the employee must have knowingly and deliberately done or failed to do what was expected of them. Conduct that is accidental or involuntary is not considered behaviour. Some examples of behaviour misconduct are:

Fraud and theft

- Falsified processes to record work time
- Theft of cash or property of the employer

---

115   B. Garner, ed. *Black's Law Dictionary*, 10th ed. (St. Paul, MN: West Group, 2014).

Alcohol or drug abuse

- Being under the influence of alcohol during working hours. (If the drinking is due to alcoholism, this behaviour is attributed to a recognized illness and is therefore not seen as behaviour.)

Recklessness:

- An employee's behaviour was so reckless as to amount to behaviour misconduct.

Conflict of interest or breach of trust:

- An employee is guilty of behaviour that seriously affects a position of trust they hold with the employer and/or the employer's clientele or puts themselves into serious conflict of interest with the employer.

Failure to follow the organization's policy

- An employee breaches the policy that prohibits the use of office technology for personal purposes.

When it comes to identifying misconduct that involves a failure to follow organizational policy, the following criteria should be satisfied to meet the test of behaviour misconduct. The rule or policy must:

- be clear and unequivocal

- have substantial impact on the employment relationship (except perhaps in cases of repeated, deliberate infractions)

- have been communicated to the employee

- be known (or ought to be known) in advance that the conduct could result in disciplinary action

- not require the employee to do anything illegal or unsafe

Wilful Neglect of Duty

Neglect means to be remiss in attending to or to fail to do. If an employee has neglected the duties of the job, they have violated a standard of conduct that the employer has a right to expect of employees. Most neglect of duty problems are *culpable*, as the employee could normally carry out the task(s) of concern. Some examples of such neglect are failure to perform assigned tasks, failure to meet expectations, lack of effort, or low productivity.

Insubordination

Insubordination is a behaviour failure to obey a supervisor or an employer's lawful orders.

In unionized workplaces, one of the most basic and widely accepted rules of *arbitral jurisprudence* holds that employees who dispute the propriety of their employer's orders must, subject to the considerations that follow, comply with those orders and only subsequently, through the grievance procedure, challenge their validity. This is a basic principle of the workplace: provided the matter at issue is legal and not demonstrably unsafe, work now, grieve later.

Apart from the circumstances in which the general principle has been found to be inappropriate, arbitrators have generally insisted that to sustain an allegation of insubordinate conduct of this type, the employer must prove that an order was in fact given, that it was clearly communicated to the employee by someone with the proper authority, and that the employee actually refused to comply.

Arbitrators have also stated that it is not possible, from one fact alone, to conclude if insubordination in a particular situation can justify dismissal. Usually, one instance of insubordination is not sufficient to instantly fire an employee. However, one instance can be enough if one or more of the following occurred:

- the insubordination was serious

- the act consisted of behaviour and deliberate disobedience of an order

- the work rules were clearly communicated to the employee

- the work rules were consistently enforced

- the work order was authorized; that is, that it came within the scope of the worker's duties

- the employee was made aware, unequivocally, that discipline was the penalty for disobedience,

- the work order was lawful and reasonable in content

- the employee had no reasonable excuse for disobedience.

In summary, all relevant circumstances must be assessed to determine if, in a particular case, insubordination justifies dismissal.

Off-Duty Misconduct

Although the employer has no direct interest in an employee's conduct away from the workplace, an employee's off-duty conduct may affect their employment obligations under certain circumstances. To determine if this is the case, ask if the employee's conduct does one or more of the following:

- harms the organization's reputation or standing in the eyes of the community

- adversely affects the public's confidence in the organization

- renders the employee unable to perform their duties satisfactorily (for any reason, including adverse public reaction)

- constitutes a serious breach of the *Criminal Code*

- leads to a reasonable refusal, reluctance, or inability of other employees to work with the employee

- makes it difficult for the employer to meet its obligations

The impact of some instances of misconduct may be considered serious enough to warrant an employee's dismissal. If an employee is charged and convicted of a *Criminal Code* violation that conflicts in any way with the employee's duty to the employer, these conflicts will be considered grounds for discipline, up to and including dismissal. These conflicts include, but are not limited to:

- Sexual offences as detailed in Part V (Sexual Offences, Public Morals and Disorderly Conduct) of the Criminal Code.

- Offences against a person as detailed in Part VII (Disorderly Houses, Gaming and Betting) of the Criminal Code.

- Illicit drug use as detailed in Part XII.1 (Instruments and Literature for Illicit Drug Use) of the Criminal Code.

- Offences against the *Controlled Drugs and Substances Act*.

An employer may suspend an employee charged with an offence under the *Criminal Code* pending the final determination of the charges, or the employer may, depending on the offence and the information available, dismiss the employee before the final determination of the charges.

Culpable and Non-Culpable Conduct

When misconduct occurs, the employer must determine whether the behaviour is culpable or non-culpable because this will determine the appropriate response.

Culpable conduct requires the presence of some blameworthy behaviour. Examples include any form of dishonest behaviour such as theft, abuse of sick leave provisions or neglect of duty, insubordination, tardiness, assault, and so on. This type of misconduct may require a corrective and/or progressive disciplinary response.

Non-culpable conduct occurs when there is no blameworthy behaviour on the part of the employee. The most common types of non-culpable conduct that worry employers are poor work performance and absenteeism. In cases such as these, non-disciplinary *corrective action* may be required.

To determine the culpability of behaviour, assess whether an employee is unwilling or unable to perform their job duties satisfactorily or to attend at work regularly. Your response will vary, depending on the nature of the conduct. If an employee is unable, because of illness or innate inability, to perform their work satisfactorily, there is little point in engaging in progressive corrective discipline since one of the purposes of imposing discipline is to correct unwanted behaviour. If the employee is not in control of the unsatisfactory conduct, the imposition of discipline will have no effect.

However, if the behaviour is in the employee's control, a corrective supervisory response may elicit a positive response. If the behaviour is of a serious nature or continues, the imposition of discipline should elicit a positive response. If a positive result does not occur, the employer will eventually be in a position to terminate the employment relationship.

It is often difficult to determine whether particular behaviour is within the employee's control. This can be particularly true with absenteeism and work performance problems. Only the employee can provide an explanation for their acts, and it is therefore the employee's responsibility to explain and substantiate the reasons for their unacceptable performance.

As an employer, you should fully investigate these explanations to help you decide how to proceed. The question that must be answered is whether, given the explanation provided by the employee and as otherwise determined, would a reasonable person conclude that the employee has control over their unacceptable behaviour or performance?

It is not always possible to determine whether an employee's behaviour falls under the category of culpable or non-culpable conduct. Culpable and non-culpable elements may be mixed together, and it is not always easy to separate them. In some cases, you may need to proceed with both progressive corrective discipline and non-disciplinary corrective action.

However, in other cases, even if you suspect the employee's behaviour is blameworthy, there may be no proof of that suspicion. Where it is unclear, it is prudent to err on the side of caution and respond to the conduct as if it were non-culpable.

Employer Response to Non-Culpable Conduct

If the behavioural or performance problem is non-culpable, discipline is not appropriate. Addressing such a problem requires a methodical approach to resolution, which includes continued observation of the employee and encouragement of performance improvement over time

Your performance improvement efforts should include:

- Communication with the employee that identifies the behavioural or performance problem, the standard expected, and the level of job performance required. Review the employee's job description and any other applicable rules, policies, and procedures.

- Providing supervisory direction to the employee to help them meet the standards, including what follow-up procedures you will be taking to ensure they comply with the standards.

- Communication with the employee intended to ensure their understanding that the behaviour or performance is unsatisfactory and of what the consequences will be of continued failure or inability to meet the required standard.

- Discussion with the employee of strategies the employee might use to correct deficiencies in their work performance or behaviour; consideration of alternate employment within the context of their competence.

- Discussion after a period of time to review the employee's progress to meet the required standards.

Remember to document your efforts, showing the ongoing communication with the employee, that the employee was given reasonable opportunities to meet the standard and that the employer made reasonable efforts to find alternate employment within their areas of competence. Consider warning the employee in writing that their employment is in jeopardy due to unsatisfactory performance. The letter must be carefully drafted so that it will not be interpreted as being disciplinary in nature and it must indicate the employee is being given time and counselling/coaching to get to the required standard.

The employee's failure to improve may result in a reasonable accommodation, such as non-disciplinary demotion and/or transfer to a job level commensurate with ability. As a last resort and after all reasonable avenues have been exhausted, the employee may be terminated.

The National Harbours Board[116] case provides eight factors to consider when an employee is being discharged for poor work performance:

- Has the employer identified in objective terms the nature of the work to be performed and the standard expected?

- Has the employer established that the employee was aware of the standard?

- Has the employer established that the work performance of the employee was below the standard?

- Did the employer provide supervisory direction to the employee to help them achieve the standard?

- Did the employer take reasonable steps to move the employee into other work that was or might have been within his or her qualifications and competence?

- Did the employer make it clear to the employee that their performance was unsatisfactory, and that dismissal might result from a continued failure or inability to meet the standard?

- For employees in a unionized setting, did the employer afford the employee a proper opportunity to challenge its assessment of their work by grievance?

- Does the evidence support the inference of a continuing inability on the part of the employee to meet the standard?

In summary, employers must assess all relevant circumstances to determine if, in a particular case, the standard for dismissal based on non-culpable grounds has been met.

Employer Response to Culpable Conduct

An employee has engaged in culpable conduct if they:

- know, or could reasonably be expected to know, what is required of them

- are capable of carrying out what is required

---

116   Drawn from *The National Harbours Board, No. C36/82 (October 2, 1982)*. See Part Three in this publication for a detailed explanation of the case.

- choose to perform in a manner other than as required

Culpable conduct may lead an employer to impose discipline. Disciplinary measures are penalties designed to make clear to an employee that their conduct must be corrected or that further penalties, up to and including dismissal, may be imposed.

In extreme cases, such as assault, culpable conduct may lead directly to dismissal from employment. However, in most situations, misconduct calls for progressive discipline. Progressive discipline is an approach calling for progressively more severe discipline until the employee either corrects their misconduct or is terminated from employment.

The primary goal of workplace discipline is to rehabilitate rather than punish. A secondary goal is to set an example for all employees that the standard of performance and conduct must be upheld.

The keys to a proper imposition of discipline are:

- clear communication of standards

- consistent application of the standards

- complete consideration of all factors

- comprehensive investigation and the fair and consistent application of discipline

Chapter 11: The Investigation – Processes and Practicalities

> The purpose of an investigation is not to find evidence to prove an allegation. The purpose of an investigation is to obtain the relevant facts and then evaluate those facts from an unbiased and objective perspective to determine what actually occurred and whether the conduct warrants a particular response.

To ensure that decisions on employee discipline are fair and sustainable, employers must adopt systems and processes that allow for the consistent and thorough investigation of discipline matters. This section provides a basic model for a discipline investigation. Since every workplace is different, keep in mind you will need to develop your own model, which should be sensitive to the particular nature and history of your workplace.

Five Cardinal Rules

A cardinal rule is a fundamental one. There are five cardinal rules to follow when conducting an investigation. The rules frame your attitudes and approaches towards the critical task that has implications for individuals and the organization where they work.

1. Focus on the task at hand.

2. Begin with an end in mind.

3. If it's going to come out eventually, better have it come out immediately.

4. Every employee must be accorded respect, understanding, courteous consideration, and fair treatment at all times.

5. Just the facts. It's not what you think—it's what you can prove.

Cardinal Rule #1
"Focus on the task at hand: fact-based, evidence-informed decision making."

In short, the goal of an investigation is to find out what happened, why it happened, gather as many details as possible, and gain insight into the motivations and integrity of the witnesses.

Checklist 1, the checklist of important facts presented later in this section, is a useful guide when bringing together the facts of a case.

It is also important to look beyond *what* happened to develop an understanding of *why* it happened. Knowing the motivation behind the events can help you assess the employee's culpability.

An investigation is the first opportunity for an employee to tell the truth and reveal any incriminating circumstances. The capacity of the employee to appreciate the nature and extent of the misconduct and to accept responsibility for that misconduct at this early stage is strong evidence that the employment relationship is viable and worth saving.

In order for the picture to be accurate, the investigation must occur as soon after the event as possible and before the witnesses can be contaminated by thoughts or guidance from third parties (well-intentioned or otherwise). The passage of time dulls the powers of recollection, and witnesses can move away from the area, making it more difficult to collect evidence.

Cardinal Rule #2
"Begin with an end in mind."

Make your decision based on the assumption that the decision may be adjudicated by a third party to ensure that your decision and its associated reasoning can withstand third-party scrutiny.

If the employer believes that misconduct has occurred, discipline may be imposed. Depending on the employment relationship (union/non-union), an employee may appeal the discipline and ask an appropriate adjudicator to determine whether the grounds for discipline existed.

In general, disciplinary sanctions should be imposed within the context of previous cases. In non-union workplaces, look to common law precedents and in unionized ones look to arbitration awards. Specifically, consider the following three questions[117]:

- First, has the employee given just and reasonable cause for some form of discipline by the employer?

- Second, and if so, was the discipline imposed by the employer an excessive response in all the circumstances of the case?

- Finally, if the arbitrator does consider the discharge excessive, what alternate measure of discipline should be substituted as just and equitable?

---

117   Adapted from the *William Scott & Company Ltd. and Canadian Food and Allied Workers' Union, Local P-162 (Weiler), July 26, 1976*. See Part Four: *Disputes and the Collective Agreement* for a detailed explanation of the case.

It goes without saying that an employer who alleges a particular form of misconduct must prove that the conduct did, in fact, occur and that it was misconduct.

The employer must show that the discipline imposed was appropriate, considering the circumstances of the case. Here, an employer has a duty to consider all mitigating factors. Ask yourself:

- How serious is the offence?

- Was the employee's conduct premeditated or repetitive, or was it a momentary and emotional aberration, perhaps provoked by someone else (for example, in a fight between two employees)?

- What is the employee's previous record—how lengthy is their service and has there been any prior discipline?

- Does the penalty imposed create a special economic hardship for the employee in light of a particular circumstance?

- Is there evidence that the organization's rules of conduct, either unwritten or posted, have not been uniformly enforced, thus constituting a form of discrimination?

- Are there circumstances that negate the intent, such as the likelihood that the employee misunderstood the nature or intent of an order given to them, and as a result disobeyed it?

Employers can consistently make good decisions only when they have reliable and complete information. This applies as much to employee discipline issues as it does to any other significant business decision.

Bad or poorly supported decisions can have damaging consequences, including money wasted on lost litigation and costly reinstatement (in a unionized environment) of employees, as well as a different kind of cost—the deterioration of management and employee morale and the erosion of management credibility.

Both supervisors and bargaining unit employees rue the return of a poor performer to the job if the result could have been otherwise. As a result, employers are under increasing pressure to ensure that they make good decisions.

Employers must carefully investigate alleged disciplinary misconduct to reach sustainable and fair decisions. Before making a serious discipline decision, they must have complete and reliable information regarding the alleged misconduct and the circumstances that surround it. They must approach a disciplinary investigation with an open mind and be prepared to embrace the innocent explanation with the same zeal with which they embrace the guilty one.

When the investigation establishes that discipline is warranted, all information relevant to the determination of the appropriate penalty should be disclosed. Therefore, employers must have current information about the employee, including the employee's economic and family circumstances. Apart from this, they must know about and consider all the potential mitigating factors that might affect the measure of discipline, and any legitimate strategic issues that might affect the penalty.

Cardinal Rule #3
"If it's going to come out eventually, better have it come out immediately."

Quote attributed to Henry Kissinger, U.S. Secretary of State when commenting about the Watergate investigation in the 1970s.

Too often supervisors gloss over or minimize events that they think are irrelevant, or that they believe may be seen as mistakes. Employers should conduct fair, complete investigations that should be open to the discovery of facts that favour the employee's position, or that explain apparent contradictions. Employers should proceed without bias or discrimination.

Effective investigations must be:

- **Timely:** Initiated immediately to gather information when it is fresh and concluded as quickly as possible.

- **Systematic:** Structured so that the investigator observes the principles of *due process*, considers the basis on which a third party will assess the decision and examines all relevant facts and circumstances.

- **Thorough:** Complete, so that every avenue of inquiry is examined.

Cardinal Rule #4
"Every employee must be accorded respect, understanding, courteous consideration, and fair treatment at all times."

It goes without saying that in all their interactions, people want to be treated with respect and fairness. When an allegation is made, and an investigation is required, such a potentially charged and stressful situation requires care and diligence. Further, when a third party (adjudicator) reviews whether your decision is appropriate, it should be clear that your decision reflects fairness, process, and equity—preserving the rights of the individual and the obligations of the employer.

- **Fairness:** Being able to depend on the organization for reasonable support and respect for the individual; objectivity; openness by the employer (investigator) to the discovery of facts; absence of bias or discrimination.

- **Process:** A series of sequential tasks directed at accomplishing one particular outcome; a set of activities that, when considered together, produce a result that will withstand the test of a neutral third party; opportunity to be heard; evidence of due consideration.

When an employee is under investigation due to a complaint or incident, and the complaint or incident causes the employee to be disciplined, the employee is entitled to due process.[118]

Due Process (natural justice) procedural fairness: requirement applicable to public bodies and domestic tribunals when making decisions that affect the rights and interests of individuals; the rules of natural justice require that persons affected by a decision are notified of the case against them and be given a reasonable opportunity of presenting their case, and that the body making the decision listen fairly to both sides and reach a decision untainted by bias; the precise content of natural justice varies according to the nature of the power exercised, the decision involved, and the consequences that flow therefrom (*Labor Law Terms: J. Sack; E. Poskanzer, 1984*).

- **Equity** Impartiality; justice; consistency of response; treating both or all sides alike without reference to your own feelings or interests.

Relatively few incidents of misconduct result in termination. As an employer, you can guard against destroying the employer/employee relationship through your attitude (prejudging the employee based on limited, incomplete, or preliminary information) or your actions (such as treating the employee differently than other employees, differently than before the investigation, or discussing the matter with others not directly involved).

An investigation of employee misconduct is a fact-gathering process. The process requires judgement about evidence and information available to the employer following a full, careful, and complete investigation that will necessarily involve the employee. Failure to conduct a proper investigation may well void what might otherwise be appropriate discipline.

---

118   Notwithstanding the legal requirement to provide due process, many collective agreements have incorporated the concept of due process. This incorporation is evident in such articles as Right to Representation; Grievance (Dispute Settlement) Procedure; Arbitration/Expedited Arbitration Process; Process Prior to Dismissal; Evaluation Process.

Remember that in these situations, you are your behaviour (actions, statements, and gestures). Your behaviour is the only part of you that other people can observe. They have no way of knowing your thoughts, attitudes, and feelings. As a result, your behaviour influences other people through their perceptions of and reactions to you.

The concept of fairness also has a legal implication: employees have the right to be represented by the individual of their choice. This right to representation must not be abrogated. Further, in a unionized workplace, the employee must be advised of this right of representation before any meeting or discussion related to the investigation is held.

Cardinal Rule #5
"Just the facts. It's not what you think—it's what you can prove."

It is important to distinguish the difference between what you think happened and what you can objectively prove happened. Don't be distracted by rumours, what you believe might have happened, what you think should have happened, or the employee's past behaviour.

If you can't establish evidence that the event happened, you will not be able to rely on this evidence to support your decision.

If you hear rumours during the course of your investigation, you should track each rumour down to its sources to determine whether it provides any information with a bearing on the allegation.

Basic Process Considerations and the Collection of Evidence

The appropriate level of discipline depends on many factors. For example, who is the employee being disciplined? Employers will have to consider this question at much greater length later in the process. But at the beginning, some routine details are mixed with potentially crucial ones, including the employee's relevant family and economic circumstances. In some cases, arbitrators have considered the inability to obtain work in the community a very important mitigating factor.

Employers should not discover crucial facts for the first time at a formal adjudicative proceeding.

Determining Precisely What the Employee Did

The first fundamental question in any investigation is: did the employee commit the alleged employment offence? This can be a difficult question, and the answer depends on a very careful and fair assessment of all circumstances.

Employers must conduct thorough and comprehensive investigations, including interviewing all relevant witnesses, and obtaining and reviewing all relevant documentary and physical evidence.

Employers often find that answering the question of whether an employee has committed an employment offence involves making a decision on credibility. Resolving credibility issues does not always mean determining whether an employee or another person is lying. Many questions are resolved by finding the credible explanation that explains an apparent conflict, or by finding information that suggests that a witness is simply mistaken. Remember the impact that perception can have on our ability to recall events ... and that perceptual errors can occur, even in the most well-intentioned and honest of individuals.

Adjudicators strive to find common ground in apparently conflicting stories, and to find witnesses to be in error rather than to be perjuring themselves. Employers have an early opportunity to ensure that they have all the facts to make fair and sustainable decisions on issues of credibility.

Identifying the Standard of Conduct

In some cases, the fact that conduct is improper may not be self-evident. The employee may claim they were not aware of the constraint. In other cases, the seriousness of misconduct will be in question. In all these instances, the investigation should identify the standard of conduct that is binding on the employee and describe how this standard was made known to the employee.

The sources of the standards for conduct are varied. Collective agreements often contain provisions that identify standards of conduct. Employer policies, rules, and handbooks are other useful sources.

Employees in certain sectors may be bound by statutes that establish specific standards and codes of conduct. Decisions in other cases involving the organization or its industry can be persuasive on standards where these awards are or should be known to employees.

Finally, knowledge of the standard and its seriousness may have been imparted to the employee in previous disciplinary or non-disciplinary settings. Whether or not an incident or communication forms part of a formal disciplinary record, employers should determine whether a previous communication brought to the employee's attention that certain conduct was required.

Ideally, cases should not turn on a close question of what standard applied to the employee. This issue should be resolved as early as possible in the investigation process.

Previous Opportunities to Remedy Misconduct

Few determinations are more critical to a disciplinary outcome than whether the employee knew the conduct was improper. The investigation should include a complete cataloguing of all previous correspondence and discussions that involved the kind of misconduct under investigation.

This cataloguing is different than assessing a discipline record. It may not be possible to refer to certain incidents in formal proceedings because of agreement provisions; i.e., sunset clauses that remove discipline based on the passage of time. This clause may eradicate previous discipline, but it does not change the question of whether, through previous discipline or otherwise, an employee should have been aware that conduct was improper. When an employee denies having been warned or instructed about the proper standards, an adjudicator can admit evidence of expunged discipline to contradict the employee.

Equally critical to the outcome is the question of whether the employee's misconduct breaches a commitment previously made by that employee. One of the fundamental purposes of the disciplinary process is to correct misconduct in a progressive way. Successful correction often requires a commitment from the employee. Both employers and adjudicators will be called on to consider the significance of a broken commitment, and to predict from this breach whether any penalty short of the chosen penalty will be useful.

The employee may have been warned against the misconduct during previous training and experience. The basic education of nurses, teachers, peace officers, and many.other technical and professional employees often provides conclusive evidence of the applicable standards and the importance with which they were imparted to the employee.

Finally, the investigation should consider the accessibility of resources to the employee in the workplace. For example, the following types of questions may apply in the context of a particular case:

- Is it relevant that an employee with alcoholism knew of, but never used, an employee assistance program?

- Does the employee who has performance issues lose credibility if it is established that the employee did not show interest in relevant education courses that were made available by the employer on the employer's time?

Impact of Misconduct

Adjudicators wish to understand the impact of misconduct on the employer. They accept that certain kinds of misconduct can threaten the business, and with it the employment of all other employees. Employers should be prepared to pay special attention to this very important factor over the course of an investigation.

Employers must consider the impact of the misconduct on the organization's reputation in light of the unique nature of the organization's business, such as patient abuse in the health care field, theft by a security company employee, or sexual activity with a student by a teacher.

Many other examples include much subtler relationships between misconduct and reputation.

Another area of investigation is the impact of the misconduct on other employees. Depending on the circumstances, the following questions can be vital.

- Does the misconduct cause employees to lose morale?

- Does the misconduct cause employees to fear for their personal safety or belongings?

- Do employees refuse to work with the employee due to the alleged misconduct?

Question that speak to the broader organizational impact can also be relevant. These questions include:

- What other impact does the conduct have on operations?

- What chain of events is started by the misconduct?

- What resources are used to guard against the misconduct?

The list of factors dealing with impact varies widely, depending on the employer, the industry, and perhaps even the community.

Non-Disciplinary Work Record

The employee's non-disciplinary work record is relevant when determining an appropriate penalty. It can be particularly important in dismissal cases, where the grievor asks the arbitrator for reinstatement. Where the employment history is characterized by negligence of duty and disrespect for authority, reinstatement is less likely. By the same token, a work history characterized by loyal and diligent service will increase the prospect of the relationship continuing.

Mitigating Factors

Mitigating factors are facts, while not negating a wrongful action, tend to show that the individual in question may have had some grounds for acting the way he/she did and that would tend towards reducing their guilt or culpability. The decision of the Labour Relations Board in the *William Scott and Company case* (1977) is instructive and perhaps cited most often in BC's labour relations community. It sets out the test that arbitrators apply to discipline cases in BC and identifies many so-called mitigating factors. These factors come from the William Scott case and have been supplemented with others from subsequent decisions. Since the law is evolving, the list can never be exhaustive.

In any dismissal case, employers should ensure that they have reviewed the relevant factors before reaching a decision on the appropriate discipline. Indeed, a careful review of the mitigating factors will sometimes point to a clear result for both employers and arbitrators.

Fairness

Fairness is the state, condition, or quality of being fair, free from bias; even-handedness. Dismissal is often characterized as the capital punishment of the workplace. Given the seriousness of the consequences of dismissal, arbitrators insist on a high standard of proof and rigorous adherence to procedural safeguards. Employers who investigate without a clear understanding of the procedural requirements of the collective agreement risk losing the right to discipline employees at all.

Adjudicators expect employers to conduct fair investigations. Similar offences should receive similar penalties if they are not significantly different in other ways.

Employees should never be able to complain that they were denied the opportunity to be heard. It is arguably always to the employer's advantage to hear from the employee. In unionized workplaces, the collective agreement may provide specific requirements. You should ask:

- Does the collective agreement require the presence of a union steward or representative, and under what circumstances?

- Must the decision be communicated to the employee in a specific way or at a specific time?

- Apart from the usual right to grieve, does the collective agreement provide any other opportunities for appeal or reconsideration?

- Does the agreement prohibit or restrict the use of documentation or evidence?

- Do any other collective agreement provisions bear on this issue?

Generally, investigations should be fair and be perceived as fair. Fairness is a situational and subjective term, so even a managerial focus on the importance of fairness will not eliminate this concern. However, an investigative process that does not consider fairness to be its fundamental basis is unlikely to survive a challenge through arbitration.

Strategic Issues

Serious discipline cases are not routine in most operations. They raise important and often strategic concerns. Can the employer afford to dismiss the employee at this time and risk an expensive and protracted case at litigation? Are witnesses available? Can the morale of the workforce survive if the case is not pursued? Is there a better and more conclusive way to achieve the objective? What is the objective?

These and other strategic concerns may dominate the final stages of the investigation, and the application of any number of valid concerns may modify the results. A comprehensive investigation checklist is included in Appendix A for use as a guide. Employers will have little difficulty listing their own important concerns in each particular case, specific to their organization.

Collecting Evidence

It is generally preferable to collect documentary and other physical evidence before conducting investigative interviews. The more evidence you can collect before questioning those involved, the better. The evidence gathered at this stage is useful in preparing for the interview(s), particularly with respect to generating questions. The employer should also identify any contractual or statutory restrictions on the use or availability of the evidence, such as covert surveillance.

Privacy Legislation

Under freedom of information and protection of privacy statutes,[119] individuals have the right of access to and the right to request correction of their own personal

---

119   Since 1993, British Columbia public bodies, including crown corporations, health authorities, boards of education, and municipalities, have been subject to the Freedom of Information and Protection of Privacy Act (FIPPA). The FIPPA regulates the collection, use, and disclosure of personal information by public bodies. It also regulates access to records in the custody or under the control

information. There is also a right of general access to records in the custody and control of public bodies, subject to certain exceptions set out in the *Freedom of Information and Protection of Privacy Act.*

In the context of workplace investigations, personal information (i.e., information about an identifiable individual) may be collected from various employees. For example, if you interview a witness to a workplace incident, you will, as a result, collect personal information about the employee(s) involved in the incident and, potentially, the witness's personal information as well. This personal information is then used to assess the incident, and may be disclosed to others who have a need to know about it in the course of their ongoing employment responsibilities.

When collecting, protecting, retaining, using, and disclosing personal information during an investigation, you must consider and comply with the requirements of applicable privacy legislation.

Responsibilities of an Investigator

An investigator should:

- limit collection and use of personal information to the extent necessary to conduct and complete the investigation

- limit disclosure of personal information to those who have a need to know

- collect and record personal information that is relevant, factual, objective, and necessary for the purposes of the investigation

- inform witnesses that information they provide will be treated confidentially, to the extent permitted by law

- clearly record on investigation documents, such as the investigator's notes, witness statements, etc., that the information is being provided in "confidence." If there is a request to access this information, this may support withholding the release of all or part of the information in the record.

- When taking notes, investigators should:

- be objective and avoid subjective comments

- only record information directly and necessarily related to the investigation

of a public body. The Personal Information Protection Act (PIPA) governs the collection, use, and disclosure of information by private sector organizations, such as provincially regulated businesses, non-profit organizations, and charities.

- limit notes to recording facts

- avoid personal opinions and irrelevant information

- be aware of the impact of combining various individuals' personal information in one report; separate documents are preferable

- keep in mind that access requests can be made.

Documents

At a minimum, this information would include a review of the accused employee's personnel file to gather information potentially relevant to the specific allegation and applicable policies.

Other evidence in document form might come from company records or other sources such as security/entry card records, computer time-stamps, phone or fax records, timesheets, credit card charges, receipts, parking/speeding tickets, fare stubs, schedules (bus, ferry, plane, television schedules), weather statistics, court or tribunal transcripts or exhibits, or any other records that may serve to corroborate or refute an employee's explanation of events. Be inquisitive and seek out as much relevant information as possible.

Electronic Evidence

Additional steps should be taken to secure all relevant electronic evidence. In a typical workplace, employees have access to computers, email, and the internet, as well as other telecommunications systems.

The jurisprudence[120] has generally supported the employer's right to use the tracking and recording capabilities of these technologies to investigate suspected employee misconduct, so long as the employer's investigation is reasonable in all the circumstances. However, the employee may assert that they had a reasonable expectation of privacy respecting the use of the technology in the particular circumstance.

Other Physical Evidence

In some cases, physical evidence is important for determining whether misconduct occurred or assessing the severity of the misconduct. For example, if a student has an injury that is alleged to have been caused by an employee, take photographs of the

---

120   For example, in International Association of Bridge and Structural and Ornamental Ironworkers, Local 97 and OTEU, Local 15, [1997] B.C.C.A.A.A. No. 630 (Bruce), the employer searched the hard drive of an employee suspected of performing personal work and storing personal files on her work computer. The arbitrator confirmed that the computer equipment belonged to the employer and that there was no reasonable expectation of privacy in respect of this office tool.

injury and the physical location where the injury is alleged to have occurred. These photographs serve to freeze the evidence and the environment at the time the events occurred. By taking appropriate photographs immediately after the event, the parties will be in a position to recreate the event more accurately. When taking photographs, record the date, time, and name of the photographer.

Physical evidence might also include such things as empty bottles (if the employee is alleged to have consumed alcohol on the premises), property, equipment, or items that were alleged to have been damaged by an employee.

It is important to maintain continuity of possession of any physical evidence. The person seizing the evidence should be the one who either keeps continuous possession of it or places it in a secure place that is not accessible by anyone else.

It is particularly important to properly handle any physical evidence that is a prohibited substance. Follow these common-sense guidelines:

- If you find an employee in possession of a prohibited substance, seize the substance and immediately advise the appropriate authorities so they can take possession of the substance. The police are properly trained in how to handle prohibited substances, so these matters are best left to them.

- Maintain continuity of possession of any prohibited substance between the time it is seized and the time it is taken by the police.

- Do not mix any substances you find. If physical evidence of a particular substance appears at two different locations, the substances must be kept separate until they are taken over by the police. For example, if you seize physical evidence of drugs on a table in the lunchroom and find evidence of a similar substance on the floor beside the table, the two substances should not be mixed together, but should be kept separate. In cases where employers have mixed substances, the criminal court has dismissed charges on the basis that the mixing of substances resulted in a reasonable doubt about the source of the prohibited substance.

- If you are not able to seize physical evidence of a prohibited substance but suspect that an employee is in possession of such a substance, ask the police for advice on determining whether the employee is in fact in possession of a prohibited drug.

Video Surveillance

In the absence of an express contractual right, conducting surveillance on an employee and videotaping the employee's conduct without their knowledge or consent will amount to a breach of the employee's right to privacy, unless the employer can justify what is considered intrusive conduct. The onus of establishing that the surveillance was justified rests with the employer.[121]

Different circumstances will attract different expectations of privacy and, as such, affect this balancing of interests. For this reason, it is often less difficult to justify open workplace surveillance than covert surveillance, provided the employer has sufficiently compelling business reasons for it.

Electronic surveillance in the workplace may be reasonable:

- if the employer has experienced acts of theft or has a reasonable suspicion of theft being committed by employees or an employee

- if the employer can show that it needs video surveillance to protect its property against theft or vandalism

- the extent of the problems or concerns precipitating the video surveillance is sufficiently serious to justify such an intrusive investigative tool and there is a strong probability that surveillance will assist in solving the problem

The collection of personal information by the use of video surveillance is subject to applicable privacy legislation.

Searching Employees' Property and Persons

Arbitrators have found that management has no absolute right to search employees or their property. Once again, employers must balance their legitimate business interests against employees' rights to privacy and are required to establish that they have reasonable cause to justify the search, that reasonable steps are taken to inform

---

121   The seminal case in this area of law is *Doman Forest Products and IWA Local 1-357* (1990) 13 L.A.C. (4th) 275 (Vickers). In *Doman* an employee with a very poor attendance record was absent under suspicious circumstances. The employer retained a private detective to conduct surveillance. In finding the surveillance to be unreasonable, Arbitrator Vickers stated on pgs. 281-2:

In my opinion, it is a balancing of interests that is required. The employee's right to privacy weighted against the company's right to investigate what it might consider to be an abuse of sick leave.

Questions to be answered include:

Was it reasonable, in all of the circumstances, to request surveillance?

Was the surveillance conducted in a reasonable manner?

Were other alternatives open to the company to obtain the evidence it sought?

the employees and that the search is conducted in a systematic and non-discrimina-tory manner.[122]

Planning the Investigation

When a complaint is received or an allegation of misconduct is made against an employee, a specific protocol or process should be followed to facilitate a thor-ough investigation of the complaint or allegation. The protocol should focus on gathering and analyzing information, while respecting the employee's rights and discharging the employer's obligation.

Remember that investigations are conducted within an employment law context. You should have a clear understanding of your legal obligations and the applicability of the collective agreement before undertaking any investigation. Failure to observe these legal obligations or the collective agreement may void what otherwise would have led to disciplinary action.

A timely, thorough investigation will lead to:

- the preservation of a productive employer/employee relationship

- an informed decision with respect to discipline or remediation

- effective arbitration preparation in the event the matter is referred to arbitration

The investigation protocol includes a number of steps, described below, that should be followed to ensure a thorough investigation. Throughout the process, you should maintain detailed documentation.

Preliminary Assessment

The investigation process starts the moment the employer is notified of an allegation of misconduct. It is critical that an investigation plan be in place to ensure appropriate steps are taken at the outset.

When you receive a complaint or allegation of misconduct against an employee, respond promptly. Delaying the investigation can lead to the defence that the investi-gation was procedurally flawed, especially when the employee denies the misconduct.

---

122   For example, in *Progistix-Solutions Inc.* and *C.E.P., Loc. 26* (2000), 89 L.A.C. (4th) 1 (Ont.—Newman).

Treat the complaint seriously. No matter how trivial the complaint may seem, it is better to follow standard procedures and avoid making assumptions or being influenced by irrelevant considerations.

Communicate to the complainant that the employer is treating the allegation seriously. Set up an interview with the complainant as soon as possible to get the complete details of the complaint(s), as follows:

- Who?

- What?

- When?

- Where?

- How?

- What is the motivation, if applicable?

- Witnesses?

Once you have interviewed the complainant, assess the incident by asking yourself:

- Is it reasonably likely that the incident, or elements of the incident, happened as reported?

- Does the incident, if proven, constitute misconduct by an employee? Could discipline result? (This is not a question of whether you will discipline, but of whether it *could* result.)

- If the answer is yes, check the collective agreement to see if the employee and/or union representative must be notified either verbally or in writing of the allegation and investigation.

Discuss the allegation and interview with employee's supervisor, if required.

- Establish a plan for investigating the complaint or allegation.

Identify the Alleged Misconduct

Identify the nature of the alleged misconduct at the outset of the investigation. Although the standard of proof in all discipline cases is on the balance of probabilities, in cases of serious misconduct such as those involving criminal behaviour, arbitrators and courts require "clear, rational and convincing evidence."[123] This usually necessitates a more comprehensive and detailed investigation.

The nature of the alleged misconduct will dictate whether you need to notify other agencies, such as the police or agencies responsible for child welfare.

You will also need to consider other factors to establish the alleged offence. For example:

- In cases of theft, not only must it be determined if the employee took the employer's property without authorization, but also whether the employee intended to steal the property or derive some personal benefit.

- In cases where a policy breach is at issue, it must be determined, among other things, if the employee's conduct breached the policy, whether the employee was made aware of the policy, whether the policy had changed since it was communicated to the employee, and whether the policy has been consistently enforced.

Identifying these factors will ensure that you identify the facts needed to make an informed decision regarding the potential outcome.

Conducting the Investigation

When you have a thorough understanding of the complaint and circumstances surrounding the complaint, prepare your strategy for investigating the matter.

This strategy should take into account the nature of your workplace (and any collective agreement obligations) as well as internal and external reporting requirements. You will also need to decide who should conduct the investigation and whether you will use outside experts, and then plan the interviews.

Unionized Workplaces: Collective Agreement Obligations

Review the collective agreement before beginning your investigation and answer the following questions:

- Are there provisions that require you to provide notice of the investigation and/or the allegation to the employee and union representative? If so, to whom and in what form? How is correspondence dealt with?

123   Garner, B.A., *Blacks Law Dictionary*, 10th ed. (Egan Min: Thomsen West, 2014).

- Have you identified and satisfied the contractual and statutory require-ments? Failure to satisfy such requirements may result in an argument that a substantive breach of the employee's rights has occurred, which could void the consequences.

- What are the provisions related to union representation and involvement? (This is a good faith discussion on what really happened, and the employee has the right to be represented by the union.) Do witnesses have the right to union representation?

- What are the time limits?

- How have recent arbitrations dealt with the issue of delay?

- For the personnel file, is there a process for allowing the employee and union access? Are there restrictions on the use of materials filed in the personnel file when considering discipline?

- What are the guidelines of procedural fairness, in terms of the requirement to interview the employee and ensure the employee has a right to a fair hearing?

Internal and External Reporting

There are often internal and external reporting requirements in place. The matter may be need to be reported internally, to the human resources department and senior management, and/or externally, to the police, social services, risk management, etc. You will also need to ask:

- Is it appropriate or necessary to suspend or remove the individual from the worksite pending the outcome of the investigation?

- Who must be notified of the complaint?

- Who conducts the actual investigation?

- Who oversees the investigation?

- How is the information to be recorded, stored, disclosed, or disposed of?

- What statutory requirements are applicable?

Who Should Investigate?

In some cases, a collective agreement may specify that an independent investigator must be used to investigate certain types of misconduct (e.g., harassment). In other cases, the governing legislation may stipulate who can investigate.

In the absence of any contractual or statutory requirements, the choice of investigator depends largely on the circumstances. Generally, the person who investigates an incident should:

- be close to the incident

- be skilled in investigation

- have rapport with employees

- be knowledgeable of collective agreement provisions

- be a strong witness

For the sake of consistency, it is preferable that the same person or person(s) conduct all the interviews.

Using Outside Experts

Determine whether it would be appropriate for outside experts such as forensic auditors or legal counsel to conduct the investigation. Who makes that decision? Remember that the involvement of outsiders may jeopardize your relationship with the union (if this applies to your workplace). Although this is not a reason to refrain from involving outside experts, you should make this decision carefully. Regardless of who conducts the investigation, it must not be perceived as underhanded or contrived.

Suspension Pending Investigation

The issue may arise as to whether the employee should be suspended, with or without pay, pending the conclusion of the investigation. In the absence of specific contractual language, you will need to determine whether the employee's continued presence in the workplace presents a reasonably serious and immediate risk to the legitimate business interests of the employer, including the safety of persons and property. If so, suspension may be warranted.

The issue is not whether the employee is guilty or innocent, but rather whether the presence of the individual as an employee of the organization presents a reasonably serious and immediate risk to the legitimate concerns of the employer. If you are suspending an employee using management's general authority, the key principles are as follows.[124]

1. The onus is on the organization to prove that such a risk exists. The simple fact that a criminal charge has been laid is not enough. The

---

124   *Ontario Jockey Club and Mutuel Employees' Association, Service Employees' International Union, Local 528* (1977), 17 L.A.C. (2d) 176 (Kennedy).

organization must also establish that the nature of the charge is such that it is be potentially harmful or detrimental to the organization's reputation or product, that it will render the employee unable properly to perform their duties, that it will have a harmful effect on other employees of the organization or its customers, or that it will harm the general reputation of the organization.

2.   The employer must investigate the criminal charge to the best of its abilities in a genuine attempt to assess the risk of continued employment. In this area, the burden on the organization is significantly less if the police have investigated the matter and have acquired the evidence to lay the charge rather than if the organization has initiated proceedings.

3.   The employer must show that it has taken reasonable steps to determine whether the risk of continued employment might be mitigated through such techniques as closer supervision or transfer to another position.

4.   There is a continued onus on the part of the organization during the period of suspension to consider objectively the possibility of reinstatement within a reasonable period of time following suspension in light of new facts or circumstances that may come to the attention of the organization during the course of the suspension. These matters, again, must be evaluated in the light of the existence of a reasonable risk to the legitimate interests of the organization.[125]

Should You Await the Outcome of Criminal Proceedings?

If the employee is alleged to have committed a criminal offence and the police are involved, you need to decide whether to conduct an internal investigation or wait for the outcome of the criminal proceeding.

This decision is generally based on the seriousness of the criminal charge and whether:

- the employer can obtain the evidence underlying the criminal charges

- the witnesses in the criminal case will cooperate with the employer's investigation

- an investigation by the employer would interfere with the police investigation

If, for example, the alleged misconduct occurred during the course of work, the employer would usually be able to thoroughly investigate the situation and decide

---

125   Ibid, pages 178,179

whether to discipline the employee.[126] However, if the employer is made aware that the employee has been criminally charged for conduct outside the workplace, it may be more difficult for the employer to obtain evidence from the criminal investigation.

If an employee is charged with a criminal offence (and is not incarcerated pending trial), the employer must balance the employer's interests in protecting its reputation and maintaining its ability to provide services, with the employee's interest in keeping his or her job. Consider whether the employee's:

- conduct could reasonably be expected to harm the employer's reputation or product

- behaviour rendered them unable to effectively perform their duties (e.g., bail conditions may restrict the employee's movements or contacts)

- actions represent a serious breach of the *Criminal Code*, thus creating a reasonable apprehension on the part of other employees or the clients

- conduct jeopardizes the ability of the employer to effectively carry out its operations

If you decide to conduct your own investigation before the outcome of the criminal proceedings, the employee is likely to invoke the right to remain silent and refuse to answer questions about the alleged misconduct. In these circumstances, it is best to present the employee with the information you have gathered and ask them whether there is any additional information you should consider that might be exculpatory.

The employee must be told that if they do not provide you with any further information, you will make your decision concerning the investigation's outcome based on the information you have before you.

Finally, it is usually preferable to conduct your own investigation if possible and not rely on the outcome of the criminal proceedings to justify any disciplinary penalty for the misconduct.

There are several reasons for this. First, criminal proceedings usually take a lengthy period of time to conclude. Second, the employer has no control over the criminal proceedings or the evidence the prosecution decides to use to prosecute the case. Third, the standard of proof in a criminal proceeding is higher than in an arbitration hearing. As a result, it is possible to conclude that the employee engaged in the misconduct even if a court has found that there was insufficient evidence to prove a conviction. If the court acquits, and the employer has not completed its own investigation, it must live with the outcome of the criminal proceedings to determine whether discipline is justified.

126   *HEABC and BCNU,* May 21, 1999 (unreported), (McPhillips).

The Investigative Interview

Don't make the mistake of rushing into investigative interviews with little or no preparation. The investigative interview process may be the only opportunity to gather critical information concerning the alleged misconduct.

Proper preparation is key to making the most of this opportunity

Plan to conduct the interviews when you have a period of uninterrupted time to complete the process. If there is a possibility that the employee will become emotional, it may be appropriate to conduct the interview at or near the end of the day. Ensure the privacy and dignity of the witnesses and hold the interview in a place out of sight from coworkers and in a location where the witnesses can feel relatively comfortable speaking openly with the investigators, without fear of being overheard or interrupted. See Part Five: *Interactions with Purpose: Skills, Techniques, Considerations* for more detail on how to conduct an interview.

Planning the Interviews

Based on the nature of the complaint or allegation, and the decision you make based on the preliminary considerations, determine how you will proceed. If you are conducting the investigation, what will you do first?

When planning the interviews, answer the following questions:

- Who will be interviewed?

- Who will be interviewed first?

- Will a recorder be necessary?

- Where will the interviews take place?

- Will anyone else be present during the interview?

With respect to interviewing witnesses, answer the following questions:
- What will I ask?

- How will I ask my questions?

With respect to the accused, answer the following questions:
- What will I ask?

- How will I ask the questions?

- When will I conduct the interview (after analyzing the statements of other witnesses)?

- Are there union representation considerations? (You should insist on union representation).

The degree of preparation will depend on the nature and extent of the complaint or allegation. A typical investigation should be complete within 48 hours.

The following checklists can help you plan for your interviews. You will want to make sure you have covered these questions when interviewing witnesses and the employee.

Checklist 1: Checklist of Important Facts

Checklist 1: Checklist of Important Facts
Develop a chronology of events

	When did the event occur? date, time of day, duration of event
	Where did it happen? specific location (visit the site and diagram, if necessary)
	What happened? • description of an individual's actions and reactions • description of the event in chronological order

Determine the parties involved	
	Who was involved in the event? • other employees • supervisors or managers • other individuals (not employees)
	Did witnesses observe the event? • was the witness present? • was the event witnessed directly?

Checklist 1: Checklist of Important Facts

Identify extenuating, unique, aggravating, enhancing or unusual circumstances

	Weather—surrounding circumstances, such as weather in a motor vehicle accident that should be taken into account.
	Warnings—in a matter concerning employee discipline, the previous record of an employee.
	Working conditions—are there unique or unusual circumstances in the workplace that should be taken into consideration?

Identify possible motives for conduct

	Why does the interviewee think the event happened, and how does the interviewee know? Can a motive be identified?

Reference authority and related documents

	Written records or materials related to the issue—policies, rules, regulations, job descriptions, performance standards, handbooks, prior directives, guidelines, letters of discipline, letters of commendations, documented evidence of training or help given, documented evidence of the impact of the employee's conduct on others, work schedules, time sheets, application forms, evaluations.

Identify other information and related documents

	Miscellaneous—other information that might be relevant, such as the demeanour of the employee, the mood of the supervisor, or personal problems or circumstances. An acknowledgement of wrongdoing now or in the past; acknowledgement or indication that this is a sign of a pattern, or a single event; workplace practices.

Note Taker

Decide who will ask the questions and who will take the notes. The note taker will likely be a witness in formal proceedings if for no other reason than to introduce the notes of the investigation.

- Will that person be a good witness?

- Will that person be required to give evidence for some other aspect of the case?

- Is the note taker someone who has a demonstrable bias, a so-called *hidden agenda*, which may be exposed in a cross-examination?

Preparing for an Investigative Interview

It is important to prepare a script prior to the interview to ensure your interview is well-organized and that you are not omitting issues of importance.

Further, drafting the questions in advance allows you to reflect on the intended path of the interview and make any changes as needed.

A script is an aid, not a boundary, in an investigation. Don't let yourself be constrained by the prepared script. If unanticipated issues arise, explore them thoroughly, even if they are not in the script. An interview must be flexible, and you should deviate from the planned path if new information arises or new lines of inquiry emerge.

When drafting the script, remember that others, including the courts or an arbitrator, may review your material. Avoid including editorial comments in the script: at the time, this may seem appropriate, but months later these comments may exhibit bias or a predetermined result. Avoid sarcastic or judgemental comments or marginal notes when preparing the script. An employer must not only be fair and thoughtful in its determination, it must be seen as such.

Interviewing Witnesses

Witnesses are interviewed to get all the information they have that will help the employer make a decision. This includes evidence supporting and opposing the complaint or allegation. It goes without saying that you cannot ask too many questions.

Interview witnesses who are directly involved—they need to have seen or heard something, not been told something by a third party. The exception would be a parent or staff member who is relaying a disclosure from a minor.

Prior to a formal investigative interview with any witness, you must have an appreciation of the facts surrounding the event and as much information as possible as to the role the witness may have played in the event.

- Is the witness the suspect, a bystander, or a person with a particular agenda?

- Do you think the person may have a bias for or against a certain result?

- Can you bring anything to the investigation that you know is true, or is alleged from another source to use as control questions (questions designed to test accurateness or truthfulness, not to acquire information)?

Conduct your investigative interview of witnesses as follows, ensuring that detailed documentation is maintained.

1. **At the interview, being by identifying the purpose of the meeting.**

   - Introduce the parties present.

   - Briefly describe the interview process and explain what will happen after the interview.

   - Emphasize the need for confidentiality.

   - Stress the need for the individual's account of the incident to be as complete as possible.

   - Underline the importance for the individual to answer your questions directly and honestly.

   - Attempt to put the individual at ease—develop a rapport.

Ask if there are any questions before you begin.

2. **Listen to the witness's account of the event without interrupting. Persistent questioning at the beginning of an interview forces the witness to frame events in the context of your questions. Listen so that you can learn about the issues from the witness's perspective.**

   Follow these guidelines:

   - Do not interrupt or attempt to clarify.

   - Listen to the individual's account as they remember it.

   - Do not immediately challenge the individual's account of the events. Make notes beside matters that may require investigation, and write down questions you will ask for clarification after the interviewee is finished.

3. When the witness finishes their initial presentation, review the interview notes and ask for clarification in areas you have noted. At this time, also ensure that the following points have been covered by your interview:

   - Prior events, to see if they impact the incident (both immediately prior to incident and the history between the parties).

   - Have the scene re-enacted, especially if physical action is involved.

   - The physical layout, if pertinent.

   - How the behaviour impacted or affected the witness. This often is the most powerful evidence you get.

   - Confirm whether anyone else has seen the incident or has relevant information.

   - Watch for information that can be corroborated, such as any paper trail or any facts that can be checked with a third party. Get details so these can be checked.

   - Question any inconsistencies in their statement or inconsistencies with other witnesses.

4. **Summarize your discussion with the interviewee presentation to ensure that you both understand the following:**

   - Events leading up to the incident.

   - Reasons for the incident.

   - Specific matters in the incident.

- Individuals present during each phase of the incident.

- Events or facts on which the parties differ.

5. **In this final stage, you should also ask some catch-all questions, such as:**

- Is there anything else you would like to say?

- Is there any part of your evidence that you would like to change?

- You understand the importance of honesty in our deliberations?

- Do you have any explanation for these events?

These questions are helpful, as you will be able to point to the fact that the individual had an opportunity to add additional comments and that the importance of honesty was yet again underlined.

6. **At the end of the meeting, cover the following with the individual:**

- Have the witness review their statement for completeness and accuracy and sign the statement. The general rule to follow when reviewing a statement is, "Would you understand what happened from reading this statement at a later date, for example in three years?"

- If the witness refuses to sign the statement, the interviewer should sign the statement indicating that it is a transcript of a conversation that took place on a specific date.

- Ask the witness to contact you without delay if additional information comes forward.

- Ensure the witness understands that this is a confidential matter that should not be discussed with anyone except you, a senior member of management, or the authorized union representative.

- Let the individual know if they will be advised of the outcome.

- Discuss privacy considerations.

7. **After the interview.**

- Check your notes for any inconsistencies with previous interviews and with any written statements you have.

- Repeat the interview process with all individuals identified as being involved in the matter.

- Complete the investigation.

- Determine if misconduct occurred

- If misconduct did occur, recommend appropriate action

Checklist 2: Checklist for Interviewing Witnesses

Checklist 2: Checklist for Interviewing Witnesses	
Preliminary Considerations	
	Do not delay a prompt response. Communicate to the complainant that the employer is treating the allegation seriously. A delay in the investigation opens the way for a defence that the investigation is procedurally flawed. The ability to recall events may be critical, especially when the misconduct is denied.
	Treat the complaint seriously. No matter how trivial the complaint may seem, it is better to follow normal investigative procedures and avoid making assumptions or being influenced by extraneous considerations.
Before the Interview	
	Outline areas to question.
	Arrange for the interview to be held on neutral territory.
	Establish a plan or strategy.

Checklist 2: Checklist for Interviewing Witnesses	
During the Interview	
	Establish rapport.
	State the purpose of the interview and review the collective agreement.
	Obtain basic personal and employment data, such as name, job title, function, length of service, training, or other background information.
	Confirm the complaint/allegations (a written statement may be appropriate).
	Practice effective questioning techniques, as follows: • ask open-ended questions • ask probing questions; don't cross-examine or ask leading questions • clarify when unclear • maintain eye contact as much as possible
	Keep accurate notes of questions and answers, and record any body language.
	Explore the impact of the complaint. (Be sensitive.)
	Obtain the names of possible witnesses.
	Obtain any relevant documents.
	Outline the process of the investigation.
	Be sensitive to the needs of the note taker.
	CYA: check your assumptions and assume nothing.
	Emphasize the need for confidentiality and the potential need to re-interview.
After the Interview	
	Visit the worksite, if appropriate.
	Type of interview notes as soon as possible following the interview.
	Ask whether the information you have gathered raises any additional questions and determine if your investigation is complete.
	Analyze the facts in response to the allegations • separate facts that are corroborated, • determine if credibility is an issue, and • when possible, confirm facts on an objective basis.

Interviewing the Accused Employee

This interview should be conducted in the same manner as witness interviews. This includes having a plan (see Part Five: *Interactions with Purpose*) and the development of a script. Remember that the timing of the meeting is in your control.

In unionized workplaces, check the collective agreement to determine the rights of the employee regarding union representation.

Statements of the employee are admissible as evidence; therefore, make careful notes of what the employee says. Note their words and not your interpretation of their words. If there is a possible misunderstanding, ask the same question in a different way or read back the question and answer.

Statements of the union representative are not admissible in evidence, so get the story from the employee or get the employee to affirm what the union representative said by asking the employee, "Is that right?"

Your script should include a prepared statement that you will read to the union representative to remind them of their role in the investigation and to emphasize the importance of honesty in the investigation.

Structure of the Interview

Developing your script in advance will ensure an organized and comprehensive investigation. In addition to the introduction, include a preamble to inform the union representative (as applicable) and the *respondent* about the process, your expectations, and the general nature of the issue to be examined.

There are generally three phases to the substantive parts of an interview: opening, exploration, and summary and conclusion.

Phase One: Opening

Ask a general or open-ended question, such as, "It is our understanding that you have been on medical leave for the past month. Without disclosing the actual medical condition, could you tell us about your condition?" After that, you can eventually hone in towards the key points. You want to keep the questions open-ended so you do not suggest an answer. If you ask questions that suggest the answer, you may influence the interviewee's answers and your ability to assess the individual's honesty. By asking open-ended questions, the accused does not know what information you have and thus will not be able to make any assessments about how far to go in revealing potentially incriminating details.

A dishonest individual will make strategic concessions and admit to those points they feel the employer can prove or has knowledge of, while denying evidence they think is beyond your knowledge.

Remember that simply because the individual does not provide you with evidence that is consistent with your understanding, this does not by itself indicate dishonesty. There may be many reasons for this discrepancy, including a failed memory, perceptual errors or a different perspective. Dishonesty is when the individual says they do not know an answer when in fact they do, or provides you with misleading information they know to be untrue.

Once you have passed through the information once with open-ended questions and you have the overview of the evidence presented by the individual, you enter the second phase of the interview.

While the first phase is primarily an investigation/credibility check, in the second phase you are looking to test an individual's resolve and learn more about the information you have or believe to be true.

Phase Two: Exploration

The questions during the second phase of the interview are not open-ended; they are asked with more focus. For example, if you are questioning someone who claims to be too ill to work, yet you have surveillance that is inconsistent with the individual's expressed limitations, you might ask questions such as:

"Is that you in the video?"

"Can you tell me about the discrepancy between what we see in the video and your limitations described in this letter?" as a way of trying to solicit more info from the interviewee

At this phase you would also use some open-ended questions such as:

"What explanation do you have for this?" Note: Your aim is to get the facts. Tone is important. Defensiveness-provoking questions and behaviour on the part of the interviewer may illicit the necessary information but can be inconsistent with the fact gathering goal.

During this phase, it is important to share your information with the individual and get their explanation. If you put your case to the individual at this point and they can explain their behaviour in a way you had not contemplated and that makes sense, you will gain information and avoid disciplining an employee who, perhaps in hindsight, did nothing wrong. At the very least, the culpability of the event may be diminished.

For those employees who persist in their dishonesty, you will get their story at the interview and they will be unable to change their story during the grievance process or at arbitration without the risk of their credibility being questioned. The more of your concerns you put to the dishonest individual at the interview, the greater the story the employee must come up with and the easier it will be for you to build your case around that and demonstrate the dishonesty. In short, you need to cement their story so they have less flexibility to change their story later. You need to get their story before they have the time and the knowledge of the collateral facts to polish their evidence.

Phase Three: Summary and Conclusion

The third phase of the interview, the summary and conclusion, allows for a consideration of any mitigating circumstances. If the individual has had personal problems they claim resulted in the improper behaviour, you need to find out about those problems now, so you can consider the evidence and include it when determining appropriate discipline.

It is a problem if you do not learn about any compelling mitigating circumstances until arbitration; you need to know well before that. In this final phase you should also ask some catch-all questions for *anything else* as detailed earlier in this section.

These questions are helpful, as they often reveal remorse or an acknowledgement of wrongdoing. In addition, they will show that the employee was provided the opportunity to give additional remarks, and that the necessity for honesty was underscored.

This final stage includes the wrap-up. This is where you tell the individual their status until the issue is resolved.

Chapter 12: Now What? Post-Investigation Considerations

Establishing the Standard of Proof

> In discipline cases, the employer is responsible for proving that the employee has given just and reasonable cause for discipline. The standard of proof required is the civil standard on a balance of probabilities, as distinguished from the criminal standard of beyond a reasonable doubt.

The basic principles have been defined in a number of decisions of high authority.[127]

> The seriousness of the allegation made, the inherent unlikelihood of an occurrence of a given description, or the gravity of the consequences flowing from a particular finding are considerations which must affect the answer to the question whether the issue has been proven to the reasonable satisfaction of the tribunal. In such matter, "reasonable satisfaction" should not be produced by inexact proofs, indefinite testimony, or indirect inferences.

> Everyone must feel that, when, for instance, the issue is on which of two dates an admitted occurrence took place, a satisfactory conclusion may be reached on materials of a kind that would not satisfy any sound and prudent judgment if the question was whether some act had been done involving grave moral delinquency.

As a result of this standard of proof, you should be confident you have reliable and compelling evidence before imposing discipline for criminal or quasi-criminal conduct such as fraud, theft, prohibited substances, assault, or conduct that could seriously affect a person's ability to continue in the profession. The evidence will be subjected to closer scrutiny by an arbitrator in these cases.

Using Circumstantial Evidence

In many cases, you will not have direct evidence of the incident, but will only have circumstantial evidence. While circumstantial evidence is sufficient to warrant discipline, careful investigation is needed to determine whether there are any alternative explanations for the incident other than an act of misconduct by the employee.

---

127   *Briginshaw v Briginshaw (1938) 60 CLR 336.*

When assessing circumstantial evidence, consider and exclude alternative possibilities, and only draw those inferences from the evidence that appear to be reasonable and appropriate in all the circumstances.

When faced with circumstantial evidence, and indeed in any investigation, the investigator must pursue all reasonable alternatives, maintain an open mind throughout the investigation, and not only critically assess the subjective accounts of witnesses, but also fully explore the objective facts surrounding the incident.

Assessing Credibility

An investigation often results in different or conflicting statements from witnesses about the incident under investigation. This does not necessarily mean that you need to determine who is lying and who is telling the truth. People are often honestly mistaken. Rather, the task of the finder of facts is to assess which version of events is more probable. Fortunately, the courts have developed certain guidelines to help with this task.[128]

Consider the following factors when assessing a witness's credibility:

- firmness of memory, accuracy, and evasiveness

- consistency with other witnesses and documentary evidence

- whether the witness was a non-party or otherwise disinterested witness

- whether the evidence is consistent with the preponderance of probabilities that a practical and informed person would readily recognize as reasonable in that place and in those conditions

Your personal reflection in important. What is your impression? What was learned and revealed and how the person approached you interaction is instructive to the test of credibility. Ask yourself:

- Did the person tell the story in a forthright and straightforward manner, or did their demeanour suggest they were not telling the truth or all of the truth? Was the person evasive?

128   Opportunities for knowledge, powers of observation, judgement and memory, ability to describe clearly what he has seen and heard, as well as other factors, combine to produce what is called credibility (see *Raymond v Bosanquet*, (1919) 59 SCSR 452, at 460.).

- Does the person have a bias or self-interest that might influence their version of events; for example, does the person stand to lose something or have a special relation with the employee who allegedly committed the misconduct?

- Was the story reasonable or, in other words, in harmony with the preponderance of probabilities? Does the story make sense, and is it probable that things happened that way? If not, why not?

- Was the story consistent with other people's stories, or with other evidence obtained during the investigation? If it has been told on more than one occasion, is each version consistent?

- What was the person's opportunity to observe the incident; was the person in a better or worse position than other witnesses to the incident? Could the person in fact have observed what the person said he or she observed?

- Might something in the employment history of the person cause you to place less reliability on the person's evidence; for example, has the person been caught lying before and been disciplined for it? Be careful with this, however. Simply because someone was unreliable in the past does not mean that they are unreliable now.

Analyzing the Information Gathered

Once all the relevant documentation and physical evidence has been collected and the investigative interviews are complete, carefully review and assess the evidence as a whole.

- Compare and contrast the information gathered. Ask yourself:

  - Is there enough evidence to reach a fully informed decision?

  - Is further investigation needed?

  - Does the information I have gathered raise any additional questions?

- Do not hesitate to re-interview witnesses and/or the accused employee to obtain clarification or explore discrepancies.

- Read any documents that are relevant to the investigation and review the interview notes of the complainant, accused, and any witnesses.

- Analyze the facts in response to the allegations, separating facts that are corroborated and, if possible, confirming facts on an objective basis.

- Ask yourself if any of the evidence is circumstantial and, if so, if there are any other avenues of investigation you should explore.

- Is any of the evidence hearsay and, if so, is direct evidence available? Hearsay evidence is any statement of fact repeated by someone other than the person who knows the truth, such as a witness who says he or she heard another person say something happened.

- While you will no doubt hear lots of hearsay evidence during the investigation, it is important to cautiously consider such comments and determine what weight, if any, can be given to them.

- Do not select information to be included. The only basis for exclusion would be relevance, prejudice, unsubstantiated hearsay, or personal opinion.

- One of the essential aspects of this assessment is evaluating the credibility of the witnesses' and the alleged offender's evidence.

- Consider the information provided to you by all the witnesses, and whether there is any basis upon which you can resolve what appears to be conflicting information through further investigation and, if the conflict cannot be resolved, determine which version you are going to accept and why.

- After obtaining the relevant physical evidence and interviewing the witnesses, the final step is to determine factual conclusions, whether discipline is warranted and, if so, the level of discipline.

  O In reaching this conclusion, consider evidence that tends to clear the employee, which tends to prove guilt and any mitigating factors.

  O There should be sufficient time between the interview of the employee and the final disciplinary decision to allow for careful consideration of all the information gathered during the course of the investigation, as well as any other relevant factors associated with the employee's conduct and their past employment record.

You must be confident in your answers to the following:

- Taking the above into account, on the balance of probabilities, did the misconduct occur?

- If the alleged misconduct occurred, what is the appropriate discipline, if any?

Assessing Disciplinary Penalties

When assessing the *reasonableness* of a penalty, an arbitrator will examine both the nature of the employee's misconduct and the employer's response to the misconduct. This section reviews the areas of an employer's conduct that an arbitrator will review to assess the reasonableness of a disciplinary penalty.

Using Prior Record

Prior misconduct for which an employee has received a written warning or formal discipline will support a more severe penalty.[129] This is generally true even though there has been debate about whether the misconduct constituting the prior record, to be relied on, must be similar to the culminating incident.

Using Employer Rules

Many employers adopt rules or policies that specify the form of discipline that follows from certain misconduct. For example, a policy might state that the penalty for theft is automatic termination.

If an employer unilaterally invokes disciplinary rules, an employer is still required to justify its disciplinary response. This means that although employer rules or policies will be considered by an arbitrator when assessing a given disciplinary response, they constitute only one factor that an arbitrator will examine in making their determination.

Discriminatory Penalties

Arbitrators are concerned with fairness and therefore adhere to the basic principle that similar cases should be treated alike. If an employer imposes a harsher penalty on one employee compared to others involved in the same disciplinary incident, or if an employer imposes discipline inconsistently in similar situations, an arbitrator will peg the employer's conduct as discriminatory and refuse to uphold the discipline. If this happens, the arbitrator may either completely exonerate the employee, or reduce the discipline imposed to accord with that received by other employees.

---

129   In unionized settings, review the collective agreement. The agreement may contain a provision that prohibits the evidence from being admitted.

Delay

If an employer unduly delays invoking discipline without good reason, an arbitrator may revoke the discipline. Several rationales have been put forward for dismissing a grievance for unreasonable delay:

1. The employer will be deemed to have condoned the employee's offence. [*Re New (Borough) and C.U.P.E., Local 373 (1979), 20. L.A.C. (2d) 289 (Schiff)*]

2. The employer will have violated the requirement to procedural fairness [*Re Miracle Food Mart, Steinberg Inc. (Ontario) and U.F.C.W., Locals 175 and 633 (1988), 2 L.A.C. (4th) 36 (Haefling)*]

3. The employer has effectively denied the employee the opportunity to defend themselves against the employer's allegations [*Re Air Canada and C.A.W., Local 2213 (Mitchell) (1993), 34 L.A.C. (4th)*]

4. The arbitrator should hold that undue delay invalidates disciplinary action on the basis of general arbitral principle [*Re Manitoba Pool Elevators Brandon Stockyards and U.F.C.W., Local 832 (1993), 35 L.A.C. (4th) 2776 (Peltz)*]

Particular Employment Offences

In the context of very serious employment offences, such as theft, arbitrators have acknowledged that an employer will sometimes be justified in terminating the employee without invoking progressive corrective discipline. In other words, in some cases, summary dismissal may be justified.

However, even if an employer is justified in terminating an employee without invoking progressive corrective discipline, the principle continues to apply. A departure from the principle of progressive corrective discipline is justified only if the arbitrator finds that the employment relationship cannot be restored on the particular facts of the case, taking into consideration the employee's capacity for rehabilitation.

If the employer summarily dismisses an employee, the employer must provide "clear and compelling" evidence that its actions were reasonable.[130]

---

130   Simon Fraser University and AUCE: ..."for some offenses in some circumstances, the employer's legitimate interests will demand arbitral acceptance of the penalty of dismissal for even a single occurrence. However, implicit in the modern just cause standard is the notion that for most offenses in most circumstances, an employer will take the path of corrective discipline prior to resorting to the ultimate sanction of a severance of the employment relationship. It follows that in the usual run of cases, if an employer is going to deviate from the accepted approach of progressive corrective discipline he must at the very least come forward with clear and compelling justification for discharge as the only response reasonably available to him."

Complete a pre-discipline checklist to ensure that you have all the necessary information to inform your decision.

Checklist 3: Pre-Discipline Checklist

Checklist 3: Pre-Discipline Checklist	
Employee	
	Name
	Position/classification
	Length of service
	Relevant family and economic circumstances

Checklist 3: Pre-Discipline Checklist	
What precisely did the employee do? Is the conduct considered culpable or non-culpable?	
	Use Checklist 1: Checklist of Important Facts and Checklist 2: Checklist for Interviewing Witnesses to gather the relevant information to determine what happened
Identifying the standard of conduct	
	Collective agreement provisions
	Employer policies, rules, handbooks, etc.
	Job or classification descriptions
	Statutes
	Discipline of other employees for similar conduct, including arbitration awards (unionized workplaces) and court decisions (non-union workplaces)

	Checklist 3: Pre-Discipline Checklist
	Previously brought to employee's attention: details, including relevant previous discipline, warnings, meetings, or other occasions
	Other
Impact of misconduct	
	On the organization's business, including reputation
	On other employees
	On customers or clients
Previous opportunities to remedy misconduct	
	Previous warnings, discussions, help: When? Where? Specifics
	Specific efforts to identify the problems and remedy them
	Commitments, including promises and follow up
	The employee's own training and experience
	Availability of resources accessible to the employee
	Has the employee attempted correction but failed?
	Has the employee not attempted correction?

	Checklist 3: Pre-Discipline Checklist
Employee's non-disciplinary work record	
	Performance appraisals
	Demonstrations of attitude, etc.
	Any other communication of standards expected in the workplace
Mitigating factors, matters for consideration	
	Seriousness of the offence in terms of company policy and company obligations
	Record of the employee
	Length of service
	Whether or not the offence was an isolated incident in the employment history of the employee
	Provocation
	Nature of the offence (its seriousness)
	Evidence that organizational rules of conduct, whether unwritten or posted, have not be uniformly enforced, thus constituting a form of discrimination
	Spur of the moment misconduct?
	Systematic and repetitive misconduct?
	Premeditated, planned, and deliberate?
	Did the misconduct involve a breach of trust? • with the employer • with the public with the employee's fellow employees • with the employee's fellow offender

	Failure of the employee to apologize and settle the manner after being given an opportunity to do so
	Failure of the employer to permit the employee to explain or deny the alleged offence
	Bona fide confusion or mistake by the employee about whether the conduct was allowed

Checklist 3: Pre-Discipline Checklist	
	The employee's inability, due to inebriation or emotional problems, to appreciate the wrongfulness of the act
	Relatively trivial nature of the harm done
	The employee's future prospects for good behaviour
	Extraordinary economic hardship
Fairness: has the employer conducted a proper inquiry?	
	Inherent fairness: • openness of employer representatives to discovery of facts • absence of bias • absence of discrimination • consistency of penalty • access to personnel file or adverse documentation
	History: • opportunity to grieve previous discipline • procedural fairness: opportunity to be heard
Strategic issues	
	What are the interests at stake for the employer?
	Availability of witnesses

	Union–employer relations (unionized workplaces)
	Client relations
	Managerial morale
	Employer resolve
	External considerations ($)

Providing Reasons for Discipline

It may seem obvious that an employee should be provided with the reasons for their discipline or discharge. These reasons should include all grounds that the employer is able to discover after exercising due diligence in investigating the incident for which the employee is disciplined.

An employer may not be prevented from later relying on additional grounds of which the employer was unaware at the time, provided that the employer could not reasonably have been expected to discover them.

However, occasionally an employee is not provided with all the reasons for their discipline or discharge, usually in connection with a termination. Some collective agreements also state that written reasons for discipline must be provided, often within a specified time and/or a specific process.

Remedy

Taking all the above into consideration, if the alleged misconduct did occur, what (if any) would the appropriate discipline be? Remember that the objective is to modify behaviour.

Supervisory Responses (Non-Disciplinary)

All employees are expected to meet performance and attendance standards and behave appropriately in the workplace. There is a range of supervisory responses to workplace indiscretions and performance issues, depending on the conduct, circumstances, position, and individual involved.

Corrective action is a process of communicating with the employee to improve attendance, unacceptable behaviour, or performance. You may take corrective action when other methods, such as coaching and performance management, have not been successful. In cases of serious misconduct, you may choose to proceed straight to disciplinary action.

Reviewing the principles of just cause (non-culpable conduct) before taking disciplinary action is instructive when determining whether discipline is appropriate in a particular situation. Supervisory responses are non-disciplinary and are often used for more minor behavioural or performance issues, as discussed below.

Corrective Coaching/Counselling

Corrective coaching and counselling can help an employee improve performance. Remember that change may not be instantaneous. Performance, work habits, and conduct tend to deteriorate gradually and may take some time to improve.

Have informal conversations with the employee about their performance and/or work habits. You should keep notes of these conversations, including the date, time, name of employee, subjects discussed, actions contemplated for improvement, explanations offered by the employee, and other pertinent information. Refer to this information in future conversations. Positive reinforcement should be freely given if any improvement is demonstrated.

Document action plans in writing and give a copy to the employee to confirm. It is important to follow up on actions within a specified time frame. Inconsistency between word and action has implications for the relationship with the employee who has been the subject of what can be a stressful and difficult process. Other employees will also draw conclusions from what they view as an inconsistency between what is expected and what is done.

Setting Expectations or Directions

When people clearly know what is expected, they can modify their behaviour accordingly. An employer's expectations regarding rules of conduct should be universal, as inconsistency can be fatal to a discipline case. If expectations are known, solving issues with and coaching employees is easier, and goals and priorities make more sense.

Expectations and directions are often provided in writing to ensure the verbal directions are well defined and understood by both parties, and to make clear to the employee that administration is serious about what it says. When you set expectations in writing:

- Determine what objective(s) you wish to accomplish:

○ Use simple, clear directions.

○ Use a separate bullet or sentence for each separate direction, and group them for clarity.

○ Make it understood that the directions must be followed.

○ Add a paragraph/sentence stating, "If unsure about these directions, please contact me to discuss."

○ Anticipate the employee's reaction to the expectations or directions and review the letter to ensure it covers reactions.

○ Hold a meeting with the employee to deliver the letter.

○ Place a copy of the letter in the employee's personnel file with details of delivery.

These letters are not normally given to the union because they are not disciplinary. However, union involvement at this stage may be helpful in changing the employee's behaviour and may lessen the union's response if subsequent discipline is imposed for the employee's failure to follow directions or meet expectations.

While a supervisory response is often the only step needed to correct misconduct, if it does not get the desired change, then discipline should be utilized.

Samples of supervisory letters can be found in Appendix C.

Holding an Expectations/Directions Meeting

If practical, the letter outlining expectations and directions should be delivered to the employee in a face-to-face meeting. This is a supervisory meeting and union presence may not be mandatory, depending on the agreement. The objective of the meeting is to achieve a change in the employee's behaviour, and the following strategies may help achieve this goal.

1. Set the tone

    • Meet in a neutral location that is private and uninterrupted by calls.

    • Establish eye contact; demonstrate a confident tone of voice and posture.

    • Remain positive and considerate, but businesslike, and avoid small talk.

    • Acknowledge the employee's positive contributions to the organization.

- Get to current performance problems quickly.

2. State the facts

  - Use written documentation to highlight specific performance or behaviour problems.

3. Encourage employee response

  - Ask open-ended questions.

  - Reflect back the employee's statements.

4. Keep the discussion focused

  - Anticipate the employee's reaction based on past experience.

  - Do not be sidetracked or misled by sympathy-evoking tactics.

  - Do not let yourself get involved in the employee's personal life.

  - Do not moralize or make generalizations about performance or behaviour.

5. Discuss solutions

  - Cover your list of objectives.

  - Ask for the employee's input.

  - Explain the procedures that go into effect if performance does not improve.

  - Be consistent—do not tolerate more from one employee than you would from another.

  - Mention employee benefits such as employee/family assistance plans (EFAP) where offered—stress that it is a confidential and professional service that the employee can choose to attend.

6. Get a commitment

  - Confirm that the employee will attempt to accomplish the objectives.

  - Ensure that job expectations and the time frame are fair (expect results, not miracles).

7. Arrange a follow-up meeting

  - Schedule a specific date for review.

8.   End on a positive note

- Offer sincere encouragement.

Applying Progressive Corrective Discipline

Under common law, an employer can unilaterally terminate an employee by providing the employee with notice or pay in lieu of notice. In a unionized environment, an employee can only be discharged for just and reasonable cause.

The concept of progressive discipline arises out of the requirement to meet the test of just and reasonable cause for discipline and dismissal in unionized settings. Progressive discipline also applies in non-union settings, where the employer has considerably more discretion.

Discipline is used to modify serious misconduct and minor misconduct if supervisory strategies fail. The objective of modifying behaviour remains, but there are now consequences.

The vast majority of employees are never disciplined as they conform to policies, procedures, work standards and reasonable employer expectations. The disciplinary process deals with a "troublesome few" who do not respond to reasonable supervisory techniques.

The theory of progressive corrective discipline stems from the obligation of the employer to warn an employee of the seriousness with which the employer views the employee's conduct. Progressive corrective discipline then provides an employee with an opportunity to reform, change, and improve, while allowing each party to know where they stand with one another.

If supervisory techniques fail and progressive corrective discipline fails, it will precipitate employee termination, either voluntary or by the employer.

Steps of the Progressive Corrective Discipline Model

Discipline options progress along a continuum:

- oral reprimands/warnings

- letter of discipline/reprimand (written warning)

- short suspension

- long suspension

- dismissal/termination

Oral Reprimands/Warnings

Oral warnings are the first step in the *progressive corrective discipline* process and are of limited utility. It is faster and less stressful on the supervisor and employee to discuss the issue with the employee using a supervisory technique such as corrective coaching or issuing a letter of expectation or direction.

If you decide to use the oral reprimand, document the time, date, names of the individuals present, subjects discussed, actions contemplated for improvement, explanations offered by the employee, and other pertinent information. Include an action plan, if one is developed. Send a copy of the memo to the employee's personnel file, clearly stating that this was a disciplinary oral reprimand/warning. If applicable, check the collective agreement to determine if a copy of the oral reprimand has to be sent to the employee and union.

Letter of Discipline/Reprimand (Written Warning)

This is usually the first step in the progressive corrective discipline model and would be imposed only after a thorough investigation.

Although a letter of discipline is appropriate for minor misconduct, it is not appropriate for serious misconduct. Serious misconduct should result in a higher level of discipline, such as a suspension or termination.

A letter of discipline is not normally imposed if the employee already has a letter of discipline in their file, even if the previous discipline was for a different type of misconduct. Arbitrators have accepted that it would create severe disruption if the employer was required to follow the progressive corrective discipline process for each different type of infraction as it may mean an employee would never reach the stage of termination. An employee could constantly run afoul of the rules and expectations of the employer, but as the employee gets near the termination stage they could switch their misconduct to another kind.

The first message to include in drafting a discipline letter is to explain what the behaviour is that has led to this specific imposition of discipline. Detail the results of the investigation and how those findings have led to the imposition of discipline.

Informing an employee as to why their behaviour was wrong is the next step. This usually means appealing to an undisputed authority. Employers should look to stated work rules, policies, the collective agreement, job descriptions, or the common law duty of honesty and good faith that every employee owes their employer as examples.

Next, detail the imposed discipline, informing the employee they are being given a written warning or that they are being suspended or terminated. If you choose one of the latter two options, you must be prepared to document in the letter that either the employee engaged in similar acts in the past—and was disciplined and warned that the conduct would lead to further and greater discipline—or that the behaviour is so severe that it must automatically lead to a suspension or discharge.

Employers have a duty to weigh all the mitigating and aggravating factors in a situation before imposing discipline, and you must inform the employee of any mitigating factors used to either increase or decrease the level of discipline applied.

If the employee is not terminated, the letter should dictate what the employee must do in future to correct their behaviour. Avoid generalities: be specific and give examples and an expected time frame of when the behaviour should change. Describe clearly what the proper behaviour expected will look like. ALWAYS warn the employee that future repetition of similar behaviour may lead to discipline, up to and including dismissal.

When signing off, be courteous and indicate that you wish to help the employee improve. You may wish to state that you are available to discuss any issues that may come up at work in the future. In addition, this portion of the letter should also be used to refer the employee to an employee assistance program or professional counselling, if covered under the employer's health insurance. Finally, remember to copy the personnel file and as required the union.

Suspension

This is the next step of the disciplinary process. Losing pay and benefits communicates the escalating seriousness of the process. Except for very serious misconduct, suspensions are seen as a necessary step prior to termination. The first suspension is generally short, of one to five days, while a second suspension may be longer, of ten to twenty days.

Arbitrators usually accept that any suspension over ten days is the final step prior to termination. Normally the suspension is without pay, although there are some circumstances in which an employee may be suspended with pay. Talk to a labour relations expert if you are considering suspension with pay to ensure that the result will be accepted as a disciplinary suspension.

Termination or Dismissal

Dismissal is used when progressive corrective discipline is not appropriate or when progressive corrective discipline has failed. Dismissal may, in fact, be based on a culminating incident—a series of events and disciplinary actions followed by the last straw. An arbitrator must feel that further corrective efforts will not likely succeed necessitating the termination of the employee's employment.

If dismissal is the response because of a number of previous disciplinary actions, management must prove the previous discipline was communicated to the employee and union in writing.

Disciplinary Meeting

A letter of discipline/suspension should be delivered to the employee in a face-to-face meeting with the employee and, if applicable, a union representative. Although the union presence may not be mandatory in some agreements, the union should always be advised of the meeting and asked to attend.

Since the objective is to achieve a change in behaviour, follow the strategies set out above in the expectation/directions meeting, where applicable, and incorporate the following depending on the circumstances:

- State the nature of the discipline and why it is being assessed. (Note: if the employee is confrontational, just let them read the letter.)

- Ask the employee if they have anything to say. (Since the discipline decision has already been made, this should not be done if the employee is not accepting that they have acted inappropriately.)

- Review the history and your efforts to date.

- Restate that you are hopeful that things can be turned around.

- Offer to help.

- State future consequences if improvement is not achieved.

- Do not get into an argument or discuss personal attributes, and do not say any-thing you would not say in front of an arbitrator or senior management, such as:

  O The decision was made by   or someone else.

  O I have been building a file/case on you and this is typical.

"There's so much evidence we should put some aside for a different case."

Used with permission, The New Yorker Collection/The Cartoon Bank 2016 by Peter C. Vey

Part Four: Disputes and the Collective Agreement – How to Effectively Manage the Grievance Process

In unionized workplaces, collective agreements provide the basic rules that govern the day-to-day relationship between an employer and the union representing the employer's employees.

Negotiated through the process of collective bargaining, the collective agreement represents a codification of what the parties have agreed on to regulate their conduct and dealings over a certain period.

The collective agreement between the employer and the union:

- delineates the rights and obligations of the union and employer

- sets out employee wages and the rights and obligations of the employer under health and welfare plans and determines the standards of eligibility

- establishes procedures for settling disputes that arise during the term of the agreement

Disputes on the meaning of a provision in a collective agreement or its application to a specific situation invariably arise. Part Four: *Disputes and the Collective Agreement* provides ideas and strategies to help you gather and organize information to resolve such disputes during the term of the agreement. It assumes that the parties intend to meet and discuss in good faith the matters at issue in an effort to achieve a settlement that is acceptable to both the employer and the union.

The six chapters that follow examine the grievance process and provide concepts, ideas, and tools you can use when administering the collective agreement and the grievance procedure in the agreement. We then turn to discuss when arbitration might be required, and the final chapter looks at the legal aspects of settlement and arbitration in resolving disputes.

Chapter 13: What is a Grievance?

Collective bargaining and the agreements that flow from it require a process to assist the parties when disputes arise during the term of the collective agreement. These disputes may concern the interpretation of the agreement, the application of provisions to certain work situations, or the general administration of the terms and conditions contained in the agreement.

Bargainers often find it difficult to draft precise language on all matters. In an attempt to address all the concerns raised when negotiating a complex issue, a measure of imprecise language can emerge.

Vague and ambiguous language may, by bargaining necessity, leave the real question unsettled, creating room for potential misunderstandings and disagreement on the application and interpretation of some provisions.

The specific method for dealing with grievances is set out in the collective agreement. It is typically an internal two- or three-step procedure in which successively higher levels of both union and employer representatives review the grievance. If the parties are unable to resolve the matter at issue, the grievance is submitted to arbitration by a neutral third party for final and binding resolution.

Definition of a Grievance in a Collective Agreement

Most often, collective agreement provisions limit the definition of a *grievance* to alleged violations of explicit provisions of the agreement. However, some agreements broadly define a grievance as any disagreement between the union and employer.

Categories of Grievances

Grievances can be sorted into two broad categories: those of *application* and those of *interpretation*.

- **Application grievances.** A grievance in which we agree on what the words mean, but we disagree on how they have been applied. Grievances involving the application of a collective agreement provision dispute the facts of the situation being grieved, not the interpretation or meaning of the provision. The most common application grievances are those concerning discipline—the application of the provisions that require that the employer have just and reasonable cause to impose discipline. Grievances in this category question disciplinary warnings and suspensions, but the most serious of such grievances dispute the propriety of employee terminations.

Most collective agreements or, alternatively, provincial labour legislation, require that employees can only be disciplined or terminated for just and reasonable cause. This term has been defined over the years, mainly through arbitral case law created in deciding discharge grievances.

A grievance may challenge the facts on which management relied in imposing a disciplinary penalty. However, disciplinary grievances usually invoke a review of whether the penalty that the employer imposed in response to an employee's actions or conduct is appropriate. Arbitrators have specified a number of possible factors to consider, particularly in assessing terminations, to determine whether there was just and reasonable cause for a disciplinary penalty.

- **Interpretation grievances.** In these grievances, we don't agree on what the words mean or how they have been interpreted in making your decision. Interpretation grievances cover all other matters, such as the assigning and performance of work, scheduling, layoffs, transfers, workplace safety, wages and benefits, and use of seniority.

    Some of the interpretation principles often encountered are:

    - **The Golden Rule:** Words in an agreement are to be taken in their usual and ordinary sense. Extended or strained readings of clauses are to be avoided. Plain language should be taken to mean what it says.

    - **Read as a Whole:** The meaning of a part of the collective agreement must be seen in relation to the entire agreement. Language should neither be read out of context nor as inconsistent with the overall intent or object of the agreement.

    - **Specific over General:** A clause that specifically deals with a particular subject will prevail over a more general clause that might otherwise have dealt with the same subject.

    - **Consistency of Terms:** Particular terms or words are presumed to mean the same thing wherever they appear in the agreement unless the context clearly indicates otherwise. This is especially true if the agreement contains a definition of the term.

    - **Avoid Absurdity:** An interpretation is favoured if it avoids an absurd or impossible result and helps achieve the overall objects of the agreement.

    - **Past Practice:** The parties' conduct after the making of the collective agreement; conduct or behaviour of the parties under a collective agreement with respect to a matter in dispute; evidence relating to *past practice* is admissible at arbitration to resolve an ambiguity in the collective agreement, or to show one of the parties represented that the other party would not insist on the strict terms of the agreement.

How is Past Practice Used?

Past practice can be used at arbitration to support an interpretation of the collective agreement (if language in the agreement is ambiguous, past practice can assist in clarifying the ambiguity) or to support a claim of estoppel.

Past practice cannot be used to vary the terms of the collective agreement or to create rights not in the collective agreement.

Essential Elements of Past Practice

To be relied upon, practice evidence must reveal the following:

- No clear indication in favour of one meaning.

- The conduct by A that is clearly based on one meaning.

- Acquiescence by B in this conduct (and inferentially, this meaning).

- Acquiescence at a responsible level.

Past practice is subject to two key limits: clerical error does not establish practice and one incident does not make a practice.

Estoppel is a legal doctrine that operates to prevent inequity. It is a principle of law preventing a party from insisting on its strict legal rights where, by its words or conduct, it has represented that it would not do so and another party has changed its position to its disadvantage or detriment in reliance upon that representation.

Estoppel may be based not only on actual statements made by a party, but also on past practice, or a prior course of conduct, or even the failure of a party to grieve or object to a departure from the parties' strict legal rights or obligations. Where estoppel involves rights under a collective agreement, the requirement of detrimental reliance may be satisfied if the party asserting the estoppel establishes that, in reliance on the other party's representations, it gave up the opportunity to negotiate a change in the collective agreement.

Although estoppel can be brought to an end by notice that a party intends to revert to its strict legal rights, arbitrators have generally held that the party adversely affected must first be given the opportunity to negotiate the issue in dispute.[131]

How Does Estoppel Work?

Consider the following example of A and B wherein A has certain rights under the contract. Can the obligations under the contract be brought to an end?

1.   A and B have a contract.

2.   A has certain legal rights under that contract.

3.   By words or conduct, A represents to B that they will not enforce those rights.

       B relies on that representation and acts accordingly.

If A wishes to revert to his/her strict legal rights, they must give B sufficient notice so that B will be put back into the same position they would have been in if they had not relied on A's promise.

Essential Elements of Estoppel

The doctrine of estoppel allows a party to recover the benefits of a promise made even if a contract does not exist provided the following three essential elements are present:

Representation: A promise or assurance by A (by words or conduct, which may include silence).

Intention (can be inferred): Intended to alter the legal relations between A and B.

Detrimental reliance: A's promise is relied on by B (by some form of action or inaction) so that it would be prejudicial to B if it were revoked.

Terminating the Obligation

Estoppel can be ended by giving reasonable notice. Where the reliance takes the form of loss of opportunity to negotiate a change in the collective agreement, estoppel will normally continue until the parties have had an opportunity to bargain. The use of the doctrine of estoppel relies on how significant the promisee's loss is in the absence of the fulfilled promise.

If the parties have had the chance to deal with the matter in negotiations, the obligation may be terminated before the expiry of the collective agreement.

---

131   J. Sack and E. Poskanzer, *Labour Law Terms* (Toronto: Lancaster House, 1984).

Types of Grievances

Grievances can be classified according to where they come from, how they arise, or who is affected.[132]

- **Individual employee grievance:** Management action specifically affects the individual grievor in an immediate and tangible way. Most grievances affect only a single individual.

- **Group grievance:** A number of employees join to file a series of grievances that have the same set of facts as their basis. Several employees are affected the same way by the same complaint at some time.

- **Policy grievance:** The subject matter of the grievance is of general interest. Individual employees may or may not be affected at the time the grievance is filed. In a policy grievance, the union complains that an employer's action (or its failure or refusal to act) is a violation of the collective agreement that could affect everyone covered by the agreement.

A policy grievance normally relates to the interpretation of the agreement, rather than to the complaint of an individual or group. However, the circumstances leading to a policy grievance could also prompt an individual grievance, insofar as the union claims that the employer's action or non-action implies an interpretation of the agreement that will be detrimental to bargaining unit members.

Generally, the following criteria indicate a policy grievance[133]:

- The number of people affected. A policy grievance deals with many people.

- The number of alleged violations involved. More than one specific incident has occurred.

- The nature of the remedy sought. Generally, grievances that seek relief for individual employees cannot be considered policy grievances.

- The possible future application. A grievance raises interpretive issues that may have implications for other issues in the future.

- The specific collective agreement language. In a few cases, the use of words such as "direct" or "interest" has outlined the extent of policy grievances. These

---

132   This section assumes that a union or an employee is the grievor. An employer may also initiate a grievance.

133   Palmer, E., and B. Palmer. *Collective Agreement Arbitration in Canada* (Toronto, ON: Butterworths, 1991), 180–181.

cases are subject to the general trend of decisions that expand the scope of policy grievances and must be read accordingly.

- *Continuing grievance*[134]—Arbitration awards have emphasized the need for the parties to pay close attention to time limits. As a result, acts by one party (generally the employer) have been deemed to be beyond the scope of arbitration after fixed time periods have passed. People must be able to rely on the validity of acts.

One approach is the development of the continuing grievance. The essence of a continuing grievance is that the act about which a grievor complains must be recurring. The problem, then, has been to determine when a series of acts has occurred that may be characterized as separate occurrences of violations of a collective agreement. The results of various cases are not uniform.[135]

134   Ibid, page 187.

135   Ibid, page 189.

Chapter 14: The Grievance Process

The grievance procedure in a collective agreement is structured to facilitate discussions between the union and the employer's representatives to negotiate a settlement of disputes arising during the term of the collective agreement.

The process is activated by parties who perceive that they are aggrieved in a specific factual situation.

The various steps of the collective agreement grievance procedure are designed so that both the employer and the union can explore several avenues of settlement and avoid the need for arbitration. Generally, before a grievance is filed, the parties have attempted to resolve the dispute through informal discussions. In the first step of the process, the grievance alleging the violation of the agreement is usually filed in writing, although this can be done orally. In most cases, the local union shop steward drafts the grievance and submits it on behalf of the grievor, the party on whose behalf the grievance is filed.

As the matter at issue proceeds through the internal dispute resolution process, the grievance can be settled or withdrawn at any stage. In most cases, grievances are settled internally, avoiding the expense, delay, and potential workplace tension resulting from the arbitration process. If the matter cannot be resolved internally, it may be submitted to arbitration for final and binding resolution. This final step in the grievance process is a hearing before a neutral arbitrator or arbitration board.

Who Has the Onus to Prove What?

The onus is generally on the party making a claim or filing a grievance. In other words, the one who asserts must prove.

In application grievances, such as those cases involving discipline, if the parties do not disagree on the meaning of the provision requiring just and reasonable cause for taking disciplinary action, the burden of proving that the employer acted appropriately by imposing discipline rests with the employer.

The two seminal cases concerning employee discipline are summarized below. The William Scott and Company case establishes the standard for culpable or blameworthy conduct. The National Harbours Board case establishes the standard for non-culpable conduct.

Employee Discipline and Dismissal

The Case of *William Scott & Company Ltd. And Canadian Food and Allied Workers' Union, Local P-162*

The leading authority in discipline and discharge cases, *William Scott & Company Ltd. And Canadian Food and Allied Workers' Union, Local P-162 (Weiler)*, July 26, 1976, obliges employers to demonstrate that a disciplined or dismissed employee's action warranted the discipline or dismissal, and, in the case of the former, that the discipline applied was not excessive. This case is still regarded as the seminal case for discipline and dismissal for culpable conduct.

In this case, the grievor, Ms. Martelli, worked at a poultry processing plant, William Scott and Company. The company had been in a dispute with a competitor and the provincial government, resulting in a backlog of chickens and turkeys awaiting slaughter. The grievor called a local newspaper and made critical comments about management practices at the plant; the comments later appeared in the newspaper. The grievor's employment was terminated.

The grievor's termination was grieved, and an arbitration board upheld the discharge. The arbitration board concluded that Martelli's actions did in fact warrant discharge and her employment record did not indicate that the substitution of a lesser penalty was justified.

This decision was appealed to the Labour Relations Board. Paul Weiler, chairing the appeal hearing, reviewed the legal history of dismissal from English common law and the evolving law of arbitration, and found that the requirement that arbitrators deal with the real substance and merits of a dismissal grievance fundamentally changed the previous definitions of "cause." The Board reviewed the rationale for the discharge, in particular citing the following arbitral standard established by a leading case:

> In evaluating the immediate discharge of an individual employee, the arbitrator would take account of "the employee's length of service and any other factors respecting his employment record with the Company in deciding whether to sustain or interfere with the Company's action" (at p.117). The following is an oft-quoted, but still not exhaustive, canvass of the factors which may legitimately be considered:
>
> - The previous good record of the grievor.
>
> - The long service of the grievor.
>
> - Whether or not the offence was an isolated incident in the employment history of the grievor.

- *Provocation.*

- *Whether the offence was committed on the spur of the moment as a result of a momentary aberration, due to strong emotional impulses, or whether the offence was premeditated.*

- *Whether the penalty imposed has created a special economic hardship for the grievor in the light of his particular circumstances.*

- *Evidence that the company rules of conduct, either unwritten or posted, have not been uniformly enforced, thus constituting a form of discrimination.*

- *Circumstances negating intent; e.g., likelihood that the grievor misunderstood the nature or intent of an order given to him, and as a result disobeyed it.*

- *The seriousness of the offence in terms of company policy and company obligations.*

- *Any other circumstances which the board should properly take into consideration, e.g., (a) failure of the grievor to apologize and settle the matter after being given an opportunity to do so; (b) where a grievor was discharged for improper driving of company equipment and the company, for the first time, issued rules governing the conduct of drivers after the discharge, this was held to be a mitigating circumstance; (c) failure of the company to permit the grievor to explain or deny the alleged offence.*

The board does not wish it to be understood that the above catalogue of circumstances which it believes the board should take into consideration in determining whether disciplinary action taken by the company should be mitigated and varied, is either exhaustive or conclusive. Every case must be determined on its own merits and every case is different, bringing to light in its evidence differing considerations which a board of arbitration must consider.

Steel Equipment Co. Ltd. (1964) 14 LAC 356, at pgs. 40-41.

At paragraph 14 the LRB signaled a fundamental shift in the standards for discipline and discharge when it concluded that the arbitrator's evaluation of management's decision must be especially searching, indicating that arbitrators should pose three distinct questions:

1.   *Has the employee given just and reasonable cause for some form of discipline by the employer?*

2.   *If so, was the employer's decision to discharge an excessive response in light of the circumstances of the case?*

3.   *If so, what alternative measure should be substituted as just and equitable?*

The appeal to have the arbitration award overturned was denied and, as a result, established the standard for discipline and dismissal.

This decision has stood the test of time. Over forty years later, the *William Scott* principles continue to provide a guide for employers, unions, and arbitrators in discipline and dismissal cases.

The following checklist provides an overview of the main principles of the case that can be used as a guide.

Checklist 4: *William Scott and Company Case* Checklist

	Checklist 4: *William Scott and Company Case* Checklist
1.	**Has the employer established just and reasonable cause for some form of punitive discipline?**
2.	**Has the employer established that the penalty selected was just and reasonable or was the response excessive (considering all the circumstances of the case)?**
	The previous good record of the grievor.
	The long service of the grievor.
	Whether or not the offence was an isolated incident in the employment history of the grievor.
	Provocation.
	Whether the offence was committed on the spur of the moment as a result of a momentary aberration, due to strong emotional impulses, or whether the offence was premeditated.
	Whether the penalty imposed has created a special economic hardship for the grievor in the light of his or her particular circumstances.
	Circumstances negating intent; e.g., likelihood that the grievor misunderstood the nature or intent of an order given to him or her, and as a result disobeyed it.

	Checklist 4: *William Scott and Company Case* Checklist
	The seriousness of the offence in terms of company policy and company obligations.
	Any other circumstances which the board should properly take into consideration; e.g., (a) failure of the grievor to apologize and settle the matter after being given an opportunity to do so.
3.	**If the response was excessive, what penalty, if any, should be substituted?**

The Case of the National Harbours Board

The National Harbours Board, No. C36/82 (October 2, 1982) is one of the leading authorities on non-culpable dismissal. In his decision, Arbitrator Allan Hope outlined the eight relevant factors to consider when an employee is being discharged for poor work performance:

1. *Has the employer identified in objective terms the nature of the work to be performed and the standard expected?*

2. *Has the employer established that the employee was aware of that standard?*

3. *Has the employer established that the work performance of the grievor was below that standard?*

4. *Did the employer provide supervisory direction to the employee to assist him/her in achieving the standard?*

5. *Did the employer take reasonable steps to move the employee into other work within the bargaining unit that was or might have been within his/her qualifications and competence?*

6. *Did the employer bring home to the grievor the fact that his/her performance was unsatisfactory and that dismissal might result from a continued failure or inability to meet the standard?*

7. *Did the employer afford the grievor a proper opportunity to challenge its assessment of his/her work or grievance?*

8. *Does the evidence support the influence of a continuing inability on the part of the employee to meet the standard?*

In an interpretation grievance, where the parties disagree on what the words mean, one party, typically the union, asserts that the employer interpreted the agreement incorrectly when it acted by making a claim or filing a grievance. The burden of proving that the union's interpretation is correct rests with the union.

Steps in a Grievance Procedure

The number of steps in the grievance procedure and the manner in which the grievance is processed vary with the particular agreement. The table below summarizes the stages in a typical grievance procedure.

No matter what steps you include, the grievance must be processed in an orderly manner and be thoroughly examined at every step. Each step requires seriously exploring avenues to settlement.

Table 12: Steps in a Grievance Procedure

Step	Action	Comment
Discussion	The matter at issue is presented orally to the supervisor within the time limitations (if any) for filing a grievance.	The shop steward usually presents the issue.
Step 1	If the issue is not settled, the grievance is submitted in writing. Depending on the practice of the parties and on the collective agreement, the grievance can be a detailed statement or a simple statement indicating that the collective agreement has been violated.	In some workplaces, the shop steward prepares the written submission, and in other workplaces, employees write their own grievances. Many large unions have standard grievance forms that an employee can easily fill out.
If the grievance is not settled ...		
Step 2	The grievance is presented to more senior employer representatives.	In this step, a specialist grievance officer may act on the grievor's behalf.
If the grievance is not settled...		
Step 3	The grievance is presented to senior employer representatives and senior union representatives.	Often, several grievances are reviewed at a single Step 3 meeting, with most being settled.
If the grievance is not settled...		

Step	Action	Comment
Step 4	The matter is set down for arbitration before either a single arbitrator or an arbitration board. The arbitrator (or board chair) may be appointed on an ad hoc basis or may be designated in the collective agreement.	Both parties may choose to be represented by legal counsel. The arbitration award is intended to result in a final and binding decision, but the award may be appealed to the Labour Relations Board on narrow grounds.

Discussion: Initiating a Formal Grievance

Under most collective agreements, employees with grievances are expected to go to their immediate supervisor to state their complaint and outline what they think should be done about the complaint.

The initial stage in a grievance procedure, discussing the grievance, usually takes one of two forms:

- A shop steward and an employee inform the employee's supervisor that they are initiating a grievance at the discussion stage.

- A shop steward and an employee meet with the employee's supervisor, and as a result of the discussion, initiate the grievance process, considering the initial meeting to be the discussion stage rather than Step 1 of the grievance process.

From a management perspective, the discussion stage serves two purposes. It identifies the matter at issue and the remedy that the employee and the union are seeking, and the information presented provides a basis upon which to further investigate the matter.

When the supervisor is advised that the employee and the union wish to formally discuss a matter at the discussion stage, or the supervisor has reason to believe a meeting will ultimately result in a grievance, the supervisor should ensure that the meeting is held in a room where the discussion will not be interrupted, a second member of management is present to act as a witness and to take detailed notes of what is said, and a copy of the current collective agreement is available as a reference.

At the end of the meeting, the supervisor should advise the shop steward and the employee that they will review the matter and the concerns presented and inform them of their decision shortly.

The initial discussions may only serve to further illuminate the grievance, leaving the matter unresolved. If the matter cannot be settled, or if it is determined for strategic reasons that settlement at this stage is inappropriate, the supervisor who heard the matter at the discussion stage advises the grievor that they believe the collective agreement has not been violated. The union then has the option of placing the grievance in writing and initiating the formal process.

Step 1: Submitting the Grievance in Writing

If the union is not satisfied with the outcome of the discussion stage, the matter may be submitted in writing to the employer. This written submission advises the employer of the union's intent to convene a grievance meeting. The union should outline the provisions of the collective agreement allegedly in dispute and the remedy it is seeking.

The wording of a grievance may be no more than a simple assertion that a provision of the collective agreement was violated. However, the dispute may entail complicated issues that are difficult to describe in words.

At this point, the grievance procedure has been formally initiated. The employer representative is expected to investigate the merits of the grievance and then give an answer, usually in writing, to the grievor through the union. The grievor and the union may be satisfied with the answer, in which case the grievance is withdrawn.

If not, the grievance continues to the next step, the grievance meeting, between representatives of the union and the employer.

Step 2: Holding the Grievance Meeting

The primary purpose of a grievance meeting is to discuss the matter in dispute and attempt to resolve the issue to the satisfaction of both parties. Start the meeting by identifying the problem or issue in dispute. This is essential because different individuals become involved at different stages of the process and thus might not be privy to all aspects of it.

A grievance meeting serves the parties in a number of ways:

- Because individuals can become emotionally invested in an issue, the meeting provides participants with an opportunity to ventilate or let off steam through the telling of their story ... performing a narrative.

- It may uncover other critical issues.

- It offers an opportunity for political posturing. In essence, labour relations needs to accommodate competing political interests. For example, union representatives come to the table representing various constituencies, many with differing interests.

- Discussions are *without prejudice* to any resulting arbitration proceedings that may result.

The meeting can identify potential solutions. To encourage this outcome, arbitrators have held that the discussions between the parties and the formal replies are privileged information. As a result, neither side may use this information as evidence at an arbitration hearing to prove what the other party said during the grievance process. The only exception to this rule is when a grievor makes an admission relevant to the matter at issue.

Step 3: Holding the Top-Level Grievance Meeting

This is the last step before asking a neutral third party to resolve the matter through arbitration. A meeting at this step provides the parties with a final opportunity to attempt to resolve the issues without involving an arbitrator. This meeting follows the same format as the previous step.

Step 4: Moving to Arbitration

In step four, the matter is referred to a third party who is charged with the task of adjudicating the grievance and determining the outcome under the collective agreement.

Before going to arbitration, the employer must:

- **Understand the matters at issue:** Through the various steps in the process and discussions with involved parties the employer must have, through inquiry, deconstructed the narratives to get to the heart of the matter. What are you asking the arbitrator to do that you cannot do yourself?

- **Prepare a list of facts.** These are the facts that the employer must prove through the evidence at arbitration.

- **Prepare an impact analysis.** This is an analysis of the impact on future negotiations, the collective agreement, and the exercise of management discretion if the employer does not succeed at arbitration.

Structural Variations in Grievance Procedures

Collective agreements may allow for specific grievance processes and procedures. As the grievance process is subject to collective bargaining, the parties may negotiate a process suitable to their workplace and relationship.

The structural variations can encompass:

- Level of participation. The process can specify who may attend at which steps.

- Level of formality. Depending on the relationship between the parties, informal, unwritten procedures may be used to resolve the process. In other cases, the grievance is submitted in writing.

- Time limits. (For a discussion of time limits, see the next section.)

- Level and frequency of meetings. The process can include regular meetings to resolve grievances at a senior level.

- *Mediation* and troubleshooting. Increasing numbers of collective agreements are incorporating alternate forms of dispute resolution.

- *Expedited arbitration.* An alternate arbitration process designed to expedite dispute settlement by using compressed timelines and procedural limitations on the conduct of the arbitration hearing.

Time Limits in the Grievance Procedure

The reason for establishing time limits for the original filing and the subsequent processing of a grievance is that the grievance should proceed from one step to the next in an orderly and predetermined way.

If time limits are not set, no party can predict how long the other party will take to respond to the issue, and both parties can abuse the process by tactical delays. This is not to say that each party should always insist on strict adherence to all time limits in every case. As much as possible, the process needs to satisfy the mutual need to handle grievances expeditiously.

The time periods specified in collective agreements vary widely. Most often, limits are placed on the time that may elapse between the event that gave rise to the grievance and the filing of the grievance. Time limits or deadlines are frequently imposed for processing the grievance, both for when answers are to be given and for how quickly the grievance should be processed after receiving those answers. Finally, in most agreements, time limits are imposed on the decision to proceed to arbitration, and on the establishment, and in some cases, on the decision making of the arbitrator or arbitration board.

Difficulties arise if time limits are breached. The employer may decide that the issue in question needs to be addressed for sound labour relations reasons, and may waive the breach of the time limits and accept the grievance. If the employer waives the time limits, the grievance may be presented normally, as if it had been filed on time. In deciding to waive the time limits, the employer would have to consider whether the time period had been significantly exceeded and whether any liability with respect to compensation had resulted.

Seeking a Resolution

Although employer representatives often chair grievance meetings, union representatives should be considered the equals of employer representatives when handling grievances. This equality is a matter of law and is necessary to give any true meaning to employee representation. Employer representatives must resist reacting to this fact or perceiving grievances as attacks on their authority.

Employer representatives who chair a grievance meeting should begin by setting an objective tone for the discussions and expressing in words and deeds a positive desire to see the problem resolved. They should never allow an overzealous union representative to goad them into a negative attitude or shouting match. Instead, the grievor and union representative should be given the opportunity to fully explain the nature of the problem before management responds.

All participants must avoid committing themselves to a fixed position before all facts, views, and considerations have been aired and an effort to achieve a settlement has been made. Snap judgements and hostile reactions (even to apparent hostility) will only ensure that the grievance will become more difficult to resolve or remain unresolved.

Union and employer representatives must not make promises to their constituents that preclude compromise settlements where these may be possible. Union and employer representatives must also allow each other to save face when necessary. At times, letting something go is the right course of action. Above all, if a grievor is correct, the grievance should be granted promptly, and arrangements made to provide a remedy for the error.

Particularly in disciplinary situations, both the grievor and the employer representative are often emotionally invested in the process and both parties need the opportunity to vent their emotions (even engaging in some shouting or strong language) before turning to the matters at issue and the contractual merits of the grievance. One of the benefits of the grievance process (regardless of contractual merit) is that it provides the opportunity for employees and supervisors to express frustration and anger without fear of reprisal. It is far preferable that these feelings be expressed within this process than stored away as resentment. All participants should be permitted to tell their story.

Make every effort to avoid arguing over apparent factual disagreement details of the case. If the discussion is diverted into quarrelling over relatively minor details, the parties may never address the real problem.

It is often productive for a supervisor and a union representative to consult informally in private about the circumstances of a grievance, assuming that they trust each other sufficiently. However, some grievance procedures require that the grievor be present for all formal exchanges and settlement attempts. Both the fact and the appearance of fairness must be maintained to keep the process legitimate in the eyes of employees and the law.

In fact, any doubts that the parties share about the circumstances of a grievance can provide the basis for a settlement. If the parties accept that they cannot achieve everything they want, chances are good that they can arrive at a settlement through their discussions. If they can maintain an objective attitude, along with a willingness to admit error, compromises are easier to accept. The parties may explicitly designate such settlements as "without prejudice."[136]

Tactically, however, employer representatives should decline to commit any potential settlements to writing until the union has agreed to them. This approach will avoid union attempts to use the settlement as a lever to gain an even better settlement at higher steps in the grievance process. The union should accept the employer's stance as prudent negotiation, rather than as "bad faith."

In the final analysis, the employer should consider several factors before declining to settle a grievance, and leave the union to decide whether the case should go to arbitration.

First, the employer should be persuaded that the union is correct in terms of both contract interpretation and relevant arbitral jurisprudence.

Second, the employer should ask whether the issue is important enough to risk the cost and other potentially adverse consequences of arbitration. Even winning an arbitration, particularly on a close call, can promote resentment and damage the relationships between supervisors and employees and between the union and the employer. In addition, the delay (two to six months in some cases) that will result from submitting a grievance to arbitration may not be acceptable.

Settling the Grievance

If both parties agree on satisfactory terms for resolving the grievance, the terms of settlement should be documented in writing and both parties should sign or initial the document. A complex legal document does not need to be drawn up; in many cases, an exchange of correspondence is sufficient. However, both parties must understand

---

136 An expression used to indicate that a party making an offer or taking an action does so on the basis that the offer or action does not imply an admission of liability or that the other party's interpretation is correct.

the terms and application of the provisions of settlement. In a procedural dispute, the settlement document should include sufficient detail to ensure that both parties are clear on the specifics of the dispute and the manner in which it was resolved. In addition, the settlement agreement should indicate if the resolution was with or without prejudice.

Denying the Grievance

Employers usually use one of three main approaches when denying a grievance: brief and pointed, reasons in principle, and a hybrid of the two.

- **Brief and pointed**—The theory behind the brief and pointed approach asserts that the written answers to a grievance should be brief and pointed, essentially consisting of a denial of the grievance. The reasoning is that the employer is not committed to any one course of action, and may put forward alternative arguments at the arbitration stage.

  The drawback to this approach is that the grievor may feel that the grievance was not given full consideration if the flat denial that the agreement was violated contains no supporting rationale or explanation.

- **Reasons in principle**—This approach asserts that the written answer should contain the reasons, in principle, for denying the grievance by providing the union sufficient rationale for the decision.

- **Hybrid approach**—A third possible course of action is to provide a brief written answer and then give a detailed explanation orally during the grievance meeting or at a meeting called after you have had an opportunity to consider the union's submission.

Generally, approaches two and three help make the grievance process more effective.

Work Now, Grieve Later

The "work now, grieve later"[137] principle applies to disputes in the workplace and it means that an employee is expected to follow an order, perform the job, and rely on the grievance procedure in the collective agreement to rectify any error.

Exceptions to the "work now, grieve later" principle have emerged when the employee would be unable to secure adequate redress through the grievance process if required

---

137   D.J.M. Brown and D. Beatty, *Canadian Labour Arbitration*, 4th ed. 7:3620; *Lake Ontario Steel Co. Ltd. and U.S.W.A.* (1968), 19 L.A.C. 103 (P.C. Weiler).

to comply with management's request. The main exceptions to the principle include the following issues:

- Health and safety—Would a reasonable employee performing the work in the grievor's position believe their health and safety were at risk?

- Illegality—Employees are not required to perform acts that might result in the violation of legislative standards in which the employees would be personally subject to legal liability as well.

- Union officials—In some instances, union officials are not required to comply with this principle where they are acting in their role as union official or where they believe they must attend to their union duties to prevent irreparable harm to the interests of other employees.

When employees seek to challenge an employer's instruction and not follow the "work now, grieve later" principle, the onus falls on the employees to demonstrate that their circumstances fall within one of the exceptions, and that they have communicated the reason for the refusal to their supervisor.

Chapter 15: The Effective Grievance Administration Template

The function of the grievance procedure in a collective agreement is to resolve contract disputes without resorting to job action, and to preserve contractual rights and obligations. The operation of the grievance procedure entails discussions between union and employer representatives, with a view to negotiating a settlement of disputes arising during the term of a collective agreement. If a particular dispute cannot be resolved in the earlier stages of the grievance process, it must be resolved through arbitration.

The effective grievance administration template (the EGA template) helps settle workplace disputes by focussing on information gathering, analysis, and the exploration of options. The EGA template is a systematic approach for identifying the issues in dispute and deepening the parties' understanding of those issues and their underlying motivation. This understanding will help settle disputes or, if the matter cannot be resolved, will result in an informed decision to refer the matter to a third party for resolution.

Figure 27: Fundamental Elements that Support the Effective Grievance Administration Template (EGA Template)

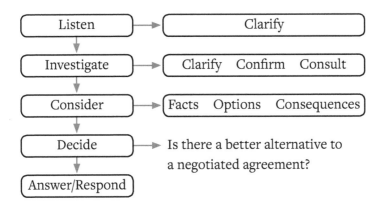

The EGA Template is designed to help realize the following outcomes:

* further understanding of workplace issues

* generation of settlement options

* settlement of disputes on their merits

- informed decisions to refer matters to arbitration

- effective arbitration preparation

Figure 28: The EGA Template

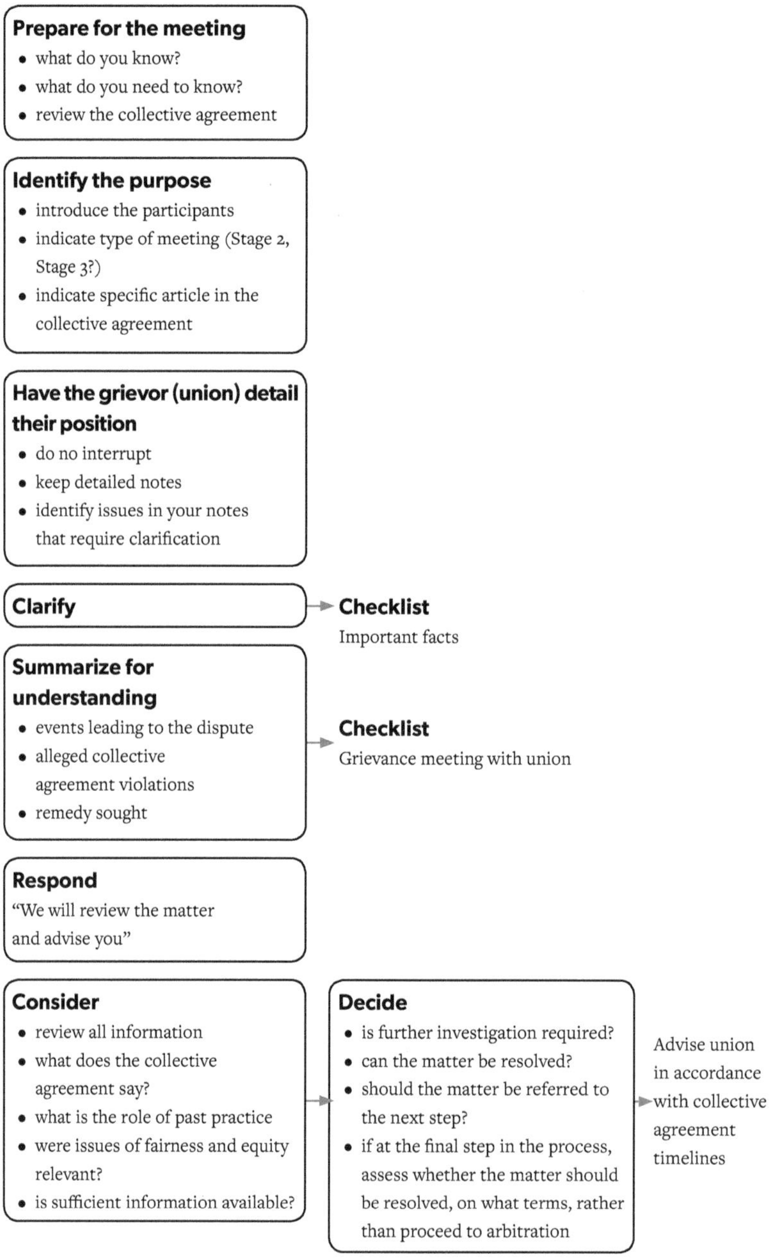

Prepare for the meeting
- what do you know?
- what do you need to know?
- review the collective agreement

Identify the purpose
- introduce the participants
- indicate type of meeting (Stage 2, Stage 3?)
- indicate specific article in the collective agreement

Have the grievor (union) detail their position
- do no interrupt
- keep detailed notes
- identify issues in your notes that require clarification

Clarify → **Checklist**
Important facts

Summarize for understanding
- events leading to the dispute
- alleged collective agreement violations
- remedy sought

Checklist
Grievance meeting with union

Respond
"We will review the matter and advise you"

Consider
- review all information
- what does the collective agreement say?
- what is the role of past practice
- were issues of fairness and equity relevant?
- is sufficient information available?

Decide
- is further investigation required?
- can the matter be resolved?
- should the matter be referred to the next step?
- if at the final step in the process, assess whether the matter should be resolved, on what terms, rather than proceed to arbitration

Advise union in accordance with collective agreement timelines

Steps in the EGA Template

In each meeting with the union representative, the employer representative needs to explore avenues for settlement and gather the information needed to allow for an informed decision. The following steps in the EGA template serve as a useful guide to follow in these meetings:

1. **Prepare for the Meeting**

   Be well prepared to ensure the meeting runs smoothly and efficiently. Gather as much background information as possible before the meeting and review the relevant collective agreement provisions and other related grievances.

2. **Identify the Purpose of the Meeting**

   The purpose of the meeting could be to:

   - have an informal discussion

   - formally initiate the discussion stage (indicate the related article of the collective agreement)

   - formally initiate the grievance committee stage (indicate the related article of the collective agreement)

3. **Listen to the Grievor's Story (Narrative)**

   The grievor or the union representative should detail the grievor's position without interruption. Persistent questioning at the beginning of an interview or meeting forces the other person to frame events in the context of your questions. You need to hear about the issues in dispute from the grievor's perspective. As such:

   - Do not interrupt or attempt to clarify.

   - Let the grievor (union representative) detail the position as the grievor remembers it.

   - Do not immediately challenge the grievor's (union representative's) account of the events. Deconstruct the narrative. Make a note of points where the parties differ, so that you can ask for clarification after the grievor (union representative) has finished the presentation.

   - Keep in mind that the meeting is not a debate.

4. **Clarify the Information**

Once the grievor (union representative) has completed the presentation, ask questions to clarify, especially if the presentation was unclear or information was not fully presented.

If they are relevant, consider the factors in the checklist of important facts (Checklist 1) introduced in Chapter 11 as you deepen your understanding of the details of the grievance. The checklist can help you gather and clarify the information.

5. **Summarize for Mutual Understanding**

Summarize the grievor's (union representative's) presentation to ensure mutual understanding of the events leading up to the dispute, the reasons for the dispute, the specific matters in dispute, and any events or facts on which the parties differ.

In particular, the parties need to be clear on two areas:

- Articles allegedly in violation—Identify the specific articles (clauses or words) of the collective agreement that are in violation from the grievor's (union's) perspective. Why does the grievor believe these articles are in violation?

- Remedy sought—Identify the remedy that the grievor is seeking. Why does the grievor feel entitled to such a remedy?

When you have determined the grievor's position and the remedy sought, you may wish to outline the employer's position, in general terms only. Remember the rule that it is not what you think happened; it is what you can prove.

When deciding on a course of action—for example, settlement or arbitration—remember the three key concepts that underlie the rule:

1. Opinions are not facts. All opinions must be specifically qualified. If a person says "Always," ask "How often and when?"

2. Hearsay evidence is not factual. Search for the original source and witnesses and obtain a first-hand account. If someone says, "Mary heard ..." or "John told me that ...," find out directly from Mary or John what happened.

3. Facts must be relevant. You need to identify the facts that directly bear on each particular grievance. Review your notes and identify the facts relevant to the case.

The employer representative should review the checklist of information to confirm during a grievance meeting (Checklist 5) after each meeting with the union representative to ensure that the needed information has been gathered.

Checklist 5: Checklist of Information to Confirm During a Grievance Meeting

Checklist 5: Checklist of Information to Confirm During a Grievance Meeting		
Discussion		Date:
Committee Stage		Date:
Ensure that the following information has been received and clarified in any meeting with the union regarding a dispute about the collective agreement.		
	Chronology of events leading to the dispute (date/time)	
	List of who is involved other than the grievor (chain of involved parties): • Other employees, managers/supervisors, witnesses (not employees)	
	Documents giving rise to the dispute: • Letters/memos, evaluation, posting number	
	Collective agreement provisions in alleged violation	
	Remedy sought	

4. **Give Your Response on the Need for Review**

   Advise the grievor (union) that you will review the matter and the concerns raised in the presentation, and that you will let the grievor know of your decision shortly. Do not make a commitment while sitting at the table. Only make a decision to settle or proceed to the next step in the process after the matter has been thoroughly reviewed.

5. **Consider the Need for Additional Information**

   Information raised in the meeting may serve only to identify information that requires further investigation. A decision can only be made to settle or to move to the next step when these additional matters have been investigated.

6. **Make Your Decision After Review**

If the matter cannot be resolved, or if it is decided that the grievance should be heard at the next stage, advise the union (either verbally or in writing) that you have reviewed the matter and believe that the collective agreement has not been violated. At this point, the union is in a position to settle if it wishes, or not settle and refer the matter to the next step in the process.

Chapter 16: Handling Grievances Effectively

Why do people go to the trouble of grieving? Why do their frame their concerns as they do? Review the section on narratives.

A complaint or workplace concern is not necessarily a grievance as defined by the collective agreement. Regardless of the contractual merit, the matter identified must be addressed. Keep in mind the variety of motivations that give rise to grievances. Consider them but don't get distracted by them. The matters at issue need to be examined and reconciled. It is a question of interests.

Grievances, Narratives, and the Mixed Motive Dynamic

More than Meets the Eye: Mixed Motives and Purposes	Adjudicative	Psychological	Communication	Political	Tactical or Strategic
Resolve a conflict or dispute, the issue(s)					
Let off steam					
Go through the motions of representation					
Set the stage for arbitration on a principle and create a record					
Establish the basis for collective bargaining and create a record					
Develop a perception of management for their constituency					
Develop and/or maintain your reputation as a (their role)					

In Part One, we examined why union–employer relations are the way they are and the concept of the emergent relationship. Within this relationship there are frames of reference, experiences, and motivations. Notwithstanding the mixed motive dynamic, when you, the employer representative, are investigating a grievance or are meeting with a union representative about a grievance, remember why you are there. What are you trying to achieve?

Clearly, you want to identify and clarify the matter at issue, and you want to resolve the matter expeditiously and preserve a productive employer-employee relationship. In addition, you want to achieve a good agreement[138] that is:

- Fair in the eyes of the parties involved.

- Efficient in that it did not take long to resolve or was unnecessarily expensive to resolve.

- Wise and in line with settlements of a similar nature.

- Durable or stable and that it facilitates compliance.

Above all, you want to validate and preserve the rights and obligations that are the foundation of the collective agreement.

Regardless of the contractual merits of a dispute, effective managers and supervisors must respond to a grievance or complaint in a way that prevents the problem from worsening. Workplace disputes often result from misunderstandings of supervisory directives or misapplications of the collective agreement. If the parties are committed to resolving problems as quickly as possible as part of their ongoing relationship, disputes can usually be resolved through informal discussions.

Dismissing complaints or grievances without adequate explanation or investigation can turn a simple misunderstanding into a substantial grievance issue or perception that the employer acts unfairly, in general. A similar outcome can result when the employer initially adopts a hardline bargaining stance. Failing to give a grievance prompt and thorough consideration can also increase the likelihood of the grievance ultimately being referred to arbitration. The resulting costs and use of resources can be considerable.

As a grievance progresses through the steps of the grievance procedure, the individuals involved may forget crucial facts. The EGA template described in this section provides a framework for gathering and organizing information. It is also recommended, especially in cases concerning workplace misconduct, that you adopt a systematic investigation protocol as discussed in Part Two: *Conflict and Work*. Proper investigation allows you to have the information required to process a grievance if an employee grieves the matter.

---

138   See Part Two: *Conflict and Work* for a detailed analysis of what constitutes a *good agreement* re. L. Susskind and J. Cruikshank, *Breaking the Impasse: Consensual Approaches to Resolving Public Disputes* (New York: Basic Books, 1988).

The grievance process is complicated by union representatives being elected officers with responsibilities to the union members and to the constituencies or groups within the membership. Employer representatives must recognize and, within reason, accommodate this political reality.

Understandably, union representatives must be seen to be doing all they can for those they represent if they expect to be re-elected to office or to achieve higher office. Therefore, union representatives may sometimes engage in a certain amount of political posturing. While accepting this political activity, employer representatives must also resist the temptation to take it personally or to act in a similar fashion.

Union representatives are often faced with members who believe they have an unlimited right to have their grievances processed through to arbitration, if necessary. These employees may threaten or actually file a duty of fair representation complaint under Section 12 (Duty of fair representation) of the *Labour Relations Code* if they believe they have been denied this right by the union. The filing of a duty of fair representation complaint, even if it is totally unfounded, can be politically damaging to the union leadership and may increase grievance's likelihood of being heard at arbitration.

These characteristics of the grievance process require that the grievance handling be as thorough and objective as possible. This requires paying attention to the needs of all participants in the process, as well as to the contractual merits.

The participants must not forget that the grievance process is only one of the activities in the ongoing employer-employee relationship. The union and the employer must continue to work together in the future, and effectively resolving a problem now will help improve future effectiveness. The opposite is also true: ineffective grievance administration invariably leads to more grievances and issues when the collective agreement is re-negotiated.

The challenge for the parties is to consistently administer the collective agreement while retaining sufficient flexibility to account for special or unusual circumstances.

Guidelines for Handling Grievances Effectively

Many situations can lead to a grievance. While each grievance has its unique characteristics that may result from the situation itself or from the personalities involved in the grievance, the general guidelines below can help you handle grievances effectively.

Guidelines for Employer Representatives

Responsible employer representatives should consider the following guidelines when handling grievances:

- Establish clear policies that both parties understand.

- Allow the grievor time to tell their full story in private and without interruption. Give them your full attention.

- Reflect on why the grievor has gone to the trouble of grieving.

- Seek to end all meetings on a positive note.

- Show your concern for the grievor's problem by promptly following through on any action required by a settlement.

- Do not consider any grievance too trivial for your attention.

Too often, employer representatives gloss over or minimize events they think are irrelevant or that may be viewed as mistakes. Whether investigating workplace misconduct or a grievance, employer representatives should remember one simple rule: that which may come out eventually must come out immediately. Employer representatives can only make good decisions when they have consistently reliable and complete information.

Guidelines for Both Parties

Successfully handling grievances requires thoroughly understanding the collective agreement and related arbitral jurisprudence, as well as insight into human behaviour. The following guidelines should be considered by responsible members of both parties when handling grievances.

The Content

- Ensure that information on the grievance is complete and accurate.

- Use the facts and only the facts. Do not base your case on hearsay. Do not allow verbal statements and hearsay to substitute for written proof and first-hand testimony.

- Know your collective agreement. Remember that it may take on a different meaning when applied to different grievance situations.

- Maintain the integrity of the collective agreement by following its terms and procedures.

The Process

- Prepare each grievance analysis as carefully, as if it were to be presented before an arbitrator or arbitration board.

- Try to settle at the earliest step in the grievance procedure. Settling as early as possible pays off in time, expense, and emotions.

- Delay can be costly as well as disruptive. Process grievances promptly and efficiently.

- Keep adequate written records to ensure consistency and future effectiveness.

- Never trade one grievance for another. Grievance settlements tend to establish precedence. Settlement on grounds other than merit may come back to haunt you.

The Relationships

- Remember that the grievance process is intended to resolve, not create, conflict. Adopt a constructive approach. Consider the differences, as shown in Table 13, below.

Table 13: Comparison of the Constructive and Adversarial Approaches

	Constructive Approach	Adversarial Approach
Atmosphere	Working with the other party; focussed on a problem *we* have	Working against the other party; focussed on the idea *you* are the problem
Stance	Prepared to explore the potential for integration through better understanding of the matters at issue.	Demonstrates that this is more than likely a zero-sum proposition. A gain for you represents a loss for me both in terms of process and substance.
Strategies	<ul><li>Exploring needs, concerns (interests)</li><li>Using objective criteria</li><li>Building on commonalities</li><li>Influencing with reasoned thinking</li></ul>	<ul><li>Position-taking, positioning</li><li>Accentuating differences; raising doubt</li><li>Coercing with pressure</li><li>Intimidation, threats</li><li>Attacks</li></ul>
Relationship	<ul><li>Goal of building, maintaining and / or strengthening</li><li>Future orientation</li></ul>	<ul><li>Seeking personal gain on the matters at issue</li><li>Potential to damage or destroy</li></ul>
Outcome	<ul><li>Goal of satisfying both parties</li><li>Long-term stability</li></ul>	<ul><li>Goal of satisfying self</li><li>Short-term gain</li></ul>

- Control your emotions. A grievance meeting is not a debate. It is not who is right, but what is right. Tantrums, vindictiveness, personal dislikes, provocations, petty jealousies, and high-pressure tactics weaken your case.

- Saving face is important to both parties. It can mean the difference between an amicable and a hostile settlement.

- Accept settlement graciously. Tomorrow you must go back to working with each other.

Remember that these guidelines only address grievance handling. Each person will use the systems and strategies that best meet their individual style and organizational objectives.

Those in closest contact with the grievance at its origin have the best chance to resolve it. Often, however, these matters are not resolved, because the individuals are emotionally invested in the issue, distracted by the narratives, and do not have sufficient experience or training to objectively manage the matter in dispute.

Assessing Outcomes and the Process

Since the resolution of a workplace dispute can considerably impact your relationship with an employee and with the union, in general, you need to review not only the results of the process (substantive/relationship outcomes), but also the process that led to the results.

In one sense, the effectiveness of a grievance process can be assessed by the degree to which the process fulfils the functions that the parties have set for it. Certainly, the extent to which collective agreement disputes are resolved without workplace disruptions is one measure of grievance effectiveness.

Procedural measures of effectiveness include how quickly a resolution was achieved, as well as at which step in the grievance process the grievance was resolved. In particular, matters of a minor or technical nature should be resolved earlier in the process through issue clarification and discussion.

The success of a grievance procedure can be measured in terms of the parties' ability to resolve issues that are most important to a particular workplace, especially to the employees for whom the grievance procedure provides a "voice."

Checklist 6: Checklist for Assessing the Effectiveness of the Grievance Procedure

Checklist 6: Effectiveness of the Grievance Procedure
Details

Checklist 6: Effectiveness of the Grievance Procedure
Who, what, where, when, why? (Are you prepared? Has the matter been thoroughly investigated and documented using the investigation protocol?)
What considerations are raised by arbitral jurisprudence?
What can be learned from your previous cases?
What are the doubts or weak points in your case?
What are the strong points in their case?
Attitudes and Roles
Are union representatives accepted as equals?
Are grievances regarded as an attack on managerial authority?
Are snap judgements avoided? (Avoid developing a conclusion and then building a case.)
Are the participants attempting to be objective?
Can anger and frustration be expressed?
Are mistakes admitted?
Do participants allow each other to retreat gracefully?
Communication
Are the participants allowed to tell their stories?
Do representatives listen actively?
Do the parties avoid arguing over details?
Do the parties understand the issues in dispute—the events that led to the dispute and the remedy that the union is seeking?
Can union and employer representatives consult informally?
Do those represented understand where they are wrong?

Checklist 6: Effectiveness of the Grievance Procedure
The Settlement
Note: These questions should be reviewed if the matter is referred to arbitration and settled through the arbitration process.
Have you communicated the settlement to those affected?
Have you changed policies, procedures, and practices to conform with the settlement?
Have you assessed the impact of the settlement on future rounds of negotiations?
Would you characterize it as a good settlement?
Lessons Learned
What worked well?
What did not work well?
How would you change your information-gathering process?
How would you change your decision-making process?
How could you avoid a similar dispute in the future? (Analyze in detail the processes and decisions that led to the dispute)
Are there relationship implications arising out of the process and this dispute?

Assessment of Management Action

When assessing the actions of employer representatives, consider the following questions:

- Have the employer representatives properly administered the collective agreement?

- Have the employer representatives consistently administered and interpreted the collective agreement?

If the agreement is silent about the issues in dispute or the language is ambiguous:

- What are the policies and procedures that relate to the issues in dispute?

- Is consistent past practice evident?

- What was the intent of the parties at negotiations?

- Have management's actions been consistent?

Chapter 17: Should You Go to Arbitration?

If the grievance proceeds to arbitration, you need to recognize that you are giving up control of the result. No matter how good your case looks and no matter how well you prepare, the arbitrator ultimately controls the result.

If you can achieve resolution without arbitration, on the other hand, you retain some control over the result.

Settlement or Arbitration?

There are no hard and fast rules about when cases should be settled. Many factors can play a part in deciding whether to settle, including:

- A genuine disagreement on the meaning or application of a provision in the collective agreement.

- The nature of the relationship between the employer and the union.

- Concern about the message that a settlement will give to the union and the employees.

- The desire to discourage the filing of a grievance by the union in order to facilitate a quick and painless settlement, regardless of the issue.

- The objective of maintaining the integrity of the grievance process to solve legitimate disputes instead of for tactical purposes such as setting the stage for collective bargaining or making a point about a supervisor's or manager's decision.

Even though no specific formula can be applied to decide whether to settle a matter or allow it to proceed to arbitration, employer representatives should consider the following questions:

- How do the costs of arbitration compare with the costs of settlement? Consider monetary costs, those associated with a potential loss in productivity, and relationship costs.

- Does the case involve a matter of principle with ongoing consequences, or is it a one-time issue, such as the length of an employee's suspension?

- How strong is the employer's case, factually and legally?

- Are you being realistic in distinguishing what you think the facts are from what you can actually prove?

- Will you be able to live with the results of losing at arbitration? Losing may have ongoing consequences in a grievance concerning collective agreement interpretation, in particular.

- What message would a loss by the organization at arbitration give to the union or the employees?

- How wide is the gap between the best result you can expect from arbitration and the terms on which the other party is prepared to settle?

- Is the other party attempting to achieve something in settling the issue that it could not receive from the arbitrator?

The answers to these questions should help determine whether to conclude a resolution short of arbitration, especially when the result of the arbitration may have ongoing operational and relationship consequences for both parties. A realistic assessment includes considering a worst-case and a best-case scenario.

Adopting the Arbitrator's Perspective

Arbitrators normally do not become involved in a dispute until the parties have exhausted all preliminary steps of a grievance procedure. The steps are designed so that the parties can mutually explore various avenues of settlement.

In many cases, arbitration can be avoided if the parties to the grievance approach the matter at issue from an arbitrator's perspective and consider the following questions.[139]

What does the collective agreement say?

The arbitrator has an obligation to interpret and apply the collective agreement as the parties who wrote it intended it to be used. Therefore, those handling the early stages of the grievance need to be sure of the intent of a particular clause—or find out the intent if they are unsure.

What is the role of past practice and precedent?

When the intent of a clause is not clear, an arbitrator is likely to consider past practices or precedents as an extension of the collective agreement. Once again, those handling the grievance should determine the nature of accepted practices in the organization. These accepted practices may differ substantially from the procedures that higher levels of the organization have developed and disseminated.

139   G.E. Phillips, *Labour Relations and the Collective Bargaining Cycle*, 2nd ed. (Toronto: Butterworths, 1981), 218.

Are the issues of fairness and equity relevant?

Most arbitrators require that the rules of due process and natural justice not be violated in the course of administering collective agreement. As a result, the parties should not overlook considerations such as previous warnings, consistent treatment, and reasonable penalties when evaluating the strengths and weaknesses of their position in a grievance.

Is sufficient evidence available?

The outcome of many arbitration cases depends on the relative abilities of the parties to produce compelling proof that something happened or that something was intended. Too often, parties proceed on the basis of what they think happened and verbal allegations, rather than on factual evidence.

Arbitration Tips

Arbitration is a formal process with a specific purpose. Consider the following tips to inform your preparation for an arbitration hearing.

The Hearing and Your Evidence

When your evidence is required, your counsel will ask you to take the witness stand. The arbitrator will administer an oath on the Bible in which you promise to tell the truth. If you do not wish to take an oath on the Bible, the arbitrator will ask you to solemnly affirm to tell the truth instead of taking the oath.

Your counsel will then proceed with *direct examination*, also referred to as *examination in chief.* In general, questions during this part of the evidence will be open-ended and not leading questions.

After the direct examination is completed, the opposing counsel has the opportunity to cross-examine you. Under *cross-examination,* the opposing counsel has great latitude to ask leading questions, or questions that suggest an answer. Cross-examination may deal with areas not covered in examination in chief, and counsel may suggest an answer or ask you to agree or disagree with a proposition. Once cross-examination has begun, you may not discuss your evidence with anyone, including your counsel.

When cross-examination is completed, your counsel can re-examine you. These questions are limited to clarifying matters raised during cross-examination. As with examination in chief, your counsel may not ask leading questions.

The Three Roles of a Witness[140]

A witness in an arbitration proceeding has three distinct roles.

1.   To give evidence, not to make argument.

2.   To testify about facts, rather than to give opinions.

3.   To answer the question, not to argue its propriety, provided the witness understands the question and has the knowledge to be able to respond to it.

General Tips on Giving Evidence

The following list has been developed as guidance for witnesses giving evidence:[141]

Answering the Questions

Answer questions, whether from your counsel, the other party's council or the arbitrator, with the following advice in mind.

- Do not attempt to memorize your answers. Give a factual, straightforward response to the questions.

- Do not answer a question unless you understand it. If the question is unclear, ask examining counsel to repeat it or phrase it in clearer language.

- Think about each question before answering, and do not supply information not requested by the question. Respond only to the question that is asked.

- Do not let anyone put words in your mouth. Use your own words.

- If your answer is not clear, clarify it immediately.

Telling the Truth

You are your credibility, tell the truth!

- You are sworn to tell the truth, so tell it. You should admit every material truth, even if not to the advantage of the party for whom you are testifying.

---

140   Adapted from B. Finlay and T. Cromwell, *Witness Preparation Manual* (Aurora, Ontario: Canada Law Book, 1991), 58–59.

141   Ibid.

- Do not attempt to answer when you truthfully do not know the answer. Say "I don't know." Do not think that because a question is asked, you are expected to know the answer to it.

- Say what you saw, heard, and did, not what you thought, inferred, and guessed. Do not speculate on what the question may mean and then answer the question based on your interpretation or speculation. A guess or an estimate is almost always inaccurate.

- Do not exaggerate.

- If your answer is wrong, correct it immediately.

Conducting Yourself as a Witness

Your credibility will be measured by what you say, how you say it, and how you conduct yourself. Consider the following guidelines.

- Give all testimony verbally. The arbitrator cannot report gestures, such as a nod or shake of the head indicating an affirmative or negative response. If you wish to describe an event with gestures, you should give an accurate verbal picture as well.

- Listen carefully to each question, and allow counsel to finish the question before answering.

- However, if your counsel begins to speak, stop whatever answer you may be giving and allow them to make their statement. If your counsel is making an objection to the question that is being asked of you, do not answer the question until after they have made their objection, and the arbitrator advises you to go ahead and complete your answer.

- Face the arbitrator and speak to them, rather than to the counsel who is asking the questions.

- Speak up so that the arbitrator can hear your testimony. Be sure to enunciate clearly.

- Speak at a pace that enables the arbitrator to record your testimony in writing. Testimony is useless if the arbitrator cannot hear it or record it. We tend to speed up our rate of speech when nervous or speaking in public Being cognizant of timing is important here.

- Do not be a smart-aleck or a cocky witness. This behaviour will lose you the arbitrator's respect.

- Try not to be overwhelmed by nervousness.

- When you leave the witness stand after testifying, wear a confident expression, not a downcast one.

Helpful Hints for Cross-Examination

- Given the nature of questioning under cross-examination, the following hints can assist you during the cross-examination questioning.

- Do not look at your counsel or the arbitrator for help in answering a question. If the question is improper, your counsel will object.

- You may be asked whether you discussed your evidence with anyone. Tell the truth. There is nothing improper about discussing your evidence with counsel beforehand.

- Do not concern yourself with where the question is leading. Concentrate only on listening to the question asked and giving an accurate and complete answer.

- Under cross-examination, if you are asked a question that suggests an answer or if you agree or disagree with a conclusion or statement, ensure that you consider the whole statement and indicate specifically what you agree or disagree with.

- Do not be rushed into answering, although you should not take so much time on each question that the arbitrator thinks you are making up an answer. If the opposing counsel cuts you off or tries to rush your answer, politely ask if you could complete your answer.

- Do not lose your temper and self-control, and never become angry or hostile. Or, if that's not possible, don't show your anger or hostility. Remember that some counsel on cross-examination will try to wear you down so that you will lose your temper and give answers that are not correct or that will hurt you or your testimony.

- Do not argue with counsel; remain polite and natural, even in the face of aggressive questioning.

Chapter 18: The Legal Framework

Effective management and leadership in a unionized workplace require an understanding of the legal framework within which the workplace functions. Each province in Canada—and the federal government, in federally regulated industries —has its own legislation to regulate union-employer relations. The statutes establish:

- the right of employees to join the union of their choice and be represented in the collective bargaining process

- an administrative agency responsible for the statute

- a duty on both parties to "bargain in good faith" and a prohibition on "unfair labour practices"

For illustrative purposes the British Columbia *Labour Relations Code* (the Code) is detailed in this section.

As you read through the information in this guide, remember that it is not intended to provide legal advice. The *Code* is subject to legal interpretation by the Labour Relations Board (LRB). If you require more detailed information, consult the Code itself and the LRB's written decisions.

The *Labour Relations* Code

The *Labour Relations Code* is the statute primarily concerned with collective bargaining and labour-management relations in British Columbia.

The *Code* governs most aspects of the relationship between unions and employers. It contains provisions designed to promote collective bargaining and sets out certain basic standards for every collective agreement.

If the union and the employer are unable to negotiate an agreement, the *Code* permits strikes, lockouts and *picketing* (within certain legal constraints) to pursue bargaining demands. However, the *Code* prohibits strikes and lockouts during the term of a collective agreement. All disputes arising during such a term must be resolved without a work stoppage by arbitration or some other method that the parties agree to.

The *Code* provides various types of assistance to the parties to resolve both collective bargaining disputes during the negotiation of a collective agreement and contract disputes during the term of the agreement.

Excluded Employees

Not every employee in a unionized workplace in BC is covered by the *Code*. Only those who meet the *Code's* definition of an employee in Section 1 (Definitions) are entitled to exercise the right to bargain collectively with their employer for the establishment of terms and conditions of employment.

Under Section 1 (Definitions), anyone who performs the functions of a manager or superintendent or anyone employed in a confidential capacity in matters relating to labour relations or personnel is not considered to be an employee for the purposes of collective bargaining.

The collective bargaining rights of some groups are also addressed in other statutes. The *Code* applies in all other labour relations matters.

Labour Relations Boards

As administrative tribunals, LRBs derive their authority from the collective bargaining legislation they administer. These statutes not only impose rights and obligations on trade unions and employers, but also provide the structure and procedure for asserting these rights.

Although they generally report to the government through the Ministry of Labour, LRBs are regarded as having considerable autonomy from the ministry. As a rule, they are tripartite, composed of independent chairpersons, representatives of trade unions and representatives of employers, and their members are appointed for either a fixed term or at the pleasure of the government. LRBs have broad statutory powers to remedy violations of the labour relations legislation.

Prohibition of Strikes and Lockouts during the Term of a Collective Agreement

Section 1 (Definitions) of the *Labour Relations Code* defines a strike as follows:

> ... includes a cessation of work, a refusal to work or to continue to work by employees in combination or in concert or in accordance with a common understanding, or a slowdown or other concerted activity on the part of employees that is designed to or does restrict or limit production or services, but does not include
>
> (a) a cessation of work permitted under section 63 (3), or
>
> (b) a cessation, refusal, omission or act of an employee that occurs as the direct result of and for no other reason than picketing that is permitted by or under this Code, and "to strike" has a similar meaning.

Strikes, lockouts, and other labour disruptions are prohibited during the term of a collective agreement pursuant to Section 75, Notice of strike or lockout, and Section 58, Honouring of agreement, of the *Code*. Section 58 states:

> Every collective agreement must provide that there will be no strikes or lockouts so long as the agreement continues to operate and, if a collective agreement does not contain such a provision, it is deemed to contain the following provision:

> There must be no strikes or lockouts so long as this agreement continues to operate.

Possible Approaches to Dispute Resolution

When a dispute is preventing settlement of a grievance, a number of approaches to dispute resolution may be used, including:

- mediation-arbitration

- appointment of a *settlement officer*

- requests to the Collective Agreement Arbitration Bureau

- expedited arbitration

- *grievance arbitration*

Mediation-Arbitration

Under Section 105, Consensual mediation-arbitration, the parties can jointly request that the LRB appoint a mediator-arbitrator to work on an expedited basis. The mediator-arbitrator first attempts to mediate a settlement of the grievance between the parties. If this attempt is unsuccessful, the mediator-arbitrator will determine the grievance by expedited arbitration.

Appointment of a Settlement Officer

Under Section 87, Settlement officer, either party to a collective agreement can request the assistance of a settlement officer. When the steps of a grievance process prior to arbitration are completed, an LRB settlement officer meets with the parties to work towards settlement of the grievance.

Requests to the Collective Agreement Arbitration Bureau

Section 83 of the *Code*, Collective Agreement Arbitration Bureau, establishes an office of the LRB that administers arbitration provisions in the *Code.* The Collective Agreement Arbitration Bureau operates as part of the LRB and is made up of LRB employees. One of the functions of the bureau is to appoint settlement officers at the request of either party to a collective agreement under section 87, Settlement officer.

Another function of the bureau is to appoint arbitrators when the parties are unable or unwilling to agree on someone themselves pursuant to Section 86, Failure to appoint arbitration board. In these circumstances, one of the parties applies to the director of the bureau, who appoints an arbitrator with full authority to hear and decide the outcome of the grievance through arbitration.

The Collective Agreement Arbitration Bureau also administers the expedited arbitration provisions of the *Code* under Section 104, Expedited arbitration. The purpose of these provisions is to ensure that matters of urgency for one of the parties are dealt with and decided quickly.

Expedited Arbitration

As an *alternative dispute resolution* mechanism, after the parties have completed the steps of the grievance procedure in their collective agreement, and before a grievance is sent to conventional arbitration, either party can apply to the LRB with a request for resolution of the grievance by expedited arbitration pursuant to Section 104, Expedited arbitration, of the *Code*. The LRB appoints an arbitrator who has strict time limits for hearing and deciding on the grievance. If both parties agree, an LRB settlement officer can also help settle a grievance during the expedited process.

Given the compressed timelines of expedited arbitration, this approach is not recommended for complex interpretive matters

Grievance Arbitration

Because strikes and lockouts in pursuit of a demand or in response to workplace issues are prohibited, a process is required to deal with such matters during the period that the collective agreement is in force. Section 84, Requirement for arbitrations in collective agreement, establishes the requirement for a dispute resolution mechanism in the collective agreement to settle disputes that arise during the term of the agreement. Section 84 states:

> (1) Every collective agreement must contain a provision governing dismissal or discipline of an employee bound by the agreement, and that or another provision must require that the employer have a just and reasonable cause for dismissal or

discipline of an employee, but this section does not prohibit the parties to a collective agreement from including in it a different provision for employment of certain employees on a probationary basis.

(2) Every collective agreement must contain a provision for final and conclusive settlement without stoppage of work, by arbitration or another method agreed to by the parties, of all disputes between the persons bound by the agreement respecting its interpretation, application, operation or alleged violation, including a question as to whether a matter is arbitrable.

(3) If a collective agreement does not contain a provision referred to in subsections (1) and (4), the collective agreement is deemed to contain those of the following provisions it does not contain:

> (a) the employer must not dismiss or discipline an employee bound by this agreement except for just and reasonable cause;
>
> (b) if a difference arises between the parties relating to the dismissal or discipline of an employee, or to the interpretation, application, operation or alleged violation of this agreement, including a question as to whether a matter is arbitrable, either of the parties, without stoppage of work, may, after exhausting any grievance procedure established by this agreement, notify the other party in writing of its desire to submit the difference to arbitration, and the parties must agree on a single arbitrator, the arbitrator must hear and determine the difference and issue a decision, which is final and binding on the parties and any person affected by it.

Grievance arbitration is a process for settling disputes between the union and the employer during the period a collective agreement is in effect. Usually a grievance arises out of the discipline or discharge of an employee by the employer or from a disagreement over the interpretation of some part of the collective agreement. The grievance process involves attempts to resolve the difference between union and employer representatives. If the attempts fail, the parties appoint a neutral third party, an arbitrator or an arbitration board, to make a binding ruling.

Do the Parties Have to Accept an Arbitration Decision?

Yes. The decision of an arbitrator or arbitration board is final and conclusive, as provided for in the *Code* in Section 95, Effect of decision, and section 101, Decision final. Arbitration decisions can be filed in the Supreme Court and are enforceable as court orders in accordance with Section 102, Enforcement, which states:

(1) If a party or a person has failed or neglected to comply with the decision of an arbitration board, a party or person affected by the decision may, after the expiration of 14 days from the date of the release of the decision or the date provided in the decision for compliance, whichever is later, file in the Supreme Court registry a copy of the decision in the prescribed form.

(2) A decision filed under subsection (1) must be entered as if it were a decision of the court, and on being entered is deemed, for all purposes except an appeal from it, to be an order of the Supreme Court and enforceable as an order of the court.

Appeals of arbitration decisions can be made to the LRB under Section 99, Appeal jurisdiction of Labour Relations Board, on one of two narrow grounds: one of the parties did not have a fair hearing or the decision is inconsistent with the principles of the *Code*.

Appeals can also be made through the Court of Appeal on questions of general law pursuant to Section 100, Appeal jurisdiction of Court of Appeal.

Importantly, the appeal of an arbitration decision has to be grounded in the requirements and jurisdiction of Section 99, Appeal jurisdiction of Labour Relations Board, and Section 100, Appeal jurisdiction of Court of Appeal. The union's or the employer's dislike of the decision or dissatisfaction with the outcome are insufficient grounds for appeal.

Duty of Fair Representation

Labour legislation also establishes a duty for unions that represent employees, referred to as the duty of fair representation.

The LRB regulates union conduct under Section 12, Duty of fair representation. The duty of fair representation requires a union to represent all employees in the bargaining unit, whether or not they are union members, in a manner that is not arbitrary, discriminatory, or in bad faith.

Employers should be aware of the union's obligations under duty of fair representation. These obligations provide insight into why a union pursues a particular dispute through to arbitration.

Shop Stewards and Employees

When the Labour Relations Board grants a union certification through the certification process established by the *Labour Relations Code,* the union becomes the sole and exclusive bargaining agent for the group of employees designated in the LRB certificate. The union has exclusive authority to bargain on the employees' behalf and bind them to a collective agreement. In fact, the collective agreement is binding on the union, the employer, and every employee in the bargaining unit.

Typically, the group of employees elects an employee to act as the shop steward and to be a liaison between the members, the union, and representatives of the employer.

A shop steward is not an ordinary union member or employee. The steward can be seen as the cornerstone of the union and the union's liaison at the workplace. In the eyes of the members, the shop steward is the union. The success or failure of implementing the terms of the collective agreement rests with the shop steward.

The moment that union members or employees are recognized as shop stewards, they take on official duties that set them apart. Shop stewards are the union's leader at the workplace. Their job is to protect employees' rights. Shop stewards are also responsible for investigating, processing, and settling grievances, and for watching for violations of labour laws, working conditions, and the collective agreement.

Shop stewards may expect the right to the following:

- Recognition by the employer.

- Time off from their regular duties to investigate, process and settle grievances. (The collective agreement usually provides for this time off.)

- The union's protection in the event of what they believe to be victimization or attacks by the employer because of their role as shop steward.

The Shop Steward and the Duty of Fair Representation

With its designation as the exclusive bargaining agent for all employees in the bargaining unit, the union is obliged to represent the interests of these employees fairly, impartially, and without discrimination.

The duty of fair representation arises whenever employees claim they have a grievance. Because the union is the sole and exclusive bargaining agent for all employees in the bargaining unit, it has control over the processing of a grievance after the employee or the union files it.

Generally, it is not difficult for a shop steward to deal with individual grievances concerning matters that are quantifiable and specific to an individual, such as back pay, vacation entitlement, shift premiums, and pension rights. However, when the grievance involves such issues as the posting and filling of vacant positions, layoff and recall, promotion, transfer, and demotion, special attention must be given to the rights of other employees who may be directly or indirectly affected by the outcome of the grievance.[142]

Did the Union Meet Its Duty of Fair Representation?

To decide whether a union acted fairly in deciding not to process a grievance to arbitration, the LRB may seek answers to such questions as:

Questions About the Process

- Did the union thoroughly investigate the employee's grievance?

- Did the union obtain a legal opinion about the merits of the grievance?

- Did the grievance appear valid?

- Did the union attempt to settle the grievance satisfactorily?

- Did the union consult the employee about settlement of the grievance?

- What internal union appeal processes, if any, were followed?

Questions About Conduct

- Was the union candid and communicative with the employee throughout the process?

- Was the employee straightforward and cooperative with the union?

- Did the union indicate hostility towards the employee?

Questions About Related Issues

- How were other employees in the bargaining unit affected by the outcome of the employee's grievance, and was this effect considered?

- How much experience did the union officials involved in the decision have?

- To what extent would proceeding to arbitration affect the overall bargaining objectives of the union?

---

142   The requirement to notify the employee potentially affected by the outcome of the grievance is referred to as the Hoogendoorn Rule, which is based on *Hoogendoorn v Greening Metal Products and Screening Equipment Co*, (1967) 1 O.R 712, 62 D.L.R. (2d) 167,67 C.L.L.C. 14,017 (C.A.).

Duty of Fair Representation: Frequently Asked Questions

Does an employee have an absolute right to have a grievance taken to arbitration?

A union has considerable leeway in deciding whether to take a grievance to arbitration. In its decision, the union will take into account a wide variety of factors, such as the likelihood of the grievance succeeding at arbitration, the effect of the outcome on the rest of the bargaining unit, and the union's financial position.

Obviously, the grievor will have a direct interest in proceeding to arbitration, unless a favourable settlement can be reached earlier. However, other bargaining unit members may have concerns about the award's impact on other employees, as well as about the substantial costs entailed in going to arbitration. Bargaining units are made up of many individuals with varied and often-competing interests.

Before making a decision that affects an employee, the union must focus its attention on the employee's situation and consider the employee's interests in light of the interests of the other employees in the bargaining unit. The union must arrive at its decision through a fair process, taking account of valid labour relations considerations.

When critical job interests are at stake, the union must have particularly sound reasons if it decides not to proceed to arbitration.

Can an employee proceed to arbitration without the approval of the union?

Unless provided for in the collective agreement, an employee cannot go to arbitration without the union's approval. The union is a party to the collective agreement and has carriage of the grievance and final say over access to arbitration.

Is an employee's consent required when the grievance is settled?

The right of a union to settle a grievance on behalf of an employee arises from its status as a party to the collective agreement and its authority to administer the grievance and arbitration provisions. This power also reflects that the parties to the collective agreement—that is, the employer and the union—have a continuing relationship that will suffer if the union brings forward unworthy claims or adheres to unrealistic positions.

Generally, grievors are not required to consent to a settlement, but as a matter of practice the union should advise grievors of the terms of a proposed settlement and permit them to give their views on it. However, a union can override an employee's position for valid labour relations reasons—for example, if it considers that the proposal is as good as could be obtained at arbitration or that the employee is being unreasonable.

What is the Hoogendoorn Rule?

In some cases, the outcome of a grievance or arbitration affects more than one employee. In discharging its duty of fair representation, a union must consider not only the grievor, but also other employees who may be affected.

In what has become known as the Hoogendoorn Rule, an employee's (Employee B) status may be affected by the outcome of an arbitration, because in representing another employee (Employee A), the union is taking a position adverse to Employee B's interests. In such a situation, Employee B is entitled to notice and an opportunity to participate in the hearing. The union has the responsibility to provide such notice.[143]

Upon Reflection: A Union's Perspective on Grievances and Their Members

As an employer, understanding the challenges faced by union representatives provides insight into why matters are handled in the way that they are. The BC Teachers' Federation provides the following insight that gives employers a sense of how a union views its responsibilities.[144]

Grievor's Syndrome

Dealing with individual teachers who have grievances very often involves sensitivity to the personal feelings that are involved. This is sometimes acute in personnel cases where the teacher is accused of wrong doing or lack of competence. The American Federation of Teachers (AFT) has described this as "grievor's syndrome":

> *When a grievance occurs, it involves the disruption of established relationships and initiates relationships between additional persons. Both the distortion of existing personal relationships and the start or intensification of other relationships have crucial psychological dimensions which must be taken into account by the union representative in order to do effective contract enforcement work.*

> *The first psychological dimension for which the grievance representative must be prepared emerges during the initial contact with the fellow employee who has the complaint. It is essential that you be prepared for "grievor's syndrome." The grievor feels that he/she has been unfairly harmed and injured. Only the most stoic among us can maintain our equanimity when we believe that we have been wrongfully hurt. Thus, it is important that the union representative be ready for the fact that the grievor may be agitated, angry, irrational and vengeful.*

143   *The Hoogendoorn Rule* is based on *Hoogendoorn v Greening Metal Products and Screening Equipment Co* (1967) 1 O.R 712, 62 D.L.R. (2d) 167, 67 C.L.L.C. 14,017 (C.A.).

144   "BC Teachers' Federation Grievances Backgrounder Collective Agreement Administration and Enforcement" (2017). https://bctf.ca. Emphasis added.

The first task of the grievance representative will be to calm the grievor and convince the employee who has a complaint that the union will do all that it legitimately can to seek a resolution of the problem.

One of the most difficult points in grievance work is informing a co-worker that her/his complaint does not constitute a grievance under the collective bargaining agreement. The grievor's initial response may well be "the union is selling me out." Therefore, it is wise that if you believe that a complaint is not grievable, that, first you check with either the bargaining chairperson or the chairperson of the grievance committee for a concurring opinion, and then give a clear and comprehensive explanation to the co-worker who has the complaint. In these situations, it is important to inform the grievor of established appeal procedures which may be available.

During the course of processing a grievance, there are two forms of "grievor's syndrome" which are likely to manifest themselves. The first is a repetition of the anger that usually accompanies the initial complaint. The grievor may have an exaggerated sense of the importance of the case and often a desire to use the grievance procedure to get even with the supervisor. The second type of behaviour will be a desire to give up on the grievance out of fear of being harassed or punished in some other manner by the supervisor.

The solution to both types of behaviour is the same. The grievance representative must keep the grievor involved in each step of the process, explaining what is being done and that it is being done in a clear and supportive fashion. The grievor who is kept informed is less likely to indulge in behaviour that will be prejudicial to a successful resolution.

If the decision, after assessment and discussion, is to proceed with a grievance, the remainder of the process in the Provincial Collective Agreement, Article A.6 should be followed step-by-step.

In acting on the grievor's behalf, you are in an institutional role, not a personal one. You are speaking for the local. The comments of the AFT on this subject are well worth repeating:

The second crucial psychological dimension of grievance work involves what can be thought of as the "psychology of power." This involves the complexity of relationships which develop between the union grievance representative and the various management personnel who will become involved in the processing and resolution of the grievance. The first point to keep in mind when doing grievance work is that you, as the representative of the union, are the legal equal of the management person who is involved in the dispute at hand. Although this person may be your supervisor (administrator, superintendent, etc.) in your regular work situation, when you are acting in your role as grievance representative you are representing the union as one party to a legally binding contractual relationship. Your authority and responsibility is to the union, your co-workers, and the maintenance of the integrity of the negotiated agreement.

In some cases, when a teacher comes to you with a problem, it may be that a simple phone call–without any reference to the grievance procedure as such, can "get it straightened out." Don't neglect that very informal first approach if there is that chance, because it gives the employer the opportunity painlessly to correct the matter before it gets defensive and positions harden.

Remember that the point of the grievance procedure exercise is to get a useful resolution to the teacher's problem–not simply to march through the steps to get to an arbitration. Thus the possibility of informal resolution by some practical, acceptable arrangement should be explored at every opportunity–and the opportunities in the formal process should be taken seriously.

Part Five: Interactions with Purpose – Skills, Techniques, and Considerations

Conversations at work serve many purposes. While most conversations are casual and informal—discussing the work day or talking about progress on a project—others may be or transition to be quite formal and involve material issues or potentially contentious subjects.

These types of interactions can be valuable opportunities to deepen relationships with employees and resolve issues. Knowing how to have successful work-oriented interactions and conduct interviews is an important skill to develop.

How you approach difficult employer–employee interactions is illustrative of your commitment to Cardinal Rule #4 that "every employee must be accorded respect, understanding, courteous consideration, and fair treatment at all times."

Part Five explores workplace interactions from two perspectives. The first looks at how to have focussed, purposeful workplace interactions, including questioning best practices and optimal approaches to listening. The second provides specific skills and techniques for conducting interactions for specific purposes, focussing on workplace incidents such as employee misconduct.

In order for any possible conversation, discussion, or debate to occur, one must understand the rules of communication. For example, consider a discourse. Discourse is the ability to have a conversation, not a one-sided soliloquy but an engagement of two or more people in the exchange of ideas, information, opinions, and/or positions.[145] Having effective discourse involves listening and understanding other people's ideas and thoughts.

Knowing the nature of what you are going to talk about and in what context is important. As a place to start, consider—given the subject—what are you about to enter?

Now, knowing this, how should you prepare?

---

145   Susan Herbst, *Civility, Civic Discourse, and Civic Engagement: Inextricably Interwoven,* Journal of Higher Education Outreach and Engagement, (Athens, GA, University of Georgia, 2014) 7–8.

Conversation: an informal interchange of thoughts and information by spoken words.

Debate: a discussion or period of public questioning where there are opposing sides.

Dialogue: a synergistic activity through which the exchange of ideas yields knowledge not previously held by participants.

Discourse: as described above and in Part Two: *Conflict and Work*.

Discussion: a process of discussing, arguing, commenting on, or conversing about a topic.

Will this interaction likely transition to a negotiation?

Chapter 19: Purposeful Workplace Interactions

Constructive Interactions Framework

Having constructive, purposeful workplace interactions is as much about attitude as approach. The Constructive Interactions Framework codifies a purposeful approach and consists of the following steps:

- preparation

- setting the stage

- creating an agenda

- exploring issues and interests

- building agreement

Preparation

The goal of this phase is to develop and adopt an informed, reasoned, and systematic approach to the matters at issue.

Consider the following:

- What gives rise to this conversation? Why, and why now?

- What is the likely nature of the interaction?

  O contentious and/or high-conflict situation,

  O identifying, distributing something of value,

  O seeking a mutually acceptable solution to what is recognized as a shared problem, or

  O attempting to repair a damaged, conflicted relationship.

The first interaction is identified with performative discourse, the second with distributive discourse, the third with integrative discourse, and the fourth with transformative discourse. Different styles of communication are associated with each type, as set out in Part Two: *Conflict and Work*.

- For what purpose and to what end? Is the goal to gather information, investigate misconduct, or solve a problem and create alignment?

- Build the *people architecture* of the matter at issue: who is at the centre, who reports to whom, who is responsible for what, and who are the influencers, observers, and decision makers?

- What is the situation, the matter(s) at issue as you currently understand them?

   O   Chronology of events

   O   Records; documents etc.

- Review the communication pitfalls and perspectives described later in this section.

- Be prepared to differentiate between issues, positions, and interests: yours and theirs.

- Given the nature of the interaction and the purpose:

   O   Review the concept of the narrative in Part Two: *Conflict and Work* and remember that your objective is to transform the narration of stories into genuine conversation and dialogue. That transformation begins with listening and understanding.

   O   Consider whether this situation has integrative potential?

- What else do you need to know? Prepare your questioning strategy.

Setting the stage

The goal is to create a productive and constructive environment.

- Jointly establish the need for discussion and clarify issues

- Set the context for the conversation—neutral broad purpose

- Consistent with the purpose, state your intention to understand and resolve the matters at issue

- Describe your role in helping to resolve the issues

- Establish processes (guidelines, structure, and timeline), discuss confidentiality

Creating an Agenda: Subjects of Conversation

> The primary concern is the creation of an agenda listing the issues that need to be discussed and reconciled.

- Create a joint list of issues answering the question, "What would we like to resolve/achieve?"

- Identify and describe the issues

- Frame issues in a collaborative/constructive, neutral, and resolvable way

- Determine the issue to start with, note other issues and prioritize them accordingly

- At a personal level, and as you prepare for the next stage, differentiate between positions, issues and interests.

Exploring Issues and Interests and Identifying What's Important

> The goal is to give or receive information to understand each other's perspective, as well as individual and common interests

- Exchange and clarify relevant facts and figures

- Explore interests related to issues

- Identify and build on common interests

- Clarify different and competing interests

- Clarify assumptions, discuss intent and reflect

- Reframe and summarize interests

Building Agreement

> The goal is to build an informed, defensible agreement or understanding given what gave rise to the meeting. The goal for an investigative meeting is different from one seeking to solve a problem and create alignment.

For example, when seeking to solve a problem, decide on matters that meet interests to the greatest degree possible and that are consistent with what you and your constituents believe constitutes a good agreement (as outlined in Part Two: *Conflict and Work*, one that is fair, efficient, wise, and stable).

- Generate options based on both parties' interests

- Reality-test your options against interests, and apply objective criteria

- Package acceptable options into a potential agreement

- Consider your alternatives first, best and worst. Internally compare your potential agreement to your best alternatives (BATNA) and worst alternatives (WATNA)

- Proceed to finalize your agreement if it is better compared to your BATNA

- Specify terms of the agreement (who, what, where, when, and how), detail implementation processes and timelines, and follow up

- Discuss procedures in the event of agreement breakdown

- Mutually reflect on the processes and outcomes

- If no resolution is reached, discuss alternatives; be specific on next steps (including timelines), and convert understanding to writing

Learn from results. Does this constitute a good agreement? What was done to achieve those results? Critically analyze and evaluate the people, processes, procedures and strategies you employed.

Communication Pitfalls and Perspectives

When you are dealing with a workplace matter, avoid the following noise or communication pitfalls:

- **Weak, hesitant, throw-away language:** The more hesitant language you use— such as "isn't it," "like," "you know," "um mm," "I mean," "okay," and "right?"— the less likely people are to believe what you are saying or have confidence in you. Use clear, thoughtful, and purposeful language.

- **Snap judgement:** The tendency to form a first impression of others without adequate information or accept a narrative without question. Make every attempt to keep an open mind about people and situations and not draw final conclusions before you have all the facts. Develop strategies of inquiry to deconstruct a narrative as the basis to further understanding. Nobody can avoid making judgements, but you can avoid acting on premature judgements.

- **Prejudice:** A bias resulting from teachings, experience, or background when knowledge and information are inadequate or insufficient. Use solid, specific information to evaluate situations and people, and avoid generalized assumptions.

- **Projection:** A tendency to attribute to others some of your faults and motives. When communicating, avoid clouding your perceptions by projecting your values onto someone else's situation. Remember, when you talk about another person, others often learn more about you than about that other person.

- **Preoccupation:** When your mind is so cluttered with concerns, problems, and issues unrelated to the conversation, you cannot communicate properly. Being sensitive to the other person's feelings and striving to actively listen are two of the cornerstones of effective communication.

- **Sloppy observation:** Sometimes people hear but do not listen, or they see but do not observe. When talking with someone, be as aware as possible of the other person's world—even imagine living in it if you can. Expand your awareness of others by observing accurately and listening actively, not passively.

- **Predisposition:** A tendency to draw conclusions before having the facts. Often, people see only what they want to see and hear only what they want to hear. Predispositions cause them to ignore facts that do not support their beliefs and to bend other facts so they do. Suspend your judgements so that the information you receive will not be tainted by your predispositions.

- **Failure to fully recognize the other party:** Individuals may represent others or themselves. It is essential to appreciate that reality. For example, in unionized workplaces, the union and the employer have legitimate roles to play, arising from the collective agreement between them. Institutional roles must be understood, recognized, and respected.

- **Individuals also have interests.** All people have their concerns, values, hopes, aspirations, and problems. If you do not fully recognize this, you will not be able to adequately understand or be fully aware of the other person's perspective—resulting in ineffective communication and a gap in mutual understanding.

Remember, You Are Your Behaviour[146]

Your behaviour is the only part of you that other people can observe. As far as others are concerned, you are your behaviour.

As a result, your behaviour influences others' perceptions of you (whether they like or dislike you, or trust or mistrust you) and others' reactions to you (how they behave towards you).

In managing a process that can be emotionally charged, consider the following four principles:

1. **To influence others more effectively, you must first change your perception of them.**

   When you meet someone, you instantly form an opinion of that person, commonly referred to as your first impression. Your biased, subjective, and personal perceptions of people automatically program how you seek to influence them, because perceptions determine how you feel, how you communicate and how you behave. It follows that if you do not first change your perception of the person you want to influence, trying harder will only reinforce your preconceived feelings, communication, and behaviour.

2. **People respond to their perceptions in spite of reality.**

   To speak to be understood, be sensitive to the perceptions of the person you want to influence. People filter others' communication through their own one-sided, limited, and preconceived perceptions. To influence others, listen to understand their perspective or point of view. You do not have to agree or disagree with, or like or dislike their perspective. Simply attempt to understand it. This listening for understanding suspends judgement on your part and enables you, in turn, to speak to be understood.

3. **How you say something influences people more than what you say.**

   Your tone of voice, as well as actions like raising your eyebrows, rolling your eyes, and shrugging your shoulders, can speak volumes more than your actual words.

4. **How well you communicate determines how much influence you have.**

146   These statements are adapted from R.L. Kirkham, *Pearls of Wisdom for Business and Life* (Salt Lake City, UT: American Training Alliance, 1994).

Personally and professionally, your relationships with others determine your quality of life. How well you communicate determines how well you interrelate with others and how much influence you have. People do not care how smart you are if they cannot benefit from your intelligence. Human beings do not lack for great ideas; they lack for great ideas that are understood and put to use. Therefore, how well you communicate your ideas determines how well others understand and use them.

Chapter 20: Techniques for Conducting Interactions

Effective Questioning

Physician and Nobel Lauriat Albert Einstein (1879–1955) is reported to have said,[147] "If I had an hour to solve a problem and my life depended on the solution, I would spend the first fifty-five minutes determining the proper question to ask, for once I know the proper question, I could solve the problem in less than five minutes."

Proper questions help facilitate constructive interactions.

The Public Conversations Project—the Cambridge, Massachusetts group that helps create constructive dialogue on divisive public issues—proposes the following guidelines for developing questions:

- Is this question relevant to the real life and real work of the people who will be exploring it?

- Is this a genuine question—a question to which I/we really don't know the answer?

- What "work" do I want this question to do? That is, what kind of conversation, meanings and feelings do I imagine this question will evoke in those who will be exploring it?

- Is this question likely to invite fresh thinking or feeling? Is it familiar enough to be recognizable and relevant—and different enough to call forward a new response?

- What assumptions or beliefs are embedded in the way this question is constructed?

- Is this question likely to generate hope, imagination, engagement, creative action, and new possibilities, or is it likely to increase a focus on past problems and obstacles?

- Does this question leave room for new and different questions to be raised as the initial question is explored?

---

147   A. M. Elijah, "Can I Learn to Invent?" *Invention Intelligence* 8, No. 8, (August 1973). Einstein died in 1955, and by 1973 a version of the saying had been assigned to him in the article. No supporting data for the attribution was given.

A powerful, well-crafted question:[148]

- is appropriate to its intended purpose

- generates curiosity in the listener

- stimulates reflective conversation

- is thought-provoking

- surfaces underlying assumptions

- invites creativity and new possibilities

- generates energy and forward movement

- channels attention and focusses inquiry

- stays with participants

- touches a deep meaning

- identifies and or/clarifies the matters at issue

- reveals interests

- evokes more questions

Well-crafted questions have the capacity to spread beyond the place where they were posed into larger networks of conversation throughout an organization or a community. Powerful questions that travel well are often the key to large-scale change.

Questions need to be designed to help the other person reach a conclusion, or to provide information and insights helpful to a discussion.

What is the purpose of your inquiry and how should you frame your question? Consider the following suggestions.

148   Adapted from the *Faculty Center: Development, Assessment and Research* (Honolulu, HI: Chaminade University of Honolulu, 2015).

Table 14: Suggestions for Effective Questioning

Plan your questions	Before your meeting, outline your information goals and a sequence of related questions to help you follow the conversation.
Know your purpose	Every question you ask should help you gather either facts or an opinion. Know your goal: to gather information, investigate misconduct, or solve a problem and create alignment. Know which kind of information you need and frame your questions accordingly. (See the next section for an analysis of question types)
Open a conversation	Unlike simple yes-or-no questions, open-ended questions invite the respondent to talk—and enable you to gather much more information. "What do you like best about this organization?" is likely to generate more valuable information than, "Do you like this organization?" Another tactic is to ask a question in the declarative format—"Tell me about that." People who won't answer questions sometimes respond better to a direct order.
Speak your listener's language	Relate questions to the listener's experience and use words and phrases that your listener understands. Avoid industry or sector jargon when you're interacting with someone outside your industry. If someone doesn't seem to understand what you're asking, try rephrasing.
Use neutral, non-specific outcome engendering wording	Avoid leading people to an answer you are seeking. Answers should be authentic to be of value. Leading questions—such as, "How'd you like the terrific amenities at that hotel?"—appear to seek a positive response and are not particularly productive. Because the question expresses a glowing opinion of the venue, the other person isn't likely to say anything negative about it, even if they didn't like the hotel. A neutral question that elicits accurate information or an honest opinion—such as, "How did you like it?"—is more constructive.
Follow general questions with specific ones	Build a hierarchy of questions that begins with the big picture and gradually drills down into specifics with follow-up questions.
Ask about one matter at a time	To get more complete answers, craft short questions, each of which covers a single point. If you really want to know two different things, ask two different questions.
Ask only essential questions	If you don't really care about the information that's likely to come, don't ask the question. Respect the other person's time and attention.
Don't interrupt	Listen to the full answer to your question. The art of good questioning lies in truly wanting the information that would be in the answer.
Transition naturally	Use something in the answer to frame your next question. Even if this takes you off your planned path for a while, it shows that you're listening, not just following a script, and it ensures that the conversation flows naturally.

Types of Questions

There are a range of question types that can be used for different purposes. In general, questions can be classified by the amount of information they seek to elicit. Some questions provide structure, others direct flow, and some help us to reach closure. Question types include:

- open-ended questions

- leading questions

- deflective questions

- closed questions

Questions are not neutral. Questions that are really statements of assumptions put in the form of a question can be aggressive, which often leads to hostility.

Asking leading questions when you are seeking information closes off options, whereas asking open questions when you are intending to move a person towards the conclusion you want them to reach can be counterproductive.

Hypothetical, reflective, and leading questions help generate ideas, motivate people, and develop insights. Other question sets are designed to gather information.

To be effective, you need to know the objectives of the questions you are asking and then design the questions to support the objective, which could be information gathering, investigating an employee workplace incident, or trying to solve problems and create alignment.

Open-ended questions gather information and facts. For example, "What are your concerns and worries about this situation?" Open-ended questions allow the interviewee to select either the subject matter for discussion, or at least the information related to the general subject that the interviewee believes is pertinent and relevant. Open questions have the following characteristics, including:

- ask the respondent to think and reflect

- give you opinions and feelings

- hand control of the conversation to the respondent

Variants of open-ended questions include:

- Recall and process questions require something to be remembered or recalled and process questions require some deeper thought and/or analysis.

- Probing questions help you gain additional detail; e.g., "Can you explain why that matters?"

- Hypothetical questions suggest an approach or introduce new ideas. An example might be, "If you could get additional funding or resources, how might that help?"

- Reflective questions check understanding, such as, "Can you tell me how you would prioritize the most critical areas for attention first and make sure that everyone knew what was most important?"

Leading questions help a person reach a conclusion or have an idea that you feel will be beneficial; a few well-planned questions can very often lead the person towards the idea and instead of responding to your request, they have their idea of how to help you be more successful. A leading question, usually subtly, points the respondent's answer in a certain direction.

Leading questions are structured to elicit information you as the interviewer believe is pertinent and relevant. These questions make a statement, setting out the relevant information, suggest that the interviewee should affirm that the statement is valid, and suggest what the answer should be. Variants of leading questions include:

- Funnelling questions are a form of leading question that essentially funnels the respondent's answers, with the questions becoming more (or less) restrictive at each step. The funnel starts very wide, with open questions, to consider a broad range of possibilities, and it then uses probing and hypothetical questions to fill in missing information, increase understanding, and suggest additional ways of thinking about the situation.

  Finally, the question funnel focusses things down by using reflective questions to ensure that all the main issues have been considered. It ends with closing questions to produce an agreed way forward.

- Narrow questions not only select the general subject matter, but also choose which aspect of the subject matter should be discussed. For example, "When Mr. X entered, where were you standing?" This question limits the subject matter to the time of the Mr. X's entry and restricts the response to the activity of the interviewee and to a particular kind of activity, standing.

Deflective questions are hybrids of open and leading questions designed to defuse an aggressive or defiant situation by redirecting the force of the other person's attack instead of facing it head-on. Attacks are synonymous with dissatisfaction or resistance and prevent you from moving forward. Dealing with a strong objection by responding with similar force creates conflict. Deflective questions help to transform the negative situation into a collaborative problem-solving occasion. Some examples include:

- Dissatisfaction: "I'm not happy with this project!"

    O   Response: "What specifically?"

- Refusal to take an action: "I have major concerns. I won't do it!"

    O   Response: "How can we address your concerns?"

- Resistance: "I disagree with the approach!"

    O   Response: "If you were to do it, what would be your approach?"

Closed or yes/no questions bring agreement, commitment, and conclusion. Yes or no questions are constructed so that the interviewee can respond with a simple, dichotomous yes or no. Yes or no questions are similar to leading questions because they severely restrict the range of response. However, they do not suggest the answer as a leading question does. Closed questions:

give you facts

are easy and quick to answer

keep control of the conversation with the questioner

Questions for Information Gathering

To solve a problem, you must inquire and become informed. Consider the following guidelines. What is the purpose of your inquiry and how should you frame your question?

Table 15: Purpose and Question Framing

Purpose	Questions
Identify an issue	• What seems to be the trouble? • What do you make of _____? • How do you feel about _____? • What concerns you the most about _____? • What seems to be the problem? (not, in what may be interpreted as more accusatory: "Why did this go wrong?") • What seems to be your main obstacle? • What is holding you back from _____? • What do you think about doing ( ) this way?
Elicit additional information	• What do you mean by _____? • Tell me more about _____ • What else? • What other ways did you try so far? • What will you/we have to do to get the job done?
Outcome-focussed **To help resolve a conflict once the issues are understood**	• How do you want _____ to turn out? • What do you want? Or what is your desired outcome? • What benefits would you like to get out of X? • What do you propose? • What is your plan? • If you do this, how will it affect _____? • What else do you/we need to consider?
Elicit action	• What will you do? • When will you do it? • How will I know you did it? • What are your next steps?
Define a risk, issue or problem	• What is the uncertainty? • How uncertain is it? • Why does it matter? • How much does it matter

Questions to Investigate an Employee Workplace Incident

Investigative questioning is a specialized form of inquiry.[149] Remember, when an incident occurs, one that may be misconduct, the employer must determine whether the behaviour is culpable or non-culpable in order to determine the appropriate response and to make a fact-based, evidence-informed decision.

This necessitates a series of planned, focussed interviews.

Conducting workplace investigations involves gathering firsthand information from employees who are involved or are witnesses to the subject of the investigation. Remember people in conflict create, structure, and perform conflict-problem narratives as a way of organizing the events and characters involved in an incident or circumstance. The purpose of the investigative interview is to reconcile the competing narratives and assemble a complete fact base to inform your decisions. Consider the following five foundation questions.

Table 16: The Five Foundation Questions

Question	Purpose
In your own words, what happened?	This question takes into account both what was witnessed and what was perceived. An overview of the incident from the mind of the person interviewed can be helpful to understanding future answers.
Where and when did this take place?	Determining the exact timing and location is important to constructing a chronology of events. This can also lead to other sources for gathering information.
What did you personally witness?	This drills down from the first question and tries to separate perception from reality. Depending on the answer, varying degrees of follow-up questions should be asked to construct a complete picture of the occurrence
Who else was present?	Witness recollections that can be corroborated by multiple parties are much more reliable to base a case on than the recollections of a single witness.
What was your response or what actions have you taken since the incident?	It is human nature to react spontaneously when offended or in a place where a defence feels necessary. While responses or reactions may or may not exacerbate a situation already being investigated, any occurrence must be documented. This can mean the difference between termination and other disciplinary actions.

---

149   This section draws in part from the work of K. Haddigan, *Conflict Resolution* (JIBC, 1999) and H.J. Finlayson, G. Johnson, and R. Dahsi, *Productive Workplace Conversations* session workbooks (Vancouver, BC: BCPSEA, 2008).

Consistency of Questioning: Maintain consistency during investigative interviews. Ask each witness the same questions. If a follow up with one witness leads down an unexpected trail, it's appropriate and necessary to go back to other witnesses to ask those same types of follow-up questions.

To protect the integrity of the investigation, ask open-ended instead of leading questions. And always consider the dignity of all involved—this can never be overstated for its importance to maintaining healthy workplace relations.

To that end, follow the following guidelines for a successful interview:

- Remember the purpose and goal of the interview, stay focussed, and have a plan.

- Focus on the primary goal: to hear the individual's side of the story and obtain a clear understanding of what happened.

- Use an appropriate question strategy.

- Do not dominate the discussion: allow the interviewee to speak.

- Listen and observe: body language can give you insights into the interviewee.

- Caucus or take a break if necessary.

- Clarify, but only when appropriate.

- Allow the union representative to speak (as applicable in the context).

When conducting an interview, avoid:

- Interrogating or asking leading questions. You are not conducting an interrogation, but are facilitating a discussion to find out what happened.

- Ever denying a participant in the interview the opportunity to speak.

- Letting your emotions take control.

- Evaluating or judging the interviewee or the situation. Remember, the purpose is to gather information that will form the basis of a decision at some point in the future; the moment you start evaluating or judging the situation, you stop listening and learning from the interview.

Questioning to Solve Problems and Create Alignment:

Questioning can be a powerful technique to help solve problems and build consensus on a course of action.

The starting point is always to ask open questions to frame the problem. The third story technique—the one an impartial or neutral observer, such as a mediator, would tell, a version of events both sides can agree on—is particularly helpful. Once the underlying reasons are agreed upon, the questioning can progress towards confirming the agreed solution or the requirements and capabilities to be developed.

When working to solve a problem or create an alignment of efforts, skeptics can emerge. Skeptics ask a lot of questions and the right type of skeptic can be very useful, especially during the planning phase, where they help teams develop a strong plan and anticipate problems by challenging commonly held beliefs. But beware; there are two types of skeptic, loyal and negative.

- **Loyal skeptic:** Asks the questions others avoid and forces debate until problems are resolved. Their focus is on scrutinizing everything to develop a robust understanding that will succeed and once satisfied, they will support the outcome they have helped create as they work towards success.

- **Negative skeptic:** Quick to identify the problems with proposed options. Often fast to pinpoint the shortcomings of a course of action but unable or unwilling to provide alternatives. Negative skeptics criticize everything, revisit previous decisions, and continuously make dire predictions. If left unchecked, this negative influence will demoralize the project team, slow progress, and eventually derail the project. Negative skeptics are driven by personal power, fault finding, and finger pointing.

Skeptics are useful and should be allowed to test the scenario during planning. It's better to deal with the hard questions before committing to a suboptimal course of action. This is a valuable contribution to the long-term success of the work and should be actively encouraged at the right time. But the questioning needs to be positive and rooted in active listening. The negative skeptics and their stories of failure and pessimism need to be removed from any position of influence as quickly as possible.

What to Expect in Response

Just as there are many questions and question types, so too there are many possible responses. Part of your questioning strategy includes reflecting on how questions may be answered and how best to react. The types of responses include:

- **A direct, complete, and honest response:** This is what a questioner would usually want to achieve by asking their question.

- **A lie:** The respondent may lie in response to a question. The questioner may be able to pick up on a lie based on plausibility of the answer, but also on the nonverbal communication that was used immediately before, during, and after the answer is given.

- **Out of context answer:** The respondent may say something that is totally unconnected or irrelevant to the question or attempt to change the topic. It may be appropriate to re-word a question in these cases.

- **Partially answering:** People can often be selective about which questions or parts of questions they wish to answer. This response necessitates narrowing further questions or funnelling.

- **Avoiding the answer:** When asked a difficult question that probably has an answer that would be negative to the interviewee, avoidance can be a useful tactic. Answering a question with a question or trying to draw attention to some positive aspect of the topic are methods of avoidance.

- **Stalling:** Although similar to avoiding answering a question, stalling can be used when more time is needed to formulate an acceptable answer. One way to do this is to answer the question with another question.

- **Distortion:** People can give distorted answers to questions based on their perceptions of social norms, stereotypes, and other forms of bias. Their answers will be consistent with what has become their narrative. Different from lying, respondents may not realize their answers are influenced by bias or they exaggerate in some way to come across as more normal or successful.

- **Refusal:** The respondent may simply refuse to answer, either by remaining silent or by saying, "I am not answering."

Listening and Responding

Listening is an active process in which a conscious decision is made to listen to and understand the messages of the speaker. It is a skill that can be practiced and learned. Your goal as a listener is to fully understand the other person's experience and point of view.

Active listening is defined as a communication technique that requires that the listener fully concentrate, understand, respond, and then remember what is being said. As the name suggests, active listening involves fully focussing on what is being said rather than just passively hearing the message of the speaker. It involves listening with all senses. As well as giving full attention to the speaker, it is important that the active listener is also "seen" to be listening—otherwise the speaker may conclude that what they are talking about is uninteresting to the listener.

Interest can be conveyed to the speaker by using the transformative discourse tips outlined in Part Two: *Conflict and Work,* specifically attending, inviting, confirming, and summarizing behaviours. By adopting these suggestions, the person in the conversation will usually feel more at ease and therefore communicate more easily, openly and honestly.

Some common mistakes made by people who think they are actively listening, but really aren't, include:

- **Cursory listening:** just going through the motions but the listener is either multi-tasking or not really interested in what's being said.

- **Shallow listening:** the listener believes they already know what the speaker is leading to and already knows the answer or what they are going to say next. This type of listening is often underpinned by arrogance and the listener fails to hear what is actually being said.

- **Listening to respond:** where the listener spends their listening time focussing on how to formulate a response to what is being said, rather than listening to understand fully.

Active listening—the communication technique that requires that the listener fully concentrate, understand, respond, and then remember what is being said—requires a number of core elements.

Table 17: Essential Elements of Active Listening

Preparation	Be an informed listener. Build your background knowledge of the subject before listening; have a specific purpose for listening and attempt to ascertain the speaker's purpose.
Use of non-verbal communication	Be aware of what you communicate with your body; your posture and expressions can convey your attitudes towards a speaker even before you say one word. Use body language to show the speaker you are engaged in the conversation and open to hearing.
Recognition of your own prejudices and biases	Be aware of your own feelings towards the speaker. If you are unsure about what the speaker means, ask for clarification instead of making assumptions.
Listen to understand the underlying feelings	People in conflict create, structure, and perform conflict-problem narratives as a way of organizing the events and characters involved in an incident or circumstance. Use your heart as well as your mind to understand the speaker. Notice how something is said as well as the actual words used.

No interruptions	Be sure you think carefully before you speak. As a listener, your job is to help the speaker express himself.
Suspend judgement	A speaker who feels you are making judgements will feel defensive. Avoid making judgements and instead try to empathize and understand the speaker's perspective.
Resist the temptation to give advice	Keep in mind that the best resolutions are those that people arrive at themselves, not what someone else tells them to do. If you feel it is appropriate, and only after you have encouraged the person to talk, offer some ideas and discuss them.

Responding

After you have listened and *really heard*, respond by conveying your interest and respect:

- **Empathize:** Put yourself in the other person's shoes and try to understand.

- **Validate:** Acknowledge that the person's feelings are valid. This is a very powerful tool because you are recognizing the person's right to feel that way, regardless of whether you would feel the same way.

- **Restate what the other person has said:** This allows you to make sure you understand the feelings and shows you are listening.

- **Clarify:** Ask questions to get more information about the problem.

- **Summarize:** Paraphrase the main points you have heard so you can make sure you understand all the issues.

- **Confirm:** Based on what we know and what we have committed to do, what are our next steps?

Constructive Interactions Skills Summary

There are a series of approaches that, when combined with the essential skills of active listening, can assist in making interactions more constructive.

Table 18: Constructive Interaction Skills

Skills	Purpose	To do this...	Examples
Paraphrasing	• To demonstrate interest in and respect for the speaker's point of view. • To check your understanding and interpretation of meaning.	• Restate the speaker's message in your own words.	• "If I understand, your point is ..." • "In other words ..." • "So what you're saying is ..."
Empathizing	• To demonstrate your understanding of both meaning and feeling in the speaker's message.	• Reflect your perception of the speaker's feelings and meaning.	• "You feel hurt by ...?" • "When ... you felt ...?"
Clarifying and questioning	• To help you understand what is said. • To get more information.	• Ask open questions.	• What do you mean when you say ...?" • "What's your view on ...?"
Descriptive language	• To accurately convey experiences or behaviours.	• Describe specific, observable experiences and behaviours.	• "When you walked away, I ..." • "Here's a specific example ..."
Summarizing	• To pull together key issues, needs, and concerns, etc. • To establish a basis for further interaction.	• Recap major points expressed over a period of time.	• "So, in essence, then ..." • "To sum up what we've covered so far ..."
Reframing	• Positive expression of future focussed needs.	• Use neutral language and non-positional, specific outcome engendering language.	• "What's important to you is ..." • "Moving forward the needs you want addressed are ..."

Chapter 21: In Search of Common Ground: Workplace Mediation

Note: This section describes an approach that can be used to reconcile Level 1: Low Intensity Conflicts and Level 2: Moderate-Intensity Conflicts. Due to the complexity and the people/positions involved in some Level 2 and Level 3: High-Intensity Conflicts, external mediative, adjudicative resources can be required. That said, the principles set out in this section are equally applicable.

> At work, many disputes arise out of a failure to communicate, understand, or consider the needs and interests of the other person. People often fix their attention on the question, "Who is right and who is wrong?" In so doing, they become blind to the possibility that both may have a legitimate point of view. Conflict between colleagues can be damaging and, if ignored, can damage morale, reduce productivity, and may lead to increased costs and even legal issues for the organization.
>
> Human resource practitioners are often relied upon to mediate matters at issue between individuals or groups of individuals. A mediator is a *process mechanic*, helping through process to find a way forward where their processes and approaches have failed.

Workplace mediation[150] is a process whereby an agreed-upon third party assists parties to come to an agreement through collaborative engagement. Mediation is most effective when used as early as possible, before a conflict becomes too entrenched. It is a meeting between two or more parties who are experiencing conflict, with the goal of reconciling the matters of issue. The individual in the role of mediator should be someone who is independent to the issues being discussed and preferably independent to the parties in the mediation.

Mediators do not make judgements or determine outcomes—they ask questions that help to uncover underlying problems, assist the parties to understand the issues, and help them clarify the options for resolving their difference or dispute.

The overriding aim of workplace mediation is to restore, improve, and maintain working relationships wherever possible. This means the focus is on working together to go forward, not determining who was right or wrong in the past.

The goal of mediation is to establish a "zone of potential agreement," which for both parties is preferable to the risks and consequences of other options. A mediator helps

---

150   Various mediation models exist, although it is common for mediators to draw on more than one. Other models include evaluative, transformative, transactional and directive approaches. This section is based predominantly on the facilitative mediation model.

the parties move from the narration of their respective stories to a genuine conversation and the exploration of integrative potential. It may not become clear whether such consensus exists until the process has been explored.

Subject to the matters at issue and organizational norms, there are different options for introducing mediation into an organization: one is to develop an in-house capacity, with trained internal mediators. Another possible approach is to call on the services of external mediators when necessary, possibly as part of an arrangement where a contract is agreed with a provider to provide their services as and when necessary. These two approaches are not mutually exclusive and can be used in combination.

Principles of Mediation

Mediation helps parties understand the reasons behind a disagreement or discord and agree on ways of future interaction and behaviour. Mediation principles include:

1. Voluntariness

The voluntary commitment of both parties is essential for the mediation's success—both parties are free to leave the process at any time, at which stage the mediation will end. Both parties are then free to use the other dispute resolution options available to them, if they wish.

2. Impartiality

The mediator always remains impartial and does not take any side or make judgements—any agreements are made by the parties themselves. Mediation is not about disputing parties blaming each other and it is not about who is right or wrong—it is about understanding what has happened, where things may have gone wrong, and agreeing on a way forward.

Workplace mediation is not about finding fault. Sometimes the parties in a workplace mediation want for someone to be labelled right and the other person to be labelled wrong. Mediation is not designed to determine facts and make findings on exactly what happened and make a ruling on who is right or wrong.

3. Confidentiality

Discussions during the mediation process and any agreements remain confidential at all times unless both parties agree otherwise.

4. Process Clarity

Workplace interactions are considered a practical affair and have become conventionalized. However, mediation entails a unique form of interaction, resulting in the necessity to have a meeting of the minds on how matters will proceed:

- Individuals will come to the mediation with different backgrounds and experiences and expectations.

- Speakers may assume and anticipate that they have certain rights and are subject to certain obligations for giving, getting, taking, and surrendering turns.

- Rules of politeness may be assumed.

The Benefits of Mediation

Mediation can yield a variety of benefits both in terms of substance, the matters directly at issue, and process, how the parties are engaged to solve their problem. Specifically the benefits include:

- Reconciliation of matters is under the control of the parties, not an individual external to the relationship or workplace. Any agreement comes from the parties themselves, not the mediator.

- Parties can have ownership of the reconciliation process.

- Parties take responsibility for the development and implementation of their own agreement—this increases the parties' levels of satisfaction with the outcome and leads to more sustainable resolutions.

- Reduces the risk of losing good employees, who may leave their employment due to the stress they face in the workplace.

- Increases the skills of parties so they will be able to handle any future conflict more effectively.

- Allows the parties to maintain dignity and gain respect for each other in a safe environment—this leads to better relationships between the parties in the long term.

- Can be used to create a workplace culture of fairness and equity, and to support Human Resources policies in the areas of conflict resolution and performance management.

A mediation is most likely to result in a successful outcome when participants:

- believe the dispute can be resolved

- are willing to attempt to resolve it and have an openness to the possibilities of the process

- have insight and a capacity to self-reflect

- are ready to move beyond the dispute

- have the capacity and willingness to listen to the other's perspective

Done effectively, at the end of mediation, participants will be able to:

- Understand their own involvement and take accountability for their actions.

- Establish and act upon agreements based on their own understanding of the conflict.

- Better understand internal policies and standards of conduct.

- Handle future situations with developed problem-solving and conflict resolution skills.

- Create and contribute to a respectful work environment.

Issue Suitability for Workplace Mediation

There are situations where the Workplace Mediation approach can be particularly helpful:

- Level 1: Low-Intensity Conflicts and some Level 2: Moderate-Intensity Conflicts.

- Relationship breakdown.

- Bullying and harassment[151] and perceived discrimination issues. Each situation needs to be judged on a case-by-case basis. Serious cases of bullying and harassment, and clear cases of discrimination, may need to be dealt with by more formal procedures as these issues have become increasingly complex— requiring expertise that cannot be easily gained with internal resources.

---

151   Includes any inappropriate conduct or comment by a person towards a worker that the person knows or reasonably ought to have known would cause the worker to be humiliated or intimidated, but excludes any reasonable action taken by an employer or supervisor relating to the management and direction of workers or the place of employment (Worksafe BC, 2018).

- When supervisors are not well-placed to deal with a conflict:

  ○ This may be because an intervention from a supervisor may be perceived as biased, or as favouring one side over another.

  ○ It may be that the supervisor has insufficient skills in handling interpersonal conflict.

There are situations where it may not be appropriate to use mediation, but it is often not clear cut and it will be up to the mediator or whoever is overseeing the mediation process to make a judgement on a case-by-case basis. Mediation may not be suitable if:

- It is used as a first resort; people should be encouraged to speak to each other and talk to their supervisor(s) before they seek a solution though third-party mediation.

- It is used by a supervisor to avoid their managerial responsibilities.

- A decision about right or wrong is needed; for example, where there is possible misconduct, the individual bringing a discrimination or harassment case wants it investigated.

- An individual is particularly vulnerable.

- The parties do not have the power to settle the issue.

- One side is completely intransigent and using mediation will only raise unrealistic expectations of a positive outcome.

The Workplace Mediation Process

Mediation, the process to help parties understand the reasons behind a disagreement or discord and agree on ways of future interaction and behaviour, by its very nature will be fluid given the individuals involved, the matters at issue and the mediator's approach. That said, there are foundation stages to any mediation.

Stages of Mediation

1. **Setting the stage: matters at issue, people involved**

   - What level of conflict does this circumstance appear to be and does it meet the test of mediation suitability generally and mediation of this type specifically?

○ Specifically, confirm that this is not the first resort and that discussions have taken place. What process was followed and what was learned? Note that this will be a narrative of narratives, necessitating the mediator begin to deconstruct the narratives to facilitate the process of understanding and reconciliation.

- Be an informed participant; what do you know, what do you need to know?

- Develop an inquiry, questioning, and facilitation strategy; based on what you know is this matter suitable for mediation, in particular, this type of mediation?

- Confirm the parties' acceptance of the need for the assistance of a third party, the mediator, and general outline of ground rules by which the meeting will abide (for example, respectful language).

○ Detail roles

○ Articulation of process expectations and rules of engagement

2.   **Separate meetings**

- First formal contact with the parties—the mediator will meet parties separately

○ The aim of this first meeting is to allow everyone involved to tell their story, without interruption and clarified as required and find out what they want out of the process.

○ De-construct the narrative following the processes set out in Chapter 3.

- During the mediation, private meetings between the mediator and either party can take place at the request of either party or the mediator.

○ These private meetings are used for clarification, to ask questions, and to coach the parties through the process.

3.   **Joint meeting**

- At the joint meeting, the mediator's role is to oversee the process, assist communication between the parties, support them in identifying their issues and needs, and facilitate the parties to reach a mutually satisfactory agreement.

- The joint meeting is where the parties will narrate their stories and the mediator will facilitate the transition from narration to the basis of a genuine conversation and a meeting of the minds on a way forward.

- The mediator provides a process that is safe for both parties and that allows them to communicate their interests and needs to each other.

- The parties' role is to collaborate with each other and explore the issues and how they could be addressed to find a way forward.

- Start the joint session

  - Frame the process; re-confirm the roles and responsibilities of the participants and the mediator.

  - Use the third story technique to outline the matters at issue.

- Hear the issues

  - The mediator generally brings the participants together and invites them to put forward their side of the story without interruption.

- Understanding the issues

  - Following each party's comments, the mediator may prompt the other party to articulate what they heard—they may direct the individual to look directly at the other party when describing their understanding.

  - The mediator will then confirm with the speaking party that what they were trying to convey has been conveyed, based on the other party's understanding.

- Identifying the issues in conflict

  - At the end of each party's comments, the mediator will summarize the main areas of conflict from that individual's point of view, as the mediator sees them.

  - Once both parties have told their stories, the mediator will summarize areas of agreement and disagreement and draw up an agenda with the parties for the rest of the mediation.

- Exploring the conflict

    ○ Having identified the issues to explore, the mediation is now about encouraging interaction between the parties, promoting understanding and empathy and changing perceptions.

    ○ The aim of this part of the meeting is to begin to shift the focus from the past to the future and begin to look for constructive alternatives.

    ○ Having identified and considered the alternatives a solution can be crafted.

4.   **Building and writing an agreement**

- As the process develops, the mediator will encourage and support joint problem-solving by the parties, ensure the solution and agreements are workable, and record any agreement reached.

5.   **Closing the mediation**

- Once an agreement has been reached, the mediator will bring the meeting to a close, provide a copy of the agreed statement to those involved, and explain their responsibilities for its implementation.

- In some cases, no agreement is reached, and other procedures may later be used to resolve the conflict.

- Unless agreed otherwise, nothing that has been said during the mediation can be used in future proceedings.

6.   **Post-mortem**

- Results are for learning; as a process, what worked and what didn't?

- Are workplace restoration processes needed? The establishment or re-establishment of harmonious, constructive working relationships amongst individuals or within a team.

- How can this situation be used to improve workplace interactions and promote problem solving?

Figure 29: Workplace Mediation

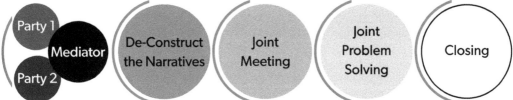

Setting the Stage	Separate Meetings	Joint Meeting	Building & Writing an Agreement	Closing the Mediation & Post Mortem
• Level of conflict & suitability • Acceptance of mediation • Questioning strategy • Ground rules • Roles	• Tell their story • Identify desired outcomes	• Frame the process • Outline the issues using the third story technique • Hear, understand and identify the issues • Explore resolutions	• Record agreements • Ensure workability	• Copies to the parties • Review responsibilities • Next steps • Learn from results

Appendix A: Comprehensive Investigation Checklist

	Appendix A: Comprehensive Investigation Checklist	
	Date/Time Completed:	
		Have you indicated the specific material facts: the date, time, location of, witnesses to the incidents documented?
		Did you factually record the action or behaviour exhibited?
		Have you been objective, recording observations and not impressions?
A.	**Getting the Facts**	
	1.	Interview complainant to get complete details of complaint(s), making detailed notes. All interview notes should have date, place, persons present, start time, and end time.
	2.	Assume information is true. Could discipline result? (Not whether you will discipline.) If yes, follow this checklist. If unsure, check with the ultimate management decision maker.
	3.	Identify the standard of conduct expected (collective agreement provisions; employer policies, rules, handbook, etc.; department/supervisor's rules; job descriptions; statutes; other employee discipline; previous verbal and written discussions with the employee; and, common sense). (Note: This material may be gathered throughout the investigation.)
	4.	Review statutes applicable to the position or profession, the collective agreement, and any other matters specific to a position or profession re: discipline. While not typical, some require a letter briefly outlining the allegation, advising the employee that you are conducting an investigation.
	5.	Before interviewing employee, interview enough other witnesses (making detailed notes) so you have a good sense of what happened. What? When? Where? How? Why (if relevant)? Who was present? Other information?
	6.	Prepare questions for the interview of the employee being investigated.
	7.	Arrange for a second management person to be available to take notes.
	8.	Advise the employee of time, etc., you wish to speak to them about the incident.
	9.	Advise the union of the meeting and ensure the representative will attend
	10.	At the interview, if no representative is present, again advise employee of their right to have a representative present and suggest that the matter be put off to get one. Make detailed notes of this discussion.
	11.	After the interview, review notes for accuracy and clarity (times, detail of circumstances, what you are quoted as saying).

	12.	Obtain legible copies of all pertinent documents (timesheets, policies, memos, etc. before they are destroyed)
B.	**Determining the Appropriate Action**	
	13.	Review the employee's personnel file. Note previous discipline matters, if any.
	14.	Discuss with the ultimate management decision maker to determine: • whether discipline is warranted • level of discipline
	15.	Does the response fit the violation, the individual, and the situation?
	16.	Will the response motivate the employee to change their behaviour? If not, is there something else that would change or improve their work situation?
	17.	Will the response maintain the morale of other employees?
	18.	Review mitigating factors.
	19.	Write the draft Letter of Discipline, where applicable.
C.	**Administering the Discipline**	
	20.	Have the draft Letter of Discipline approved in accordance with company policies.
	21.	If the discipline is more than a Letter of Discipline, review the collective agreement
	22.	Note date, time, and place of delivery of the letter to the employee and union on the copy of letter that goes to personnel file and send it to the personnel file
	23.	Is it clear to the employee that the discipline is aimed at the behaviour and is not regarded as personal punishment?
	24.	Is it clear to the employee what is expected of them in the future, and do they understand the possible consequences of continuing inappropriate behaviour/performance?
D.	**Follow Up**	
	25.	Has the employee's performance/behaviour been monitored since they were disciplined?
	26.	Has the response had the desired effect on the employee?
	27.	Is the employee receiving feedback on their improvement (or lack thereof)?
	28.	Have I attempted to overcome any resentment?
	29.	Does the employee understand that the action is in their best interests?

Appendix B: Checklist – Processes and Protocols for Investigating Misconduct

Appendix B: Checklist - Processes and Protocols for Investigating Misconduct	
1. Review collective agreements	
	What are the relevant sections?
	What is the interpretation and application of these sections?
	What are the procedural requirements?
	What is the role of the union representative?
	What policies, procedures, and protocols already exist?
	What is the role of the investigator?
	Who is notified that an investigation has been initiated? What is the form of this notification?
2. Establish a procedure and protocol for investigating complaints	
	Relate this working model to the collective agreement.
	Provide training on the collective agreement and protocol to those who will be involved in the investigations (at all levels).
	How is this protocol to be communicated?
	When a complaint is received, who is notified of the complaint?
	Who conducts the actual investigation?
	Who oversees the investigation?
	What types of complaints will be investigated?
	How is information to be stored, disclosed, or disposed of?
	What statutory requirements are applicable?
3. Determine resources required	
	Who is to be the note taker?

Appendix B: Checklist - Processes and Protocols for Investigating Misconduct

4. Define the misconduct

	What is the nature of the complaint?
	Who is affected?
	What is the impact?

5. Review the analysis in *William Scott*

	Who has information?
	What are the facts?
	How has the employer responded to previous incidences of misconduct?

6. Establish a procedure for imposing discipline

	Who imposes discipline?
	How is discipline imposed?
	What is the role of the investigator?
	What is the role of the union representative?

7. Monitor the imposition of discipline

	Who has the authority to discipline?
	What is the extent of authority to discipline?
	Who is notified of the imposition of discipline?
	What information is recorded, stored, disposed of, or disclosed?

8. Establish procedures for concluding the matter

	How does the resolution affect documentation?
	Who is to be informed of the resolution?
	What information is to be recorded, stored, disposed of, or disclosed?

Appendix C: Correspondence and Sample Letters

Purpose of Supervisory Letters versus Discipline Letters

Letters of Expectation and Direction are considered supervisory letters and are not considered disciplinary in nature. However, over time, there has been confusion regarding the actual difference in the format and wording of the letters.[152]

Letters of Expectation

While it is permissible for an employer to provide a general written statement of its expectations to an employee, an employer may not disguise discipline in the form of a letter of expectation.

The burden of proving a prima facie case that a document is disciplinary in nature falls to the union. Once such a prima facie case is made, the burden then shifts to the employer to prove it has just cause to impose the discipline. When looking at the content and character of the letter, consider whether the letter:

- is specifically directed at particular employees

- accuses the employees of misconduct of a culpable nature

- refers to possible disciplinary action if the conduct persists

- suggests that the employee's actions are ill-founded or improperly handled

- uses language that refers to communications of performance expectations rather than the identification of concerns or unacceptable or insubordinate behaviour, possibly warranting discipline in the future, if it continues

- focusses on correcting undesirable behaviour by specific employees

- addresses employer concerns in a supportive manner and whether any support is offered to improve or overcome the perceived problems

- is in a disciplinary format

152   Lisa Claxton, *BCGEU STEWARD* 2007 based on arbitration cases identifying when a supervisory letter is in fact a disciplinary letter.

The following are the differences between letters of expectation and letters of discipline.[153]

Table 19: Differences between Supervisory and Discipline Letters

Supervisory Letters Performance Expectation Letter	Discipline Letters
Purpose: to counsel and communicate, to identify or clarify expected behaviour or performance of job duties.	Purpose: to correct poor performance or undesirable behaviour—assumes discipline needed to achieve correction.
Employer's intention: helpful, supportive.	Employer's intention: disciplinary.
Examples used only as a means to clarify inappropriate or acceptable behaviour.	Nature of the employee's conduct: culpable—specific incidents or poor performance, or infraction of a rule, policy or standard.
Support is offered by way of training and/or other resources.	Should be clearly stated to be disciplinary.
Develops, with the employee's input, mutual goals to encourage the employee's commitment to change.	Does the employee have to grieve the letter to be able to respond effectively to it?
Focus: assumes behaviour will change in the future, when the employee understands what is expected and is supported in an effort to change.	Focus: expected behaviour is identified, but consequences are attached to present and any future failure to meet prescribed standards.
A review period is set to give feedback on progress of change.	May require compliance with provisions of the collective agreement, such as the presence of a union representative, when discipline imposed.
A future disciplinable offence will be treated with no reference to this letter as a foundation for any progressive discipline. This letter may only be used to show that the employee was aware of the employer's requirements.	Negative impact on the employee's work record. Part of progressive discipline—further incidents of a similar nature may be followed by further, possibly increased, discipline.

153   *Alberta Hospital Edmonton and HSAA 115 LAC (4th) 154 2003 (Gordon).*

Format of Discipline Letters

Disciple letters are business letters and should observe business letter standards.

Table 20: Format of a Discipline Letter

Format	The letter is serious; therefore use formal names. To Ms. Smith, not Cindy, and signature should be full name—Mr. Bill Smith, not Bill.
Purpose of Letter	"Re: Letter of Discipline" should be included. Replace "Discipline" with "Suspension and Termination" in appropriate circumstances.
Facts	Set out facts resulting in this discipline. Note the unacceptable behaviour as facts, not opinions, or as information received from a third party. Be specific: include dates, times, location, etc. If there are many different incidents or types of incidents, include an outline of all the different types of misbehaviour. If dates are unknown, use approximate dates: "During this fall ..." In an arbitration, the burden of proof is on the employer and the grounds are limited to those in the disciplinary letter.
Statement Behaviour Inappropriate	This can be as short as: "This type of behaviour is completely unacceptable." In order to emphasize expectations of your role, the following (or parts of it) could be considered: "This behaviour is completely unacceptable for a (position)... It jeopardizes not only your reputation as a (position) but also the reputation of the organization, profession." For example, positions of authority such as a teacher may be worded such as: Position title *occupy positions of trust and confidence, and exert considerable influence over their students as a result of their positions. The conduct of a* position title *bears directly upon the community's perception of the position title's ability to fulfil such a position of trust and influence, and upon the whole community's confidence in* organization name.
Discipline	Set out disciplinary action in detail. In a Letter of Discipline, this is not a separate paragraph, as it is covered in the "Purpose of Letter."

Employee's Record	Set out previous record relied on in determining this action. It may be a generic sentence, such as: "In arriving at this decision we have considered your entire work record, including your disciplinary record." This may include specifics of previous meeting and letters that have been given to the employee. In some situations, it may be better to reverse this paragraph with the disciplinary response paragraph. If there is no previous record being relied on this may be left out.
Directions/ Expectations (not mandatory)	Often, during the investigation, a number of issues surface that should be addressed. The employer can do this by setting out expectations or issuing directions to the employee. This can be included in this letter or in a separate letter. If there are several, or if there will be ongoing expectations or directions, then place them in a separate letter. Remember, some collective agreements require the removal of disciplinary letters after a period of time, which means the directions would go if they are in the same letter.
Warning about Future Incidents	Include something similar to, "Please be advised that any future infraction will result in further disciplinary action up to and including termination." Avoid stating what the next disciplinary step may be unless that is the step (i.e., termination).
Positive Statement (not mandatory)	A positive statement expressing hope things will turn around may be added in appropriate circumstances.
Who Gets a Copy?	The union and personnel file should always be copied.
Proof of Service	Add at the bottom:

"HAND DELIVERED TO THE EMPLOYEE ON THE DAY OF , 20XX BY THE UNDERSIGNED.

Signature _____

"COPY SENT TO THE UNION BY FAX/E-MAIL/INTERNAL MAIL SYSTEM ON THE DAY OF , 20XX BY THE UNDERSIGNED.

Signature _____

Example Letter – Notice of Investigation

Date:

Dear Mr. Smith:

Re: Notice of Investigation

*This is to advise you that pursuant to Article XX of the collective agreement, the employer is conducting an investigation that on December 10, 20XX you allegedly falsified your time card.

**You are also advised of the right to have a union representative at any interview of yourself in connection with the investigation.

Sincerely,

cc: Union, Personnel File

Hand delivered to the employee on the   day of   , 20XX by the undersigned.

Signature _____

Copy sent to the union by fax/e-mail/internal mail system on the   day of   , 20XX by the undersigned.

Signature _____

Note: *This would cover a general notice but may not be sufficient if the collective agreement requirement is to set out specifics of allegation or particulars.

**If the collective agreement makes it mandatory that a union representative be present, use the following wording in place of the above paragraph 2:

"You are also advised of the requirement to have a union representative at any interview of yourself in connection with the investigation."

Example Letter – Letter of Direction

Date:

Dear Mr. Smith:

Re: Letter of Direction

In the formal observations, a number of concerns have been raised with regard to your performance.

In order for you to improve your performance, you are directed to do the following:

1. Arrive at work during the workday at a reasonable time and be fully prepared and ready to start your shift at the scheduled start time

2. Ensure daily work plans are completed and maintained

3. Ensure work plans are formally signed off and submitted

4. Ensure your work area is maintained in an organized and orderly fashion

5. Avoid making inappropriate or unprofessional comments to co-workers

I will be monitoring your progress and reviewing these matters with you. If you are unsure about any of these directions, please contact me to discuss.

Yours truly,

copy: Union, Personnel File

Hand delivered to the employee on the   day of   , 20XX by the undersigned.

Signature _____

Example Letter – Letter of Expectations

Date:

Dear Mr. Smith:

Re: Letter of Expectations

This will confirm our discussion on November 4, 20XX concerning the responsibilities for closing and securing the store on October 21, 20XX.

It is an expectation of the company that all managers follow all the directions contained in the Company Handbook regarding store closing procedures, a copy of which is attached. In particular, I would draw your attention to the following:

1. Follow the Closing Manager's Checklist

2. Ensure employees complete store cleanliness standards

3. Prepare a closing notes plan for the store opening manager to review the next day.

If you are unsure about any of these expectations, please contact me to discuss.

Yours truly,

copy: Union, Personnel File

Hand delivered to the employee on the   day of   , 20XX by the undersigned.

Signature _____

Example Letter – Letter of Discipline

Date:

Dear Mr. Smith

Re: Letter of Discipline

On March 3, 20XX, you were absent from work without a satisfactory reason.

This was discussed with you on October 10, 20XX. This was further discussed with you on January 10, 20XX, at which time you were given a written Letter of Direction that you were to attend work on time. As indicated during these discussions, unnecessary absences create operating problems, morale problems, and employee distractions.

Please be advised you are directed as follows:

1.   You are to be at work as scheduled and on time.

2.   If for some reason you are unable to report for work, you are directed to:

   2.a   give prior notification to your supervisor, or if not possible, call your supervisor if ill or an emergency arises

   2.b   provide a satisfactory reason for your absence to your supervisor immediately upon your return to work.

I will be reviewing your record and talking to you from time to time about your attendance.

Please be aware that any further infractions will result in further disciplinary action, up to and including termination.

Yours truly,

copy: Union, Personnel File

Hand delivered to the employee on the   day of   , 20XX by the undersigned.

Signature _____

Copy sent to the union by fax/e-mail/internal mail system on the   day of   , 20XX by the undersigned.

Glossary

accommodation conflict style. Also referred to as accommodating, yielding, smoothing, obliging. Maximizes empathy and minimizes assertiveness.

accreditation. The procedure followed by a labour relations board to designate an organization of employers as the bargaining agent for a group of employers. The parallel term for employee organizations is *certification*.

alternative. A choice limited to one or more possibilities, propositions, or courses of action. A selection of one alternative precludes any other possibility.

alternative dispute resolution or **appropriate dispute resolution (ADR).** A range of techniques outside the traditional litigation process (though they may be used in tandem with it). ADR procedures are chosen by parties in conflict to try to resolve the dispute in a less adversarial way. These techniques are usually voluntarily and confidential (with some exceptions). ADR procedures range from self-help processes at one end of a continuum to binding arbitration at the other. Except for arbitration, ADR uses non-binding processes that parties can walk away from at any time. Parties remain in control of the process and the outcome. The most common processes are negotiation, mediation, and group facilitation.

anchor or anchoring. A cognitive bias that describes the common human tendency to attach (or "anchor") our thoughts to a reference point—even though it may have no logical relevance to the decision at hand and rely too heavily on the first piece of information offered (the "anchor") when making decisions. It is considered a bias because it distorts our judgement, especially when matters are unclear or otherwise unexplored.

application grievance. Grievances that involve the application of a collective agreement provision and dispute the facts of the situation being grieved, not the interpretation or meaning of the provision. The most common application grievances are those concerning discipline.

arbitration. A method of settling an employer-union dispute by having an impartial third party render a decision binding on both the union and the employer.

All collective agreements must provide for the arbitration of disputes over the interpretation of collective agreement language—for example, a dispute over the discipline of an employee for insubordination. This type of arbitration, which is referred to as *grievance arbitration* or *rights arbitration*, involves the interpretation of existing collective agreement language. It is different from interest arbitration, which is used to resolve collective bargaining disputes. In interest arbitration, an arbitrator awards new collective agreement language for specific matters at issue.

arbitral jurisprudence. The body of labour law developed by arbitrators through their decisions.

avoidant conflict style. Also referred to as avoiding, withdrawing. Low in assertiveness and low in empathy.

balance of probabilities. A legal standard, applied in many jurisdictions, for deciding the outcome of civil disputes, which requires that a dispute be decided in favor of the party whose claims are more likely to be true.

bargaining agent. Once a union is certified by a labour relations board, the union becomes the exclusive representative of all the employees in a particular bargaining unit. The employer can no longer negotiate with individual employees over terms and conditions of employment.

bargaining unit. A labour relations board will only certify a union to represent a group of employees if the board considers the group to be appropriate for collective bargaining purposes. This group of employees is the bargaining unit. Generally, labour relations boards prefer an all-employee bargaining unit, but they may certify a union for smaller groups under certain circumstances.

Whether any particular employees are properly included in that bargaining unit will be determined by whether those employees and other members of the unit have a *community of interest*. A community of interest depends on a number of factors such as similar terms and conditions of employment, similar skills and similar training.

best alternative to a negotiated agreement (BATNA). The alternative left to a party if the party is unable to reach an agreement—the "walk-away" alternative. It represents one of several paths that you can follow if a resolution cannot be reached. You walk away from the negotiation when your interests are not met. Your BATNA is what you end up with. In general, neither party should agree to something that is worse than its best alternative to a negotiated agreement away from the table. Like its WATNA counterpart, understanding your BATNA gives you a measure you can use to assess your other options in order to make more informed negotiation decisions.

bias. An inclination to present or hold a partial perspective at the expense of (possibly equally valid) alternatives. Bias can come in many forms.

business agent. A full-time officer of a local union who handles grievances, helps enforce agreements, and performs other tasks in the day-to-day operation of a union.

certification. Official recognition by a labour relations board of a union as the sole and exclusive bargaining agent, following proof of majority support among employees in a bargaining unit. Once a trade union is certified, the employer must recognize its bargaining agency.

change management. A systematic approach to dealing with change both from the perspective of an organization and the individual.

collaboration. The action of working with someone to produce or create something.

collaborative conflict style. May be referred to as collaborating, integrating, or problem-solving. Highly assertive and highly empathetic at the same time.

community of interest. A community of people who share a common interest or passion.

competitive conflict style. Also known as contending, competing, forcing, directing. Maximizes assertiveness and minimizes empathy.

compromising conflict style. Intermediate on both the assertiveness and empathy dimensions of the dual concerns model.

complainant. The individual bringing forward an allegation.

conflict. A form of friction, disagreement, or discord arising within a group when the beliefs or actions of one or more members of the group are either resisted by or unacceptable to one or more members of another group; a disagreement when people (or other parties) perceive that, as a consequence of a disagreement, there is a threat to their interests.

constructive conflict. A type of conflict in which people focus their discussion on the issue while maintaining respect for people having other points of view. It encourages people to present their divergent viewpoints so ideas and recommendations can be clarified, redesigned, and tested for logical soundness.

continuing grievance. A grievance in which the act about which a grievor complains must be recurring. The problem is in determining when a series of acts may be characterized as recurring or as separate occurrences of violations of a collective agreement. The results of continuing grievance cases are not uniform.

corrective action. See *progressive discipline*.

cross-examination. A form of examination during a hearing in which the opposing counsel has great latitude to ask leading questions. The opposing counsel may suggest an answer or ask the witness to agree or disagree with a proposition. This is distinct from direct examination, or examination in chief.

culpable. Meriting condemnation or blame.

culture (organizational). The combination of shared values and group norms often described as the characteristics of "the way we do things around here." Organizational culture fills the organization with life and ideals; it influences how roles and responsibilities are fulfilled and provides the organization with an external corporate identity. Organizational culture is evident in an individual's words and actions and in the organization's systems and processes.

decision-based fact making. Refers to an approach that starts with a decision followed by attempts to gather facts to support the decision. Whether used by default or design, this decision-making error is to be guarded against.

dialogue. Stems from the Greek words *dia* for "through" and *logos* for "words." Dialogue is a synergistic activity through which the exchange of ideas yields knowledge not previously held by participants.

direct examination. See *examination in chief.*

discourse. The noun discourse comes from the Latin *discursus* to mean "an argument. " The argument in discourse refers to an exchange of ideas—sometimes heated—that often follows a kind of order and give-and-take between the participants.

Discourse refers to an extended communication (often interactive) dealing with some particular topic, as well as the activity of communicating and conveying information. The discourse may transition to a form of negotiation—the basic means of getting what you want from others. It is the back and forth communication designed to reach an agreement when you and the other party have some interests that are shared and others that are opposed.

dual concerns model. Two-dimensional framework that postulates that people in conflict have two independent types of concerns:

- Concern for self: the degree to which you attempt to satisfy your own interests; embodied in the quality of being self-assured and confident without being aggressive (assertiveness).

- Concern for others: the degree to which you attempt to satisfy the interests of others; embodied in the ability to see the world as another person, to share and understand the other's feelings, needs, concerns and interests (empathy).

dues. Periodic fees or payments made to a union by members of the bargaining unit and/or the union.

due process. (natural justice) Procedural fairness requirement applicable to public bodies and domestic tribunals when making decisions that affect the rights and interests of individuals; the rules of natural justice require that persons affected by a decision be notified of the case against them and be given a reasonable opportunity of presenting their case, and that the body making the decision listens fairly to both sides and reach a decision untainted by bias. The precise content of natural justice varies according to the nature of the power exercised, the decision involved, and the consequences that flow therefrom. All employees have the right to:

- make complaints

- be informed of complaints made against them

- be informed of remedial actions taken

- a fair hearing

- a full investigation

- promptness

- impartiality

- consistency

- representation

- follow up

enemyfy. An expression coined by conflict mediator and peace negotiator Adam Kahane to describe an approach used by some when speaking of another party or person. Polarizing in nature, individuals or groups are not simply *people I disagree with*, but the derisive *other people. They are people who I can't work with and what I really want more than anything is for them to just go away, for them to be excluded or eliminated.*

employment relationships. Social relations among people at work; rights, obligations, expectations, values, and rewards that define interactions in the labour market—the legal link between employers and employees; exists when a person performs work or services under certain terms and conditions in return for remuneration.

estoppel. Principle of law preventing a party from insisting on its strict legal rights where, by its words or conduct, it has represented that it would not do so and another party has changed its position to its disadvantage or detriment in reliance on that rep-resentation. Estoppel may be based not only on actual statements made by a party, but also on past practice, or a prior course of conduct, or even the failure of a party to grieve or object to a departure from the parties' strict legal rights and obligations.

Where estoppel involves rights under a collective agreement, the requirement of det-rimental reliance may be satisfied if the party asserting the estoppel establishes that, in reliance on the other party's representations, it gave up the opportunity to negotiate a change in the collective agreement. Although estoppel can be brought to an end by notice that a party intends to revert to its strict legal rights, arbitrators have generally held that the party adversely affected must first be given the opportunity to negotiate the issue in dispute.

examination in chief. A form of examination, also referred to as *direct examination*, during a hearing in which counsel asks open-ended questions and cannot ask leading questions, or questions that may suggest an answer. This is distinct from *cross-examination*.

expedited arbitration. A dispute resolution mechanism that can be used before a grievance is sent to conventional arbitration, and in which either party can apply to the Labour Relations Board to request resolution of the grievance by expedited arbitration. The Board appoints an arbitrator who has strict time limits for hearing and deciding on the grievance. The compressed timelines of expedited arbitration make this approach unsuitable for complex interpretive matters. Some collective agreements contain expedited arbitration provisions available as an alternative to conventional arbitration based on the criteria established by the agreement.

fact-based or evidence-informed decision making. Refers to an approach that emphasizes the definition of the problem and the use of information and analysis to inform decisions.

grandfather clause. See *modified union shop*.

grievance. A dispute between an individual and management or between the union and management over the interpretation, application, or administration of a collective agreement. The procedure for dealing with grievances is set out in the collective agreement. If a grievance cannot be settled at the worksite level (where many of them are settled) or at any of the subsequent steps established in the grievance procedure, it must be resolved by arbitration.

grievance arbitration. See *arbitration*.

Hoogendoorn Rule. A rule applying to a situation in which an employee's status may be affected by the outcome of an arbitration. In representing a second employee, the union is taking a position adverse to the first employee's interests, and this employee is therefore entitled to notice and an opportunity to participate in the hearing. The union has the responsibility to provide such notice. The Hoogendoorn Rule is based on

Hoogendoorn v Greening Metal Products and Screening Equipment Co, (1967) 1 O.R. 712, 62 D.L.R. (2d) 167, 67 C.L.L.C. 14,017 (C.A.).

inherent rights. See *management rights*.

integrative potential. The potential for the parties' interests to be combined or elements incorporated in ways that create joint value. In other words, join forces to achieve something together that cannot be achieved independently though joining several elements, parts into a whole, focussed on creating value before claiming value. The following factors indicate the potential for integration:

- The parties cannot achieve what they need to achieve independent of one another.

- More than one issue is involved.

- It is possible to add more issues to the mix.

- The parties' interactions will recur over time.

- The parties have varying preferences across issues

interests. The things that people want to satisfy or achieve in a conflict or negotiation situation. Unlike people's positions—which are simple statements purportedly that represent their interests—the interests underlying a position answer the question "*Why* do you want that?" or "*Why* do you feel that way?" Interests must be prioritized into needs and wants. Needs are more important and usually must be satisfied before an agreement can be reached, whereas wants may be traded or given away.

interest arbitration. See *arbitration*.

interpretation grievance. A grievance where the parties do not agree on the interpretation of the wording used in making a decision. Interpretation grievances involve such matters as the assigning and performance of work, scheduling, layoffs, transfers, workplace safety, wages and benefits, and use of seniority.

Issues (conflict). Focus on what the matter is about. An issue is an important topic or problem under consideration. There can be central issues and secondary or sub-issues that comprise a topic or problem. An issue is not a position. Issues can be of three different types: substantive issues, procedural issues, and relationship issues. Issues provide an alternative to framing the conflict in terms of two opposing positions, which allows for a focus on what the problem is and not who is right. While positions can be limiting, issues can more readily lead to a discussion.

jurisdiction (union). The area of jobs, skills, occupations, and industries or sectors within which a union organizes and engages in collective bargaining. Unions may also define their jurisdiction geographically. For example, a union may state in its constitution that it has jurisdiction over all employees in a particular industry in a particular province.

jurisdictional dispute. A conflict between two or more unions over the right of their membership to perform certain types of work. If the conflict develops into a work stoppage, it is called a jurisdictional strike.

jurisdictional strike. See *jurisdictional dispute*.

just cause. Sufficient or proper reason for discipline or discharge. Fair, adequate, reasonable cause. Legitimate cause; legal or lawful ground for action; such reasons as will suffice in law to justify the action taken. A cause outside the legal cause, which must be based on reasonable grounds, and there must be a fair and honest cause or reason, regulated by good faith. As used in a statutory sense, it is that which to an ordinary intelligent person is a justifiable reason for doing or not doing a particular act.

letter of intent (letter of understanding). Letter by a party to a collective agreement that clarifies or supplements the agreement. Whether a letter of intent forms part of the collective agreement, so that it is enforceable through the grievance and arbitration procedures, depends on the manifest intention of the parties. Where a letter of intent is in writing and signed by both parties, or is referred to in the collective agreement, it will generally be held to form part of the collective agreement.

lidism. An expression coined by Paul Rogers, professor of peace studies, University of Bradford, West Yorkshire to mean measures aimed not to address the underlying issues but to keep the lid on.

lockout. The closing of a place of employment, a suspension of work or a refusal by an employer to continue to employ a number of employees, to compel the employees to agree to conditions of employment. A lockout is not permitted during the life of a collective agreement.

management rights. A shorthand expression for the principle, applied in the interpretation of collective agreements, that any rights that the employer has not expressly bargained away in the agreement are retained by management. For example, if the union cannot point to an explicit clause that prohibits management from contracting out union work to an outside company, management can contract out as part of its management rights. Equivalent terms used are *inherent rights* and *residual rights*.

master agreement. A collective bargaining agreement that serves as the pattern for major terms and conditions for an entire industry or an industry segment. Local terms may be negotiated in addition to the terms set out in the master contract.

mediation. A process that attempts to resolve labour disputes by compromise or voluntary agreement. In contrast with arbitration, the mediator does not bring in a binding award, and the parties are free to accept or to reject the mediator's recommendation.

mission. In organizational planning, *mission* refers to an organization's reason for being, what it does.

modified union shop. A place of work in which non-union workers who are already employed need not join the union, but all new employees must join, and those workers who are already members must remain in the union. Often referred to as a *grandfather clause*.

multiple proceedings (vs. double jeopardy). If the proceeding is being carried out by a different authority it is not in conflict with the principle of double jeopardy. For example, a teacher may be investigated by the police and their employer for the same issue. Each authority has different burdens of proof and expectations and penalties.

natural justice. See *due process*.

negotiation. A basic means of getting what you want from others. It is back and forth communication designed to reach an agreement when you and the other side have some interests that are shared and others that are opposed.

objective. Something aimed at or strived for; a goal. In a negotiation, an objective is a statement of what you desire as outcomes or what you hope your settlement position will contain. An objective is not your position, but rather is a description of your desired outcome.

options. Alternative courses of action. The full range of possibilities on which parties might conceivably reach agreement. Options might be put on the table. A collective agreement is better if it is the best of many options, especially if it capitalizes on all potential mutual gain.

past practice. Conduct or behaviour of the parties under a collective agreement with respect to a matter in dispute. Evidence relating to past practice is admissible at arbitration to resolve an ambiguity in the collective agreement or to show one of the parties represented that the other party would not insist on the strict terms of the agreement.

picketing. Patrolling near the employer's place of business by union members (pickets) to publicize the existence of a labour dispute, to persuade workers to join a strike or join the union, to discourage customers from buying or using the employer's goods or services, or to serve some related purpose.

policy grievance. A grievance in which the subject matter is of general interest. In a policy grievance, the union complains that an employer's action (or its failure or refusal to act) is a violation of the collective agreement that could affect everyone covered by the agreement. A policy grievance normally relates to the interpretation of the agreement, rather than to the complaint of an individual or group. Individual employees may or may not be affected at the time the grievance is filed.

positions. *What I want as an outcome*:

- An attitude toward, opinion on, or statement on a subject; a particular stand or stance on an issue or subject. Positions are developed to represent a party's demands.

- A solution introduced by a party which benefits that party but does not necessarily take the other party's interests into consideration. Usually self-serving and expressed as a solution that the other party should agree to; what is the *right* course of action.

- Sets the basis for moving from the articulation of what's *right* to defending one's own position and attacking the other's.

- Framing a matter in terms of a position personalizes it leading to a defensive posture and adversarial atmosphere.

power. The real or perceived ability, or potential, to make choices and to bring about significant change. Power can be based on a dominance of sex, age, race or ethnicity, sexual orientation, mental or physical ability, socioeconomic class, etc. Power can also be conferred on an individual or group. An inequity of power is one of the most common causes of social injustice.

preferential hiring. An agreement that in hiring new workers, an employer will give preference to union members.

probation. Initial period of employment during which the employer has an opportunity to assess the suitability of the employee. Ordinarily, a lesser standard of cause is required to discharge probationary employees, and these employees' right to challenge discharge, as well as their seniority rights and benefits, may be further restricted by the terms of the collective agreement.

procedural issues. Related to the manner, process, and procedures used to settle the matters at issue; how we talk to and treat each other—the how.

progressive corrective discipline. See *progressive discipline*.

progressive discipline. A process for dealing with job-related behaviour that does not meet expected and communicated performance standards. The primary purpose for progressive discipline is to help the employee understand that a performance problem or opportunity for improvement exists. Also referred to as *corrective action* and *progressive corrective discipline*.

ratification. Formal approval of a newly negotiated collective agreement by vote of the union members affected.

reasonableness. According to the Supreme Court of Canada in *Dunsmuir v New Brunswick*, [2008] S.C.J. No. 9 (QL): "Reasonableness is concerned ... with whether the decision falls within a range of possible, acceptable outcomes which are defensible in respect of the facts and the law. It is a deferential standard which requires respect for the legislative choices to leave some matters in the hands of administrative decision makers, for the processes and determinations that draw on particular expertise and experiences, and for the different roles of the courts and administrative bodies within the Canadian constitutional system."

reasonable person test. How a typical person, with ordinary prudence, would act in certain circumstances. The investigator must look at facts in relation to how a reasonable person would. They are not searching for extreme reactions by either overly sensitive or overly insensitive opinions. The test can change over time based on society's expectations. The acceptability of smoking in the workplace and public areas is a good example of the changing nature of social expectations.

recognition. Employer acceptance of a union as the exclusive bargaining agent or representative for the employees in the bargaining unit, without the formal process of certification by a labour relations board. Also referred to as *voluntary recognition*.

relationship issues. Matters pertaining to the relationship (power, legitimacy, respect) both individual relationships (between individuals or groups of individuals) and institutional relationships (between, for example, representatives of the employer and representatives of the union).

respondent. The individual facing an allegation.

residual right. See *management rights*.

rights arbitration. See *arbitration*.

rotating strike. A strike organized so that only some of the employees stop work at any given time, each group taking its turn.

satisficing. Aiming to achieve only satisfactory results because the satisfactory position is familiar, hassle-free, and secure, whereas aiming for the best-achievable result would call for costs, effort, and incurring of risks. In decision making examining alternatives until a practical (most obvious, attainable, and reasonable) solution with adequate level of acceptability is found, and stopping the search there instead of looking for the best-possible (optimum) solution.

seniority. Length of service of employment. Seniority is frequently used in collective agreements as a basis for calculating benefits, such as entitlement to vacation. Seniority provisions (for example, layoff, recall or promotion clauses) in a collective agreement are terms that give employees preferential job rights in accordance with their relative seniority.

settlement officer An official appointed by a Labour Relations Board or Minister of Labour to confer with both parties to assist them in reaching a settlement. Prior to proceeding to arbitration, either party to a collective agreement may request such an appointment in writing. If both parties agree, a settlement officer can also assist in the settlement of a grievance during the expedited arbitration process.

shop steward. A union official who represents a specific group of members and the union in union duties, grievance matters and complaints about employment conditions. Stewards are usually part of the workforce who represent and handle their duties on a part-time basis. Also referred to as a union steward or staff representative.

slowdown. A deliberate lessening of work effort to apply pressure for concessions from the employer. A slowdown constitutes a strike under most labour relations statutes and is legal only when a collective agreement is not in force.

status quo. The currently existing state of affairs; facts as they stand at the present time. The position/s we take and argue for during negotiations is motivated by and purportedly represents our interests. Positions are something that you decide upon. Your interests are what caused you to so decide.

step-up step-back technique. Participants should be aware of how much they are speaking. If they feel they are speaking a lot, they should let others speak, and if they find themselves not talking, they should try to contribute some comments, ideas or suggestions.

stereotype. Preconceived notions about a person or group of people based on their characteristics such as their sex, age, sexual orientation, ethnicity, religion or physical or mental ability.

stretch collaboration. A variant of conventional collaboration is *stretch collaboration*. It abandons the assumption of control, gives up unrealistic expectations of harmony, certainty, and compliance, and instead embraces the messy realities of discord, trial and error and co-creation and emphasises flexibility and improvisation.

strike. A strike includes a cessation of work or a refusal to work or to continue work by employees in combination, in concert, or in accordance with a common understanding. Strikes usually occur as a last resort when collective bargaining and all other means have failed to obtain the employees' demands. Strikes are legal only when a collective agreement is not in force.

substantive issues. The concrete content of the conflict; directly related to the matters at issue—the what.

sympathy strike. A strike by workers not directly involved in a labour dispute and is usually intended to show labour solidarity and bring pressure on an employer in a labour dispute.

unfair labour practice. A practice on the part of an employer, union or employee that violates provisions of the statutes governing labour relations.

union fees. See *dues*.

union security clauses. Provisions in collective agreements designed to protect the union. Union security clauses include the following examples: *closed shop*, *preferential hiring*, and *union shop*.

union shop. A place of work governed by an agreement that the employer may hire anyone the employer wants, but all workers must join the union within a specified period after being hired and must retain membership as a condition of continuing employment.. See also *Union security clauses*.

union steward. See *shop steward*.

vision. In organizational planning, *vision* refers to an organization's preferred future, what it aspires to.

voluntary recognition. See *recognition*.

worst alternative to a negotiated agreement. In a negotiation, your WATNA represents one of several paths that you can follow if a resolution cannot be reached. Like its BATNA counterpart, understanding your WATNA gives you a measure you can use to assess your other options in order to make more informed negotiation decisions.

Wagner Act or Wagner Act Model. The 1935 U.S. *National Labour Relations Act* also known as the *Wagner Act* established the following:

- the right of employees to join the union of their choice and be represented in the collective bargaining process

- the National Labour Relations Board as the administrative agency responsible for the Act

- a duty on both parties to "bargain in good faith" and a prohibition on "unfair labour practices"

The Wagner Act model was subsequently adopted by Canadian jurisdictions, and is the origin of collective bargaining and grievance procedures.

whipsaw. The process or strategy wherein unions use one contract settlement as a precedent for the next and force the employer to settle all contracts on that basis, effectively playing one employer off against others.

wildcat strike. A strike that is not legal because the collective agreement and the statutes governing labour relations forbid it, but the union strikes anyway.

without prejudice. Expression used to indicate that a person or party making an offer or taking an action does so on the basis that the offer or action does not imply an admission of liability, or otherwise adversely affect his or her legal rights; settlement discussions between litigating parties or between a union and employer during the grievance procedure are inadmissible in evidence, absent the consent of the parties, on the ground of public policy, whether or not such discussions are stated to be without prejudice.

working conditions. Pertaining to an employee's job environment, such as hours of work, safety, paid public holidays and vacations, rest periods, free clothing or uniforms, and possibilities of advancement. Many of these conditions are included in the collective agreement and are subject to collective bargaining.

ZOPA. A "Zone of Possible Agreement" or ZOPA describes the intellectual zone in negotiations between two parties where there is a potential agreement that would benefit both sides more than their alternative options do. Within this zone, an agreement is possible. Outside the zone no amount of negotiation will yield an agreement.

References

Anderson, C., and A. Galinsky. "Power, Optimism, and Risk-taking," *European Journal of Social Psychology*. New Jersey: John Wiley and Sons, 2006.

Argyris, C., and D.A. Schon. *Theory in Practice: Increasing Professional Effectiveness*. San Francisco, California: Jossey Bass, 1978.

Bieristo, B., H.J. Finlayson, and C. Naylor. Proceedings of *Reimagining Public Education Discourse in BC*. Vancouver, BC: Centre for the Study of Educational Leadership and Policy (CSELP), 2016–2018.

Breslin, J.W., and J.Z. Rubin, eds. *Negotiation Theory and Practice, The Program on Negotiation*. Cambridge: Harvard Law School, 1991.

Brown, D.J., and D.M. Beatty. *Canadian Labour Arbitration*, 4th ed, Aurora, ON: Canada Law Book, 2006.

Cameron, E., M. Green. *Making Sense of Change Management: A Complete Guide to the Models, Tools & Techniques of Organizational Change,* 3rd ed. London, UK; Philadelphia, PA: Kogan Page, 2012.

Cawsey, T., G. Deszca, and I. Ingols. *Organizational Change: An Action-Oriented Tool Kit* 3rd edition, Sage Publications, Los Angeles, California, 2016.

Colosi, T.R., and A.E. Berkeley. *Collective Bargaining: How It Works and Why,* 2nd ed. New York: American Arbitration Association, 1992.

Coser, L.A. *The Functions of Social Conflict*. New York: Routledge, 1956.

Cutcher-Gershenfeld, J., R.B. McKersie, and R.E. Walton. *Pathways to Change: Case Studies of Strategic Negotiations*. Kalamazoo, MI: W.E. Upjohn Institute for Employment Research, 1995.

Craver, C. *The Impact of Negotiator Styles on Bargaining Interactions*. Washington, DC, George Washington University Law School, and 35 *Am. J. Trial Advocacy* 1, 2010.

Deutsch, M. *The Resolution of Conflict: Constructive and Destructive Processes*. New Haven, CT: Yale University Press, 1973.

Falcone, Paul. *101 Tough Conversations To Have With Employees*. New York: American Management Association (AMACOM), 2009.

Finlayson, H.J. *Disputes and the Collective Agreement: Effectively Managing the Grievance Process*, Vancouver, BC: BC Public School Employers' Association with permission, 2006.

Finlayson, H.J., G. Johnson, and R. Dahsi, *Productive Workplace Conversations* session workbooks. Vancouver, BC: BC Public School Employers' Association, 2008.

Finlayson, H.J., Holland, B., and Johnson, G. *Constructive Inquiry: Investigating Workplace Incidents* session workbook. Vancouver, BC: BC Public School Employers' Association, 2011.

Finlayson, H.J. *Perspectives, Practices and Practicalities: Preparing to Negotiate a Collective Agreement,* 6th ed. Vancouver, BC: BC Public School Employers' Association permission, 2010.

Fisher, R., and W. Ury. *Getting to Yes*. Boston, Massachusetts: Houghton Mifflin Co., 1981, 2nd edition with B. Patton, 1991.

Fisher, R., S. Brown. *Getting Together Building Relationships as We Negotiate*. Boston, MA: Penguin Books, 1988.

Folberg, Jay. *Resolving Disputes: Theory and Practice*. New York: Aspen Publishers, 2005.

Folger, Joseph, P.M.S. Poole, and R.K. Stutman. *Working Through Conflict,* 7th ed. New York: Pearson Higher Education, 2012.

Freeman, R., J. Medoff. *What do Unions Do?* New York: Basic Books Inc., 1984.

Garner, B., ed. *Black's Law Dictionary*, 10th ed. West Group, 2014.

Gunderson, M., A. Ponak, and D. Gottlieb Taras. *Union-Management Relations in Canada*, 4th ed. Toronto, ON: Addison Wesley Longman, 1995, 2001.

Haddigan, K. *Conflict Resolution*. Vancouver, BC: Justice Institute of BC, 1999.

Hoggan, James. *The Toxic State of Public Discourse and How to Clean it Up*. Gabriola Island, BC: New Society Publishers, 2016.

Holbrook, James, R., and B. Cook. *Advanced Negotiation and Mediation: Concepts, Skills and Exercises*, St. Paul, Minnesota: West Academic Publishing, 2013.

Holbrook, James. "Using Performative, Distributive, Integrative, and Transformative Principles in Negotiation." *Loyola Law Review,* Vol. 56. Chicago, IL: Loyola University, 2010.

Kahane, A. *Collaborating with the Enemy: How to Work with People You Don't Agree with or Like or Trust*. Oakland, CA: Berrett-Koehler Publishers, 2017.

Kirkham, R.L. *Pearls of Wisdom for Business and Life*. Salt Lake City, UT: American Training Alliance, 1994.

Knight, T. *Effective Grievance Handling* (Instruction and Resources). Vancouver: UBC Executive Education Seminar, 1998, 1999; BC Public School Employers' Association Seminar, 1998.

Lax, D., and J. Sebenius. *The Manager as Negotiator: The Negotiator's Dilemma, Creating and Claiming Value*. Boston, MA: Little Brown and Co., 1992.

Lewicki, R.J., D.M. Saunders, and J.W. Minton. *Essentials of Negotiation*. 4th ed. Boston, MA: Irwin McGraw-Hill, 2007; Lewicki, Saunders, Barry, and Tasa, 2nd Cdn ed., 2014; 3rd Cdn ed., 2017.

Mayer, B. *Staying with Conflict: A Strategic Approach to Ongoing Disputes*. San Francisco, CA: Jossey-Bass, 2009.

McShane, S., and S. Steen. *Canadian Organizational Behaviour*. Toronto, ON: McGraw-Hill Ryerson, 2012.

Palmer, E.E., and B.M. Palmer. *Collective Agreement Arbitration in Canada*, 3rd ed. Toronto, ON: Butterworth's Canada, 1991.

Phillips, G.E. *Labour Relations and the Collective Bargaining Cycle*. Toronto, ON: Butterworths, 1981.

Program on Negotiation, Proceedings: Executive Education Series, 1994, 1995, 1996, 1998, 2006. Intra-University Consortium, Harvard University, Cambridge, MA.

Pruitt, D., and J. Rubin. *Social Conflict, Stalemate and Settlement*. New York: Random House, 1986.

Sack Goldblatt Mitchell. *Words and Phrases, A Dictionary of Collective Agreement Language*, Toronto, ON: Lancaster House, 1993.

Sack, J., and E. Poskanzer. *Labour Law Terms, A Dictionary of Canadian Labour Law*. Toronto, ON: Lancaster House, 1984.

Schelling, T.C. *The Strategy of Conflict*. Traverse City, MN: Pickle Printers Publishing, 1960, 2015.

Sloman, S., and P. Fernbach, *The Knowledge Illusion*. New York: Riverhead Books, 2017.

Susskind, L., and J. Cruikshank. *Breaking the Impasse: Consensual Approaches to Resolving Public Disputes*. New York: Basic Books, 1988.

Susskind, L. *Good for You, Great for Me: Finding the Trading Zone*. New York: PublicAffairs, 2014.

Tidwell, Alan C. *Conflict Resolved? A Critical Assessment of Conflict Resolution*. New York: Continuum, 2003.

Tjosvold, Dean. *The Conflict Positive Organization*. Boston, MA: Addison Wesley Publishing, 1990.

Ury, W. L., J. M. Brett, and S. B. Goldberg. *Getting Disputes Resolved Designing Systems to Cut the Cost of Conflict*. Cambridge, MA: The Program on Negotiation at Harvard Law School, 1988.

Walton, R.E., and R.B. McKersie. *A Behavioral Theory of Labour Negotiations*. Ithaca, NY: ILR Press, 1991.

Williams, G.R. *Legal Negotiation and Settlement*. St. Paul, MN: West Publishing Company, 1983.

About the Author

Hugh J. Finlayson

Hugh J. Finlayson is a Chartered Professional in Human Resources (CPHR) and a faculty member in the School of Business, Human Resources Management Program at the British Columbia Institute of Technology (BCIT). He is also an Affiliated Scholar with the Centre for Educational Leadership and Policy (CSELP), Faculty of Education, Simon Fraser University.

His current research and teaching builds upon his 30-year career in human resource leadership and management across multiple roles, from practitioner, manager, part-time faculty member, and director to CEO. Hugh held senior leadership positions in the K-12 public education sector at the school district level and ultimately at the provincial level as the CEO of the human resource services agency and accredited bargaining agent for the province's K-12 education employers. While there he led two other multi-employer associations, one in the post-secondary education sector and the other in the community social services sector, through governance and organizational changes as interim CEO.

An active contributor to advancing the human resource profession, Hugh served as chair of BCIT Human Resources Management Program Advisory Committee (PAC) and is a past president of the Chartered Professionals in Human Resources of British Columbia & Yukon. In 2014, Hugh was made an Honorary Life Member of the CPHR BC & Yukon in recognition of his contribution to the field of human resources and in 2018 he was designated a Fellow CPHR, a title that recognizes the most exceptional CPHR holders in BC and the Yukon.

With a management career that began in the private sector and continued through the public sector, Hugh always appreciated that people do *well* at work worth doing. Further, we only achieve what we need to achieve through the energy, creativity and commitment of those who choose to work with us. It's what we do together that allows us to achieve excellence. These ideas are reflected strongly in his writing. Excellence can be achieved together.

Notes and Ideas

CPSIA information can be obtained
at www.ICGtesting.com
Printed in the USA
LVHW01s0058260718
584944LV00005B/7/P

9 781525 531149